Praise for *The Pr*

"Reminiscent of Truman Capote's *In Cold Blood* . . . Like Capote before him, Bardenwerper brilliantly portrays not a cardboard villain, but a complicated man who was unquestionably sadistic but also manifested flashes of generosity and compassion. . . . Bardenwerper has revealed one of the greatest little-known war stories in American history."

—Andrew Carroll, *New York Times* bestselling author of *War Letters*

"In the American imagination, Saddam Hussein functions as nothing more than a two-dimensional despot, a monster who terrorized and gassed and desecrated his own people. He was. He did. Will Bardenwerper's *The Prisoner in His Palace* reveals something else about Saddam, though, something less simple than that known caricature and certainly more troubling: he was a human being, a human like all of us, a human being with hopes and dreams and regrets that woke him in the dead of night. Saddam wrote poetry and longed for his family and treated the American soldiers tasked with guarding him during his trial with kindness and generosity of spirit. This is a brave and piercing book."

—Matt Gallagher, author of the novel *Youngblood* and *Kaboom: Embracing the Suck in a Savage Little War*

"In skin-crawling detail, Will Bardenwerper effectively captures a unique time and place in an engrossing history. A singular study exhibiting both military duty and human compassion."

—*Kirkus Reviews*

"Reveals the gritty humanity of Saddam through the eyes of the young American soldiers assigned to guard him in the last months before he is hanged. A disturbing and entirely captivating piece of literary journalism."

—Kai Bird, coauthor of the Pulitzer Prize–
winning *American Prometheus* and *New York
Times* bestselling author of *The Good Spy:
The Life and Death of Robert Ames*

"Expertly examines Saddam Hussein."

—*Vanity Fair*

"In war, the enemy is always the 'the other.' What makes *The Prisoner in His Palace* so captivating is how Bardenwerper brilliantly juxtaposes the brutal acts that Saddam Hussein perpetrated against his own people, with the dignified and even tender manner in which the Iraqi dictator interacted with his American guards. What the book reveals is that our common humanity turns 'the enemy' into someone quite unexpected."

—Peter Bergen, *New York Times* bestselling
author of *Manhunt: The Ten-Year Search for
Bin Laden from 9/11 to Abbottabad*

"Takes you inside the minds of the prisoner and his protectors, whose sole task is to guard the 'Vic,' or Very Important Criminal. . . . The book is captivating . . . a study of how proximity has a propensity to be persuasive, even when the common area is a cell in the basement of a courthouse."

—*Military Times*

"*The Prisoner in His Palace* finds humanity in a singularly inhuman figure, Saddam Hussein. Through meticulous reporting and beautiful storytelling, Will Bardenwerper has crafted a portrait that is both deeply moving and deeply disturbing. This book challenges the tired constructs of 'good versus evil' that have led us into so many ill-conceived wars."

—Elliot Ackerman, author of *Green on Blue*

"Compelling."

—*New York Post*

"Will Bardenwerper has succeeded in writing a book about the Iraq War from a wholly new perspective. This superb account of the twelve men assigned to guard Saddam Hussein forces us to acknowledge that there can be honor and courage on all sides in war. Absolutism is for people who've never been there."

—Nathaniel Fick, *New York Times* bestselling author of *One Bullet Away*

"Searing . . . Bardenwerper breathes an impressive amount of life into a story that hurtles toward death from the opening page."

—*War on the Rocks*

"Thoroughly engrossing . . . We want to believe that Saddam Hussein was a monster, but reading this, you'll learn that he was quite human—which is even more chilling. I highly recommend this book to anyone interested in our recent war in Iraq, or in the heights and depths of human nature."

—Karl Marlantes, *New York Times* bestselling author of *Matterhorn* and *What It Is Like to Go to War*

"Bardenwerper gives the reader a close look at a real-life supervillain, and how easy it is for him to gather minions at his feet. . . . Tightly-constructed and engaging."

—*The Rumpus*

"A moving and perception-altering book that exposes how wrong we are in so much of what we assume about war. . . . Mr. Bardenwerper forces us to turn our gaze not only on those we have killed but on those who were there to see the task done."

—Eric Fair, Pushcart Prize–winning essayist and author of the memoir *Consequence*

"*The Prisoner in His Palace* is an affirmation of human dignity even in people who have behaved horrifically and in situations where you would least expect to find it."

—*San Quentin News*

"A searing, beautifully crafted exploration of humankind's capacity for both boundless savagery and awe-inspiring perseverance. By tracking down and listening to the soldiers who stood watch over Saddam Hussein during the dictator's final days, Will Bardenwerper has done far more than just commit a heroic act of journalism; he has also created an extraordinary work of history that should be read by all who seek to understand how evil can flourish, and how it can be defeated."

—Brendan I. Koerner, author of *The Skies Belong to Us* and *Now the Hell Will Start*

"A moving account."

—*5280* Magazine

"An important contribution . . . The stories of the American soldiers who guarded the Iraqi leader serve as a sharp reminder of war's complexities, contradictions, and costs."

—J. Kael Weston, author of *The Mirror Test: America at War in Iraq and Afghanistan*

"The book's action will pull you along like any great military adventure, but bubbling underneath is an absorbing and sometimes heartbreaking survey of young men grappling with a moral certitude that begins to shift below the desert sands they're standing on."

—Tim Townsend, author of *Mission at Nuremberg*

"Astonishing . . . Through meticulous research and a keen eye for detail, Bardenwerper does the near impossible: convinces the reader to empathize with Saddam Hussein during his sad final days. *The Prisoner in His Palace* is a deeply human book, and though we all know the ending, I couldn't put it down."

—Brian Castner, author of *The Long Walk*
and *All the Ways We Kill and Die*

"Riveting . . . Brings the reader face-to-face with the specter of Saddam Hussein in captivity. An unforgettable, essential read."

—William Doyle, author of *A Soldier's Dream:*
Captain Travis Patriquin and the Awakening
of Iraq

"*The Prisoner in His Palace* will be many things to many people. To this writer and combat veteran, it is an exhilarating, extraordinary, and damning look in the mirror."

—Adrian Bonenberger, author of *Afghan Post*

THE
PRISONER
IN
HIS PALACE

SADDAM HUSSEIN,
HIS AMERICAN GUARDS,
AND WHAT HISTORY LEAVES UNSAID

Will Bardenwerper

SCRIBNER

New York   London   Toronto   Sydney   New Delhi

SCRIBNER
An Imprint of Simon & Schuster, Inc.
1230 Avenue of the Americas
New York, NY 10020

First Scribner trade paperback edition October 2018

SCRIBNER and design are registered trademarks of The Gale Group, Inc.,
used under license by Simon & Schuster, Inc., the publisher of this work.

For information about special discounts for bulk purchases,
please contact Simon & Schuster Special Sales at 1-866-506-1949
or business@simonandschuster.com.

The Simon & Schuster Speakers Bureau can bring authors to your live event.
For more information or to book an event, contact the Simon & Schuster Speakers Bureau
at 1-866-248-3049 or visit our website at www.simonspeakers.com.

Manufactured in the United States of America

5   7   9   10   8   6   4

Library of Congress Cataloging-in-Publication Data is available.

ISBN 978-1-5011-1783-1
ISBN 978-1-5011-1784-8 (pbk)
ISBN 978-1-5011-1785-5 (ebook)

This book is dedicated to my parents,
Walter and Patricia.

That afternoon there was a party of tourists at the Terrace and looking down in the water among the empty beer cans and dead barracudas a woman saw a great long white spine with a huge tail at the end that lifted and swung with the tide while the east wind blew a heavy steady sea outside the entrance to the harbor.

"What's that?" she asked a waiter and pointed to the long backbone of the great fish that was now just garbage waiting to go out with the tide.

—Ernest Hemingway, The Old Man and the Sea

CONTENTS

AUTHOR'S NOTE

The American soldiers who guarded Saddam Hussein in his last days, the self-dubbed "Super Twelve," were forbidden from keeping a journal, or from even mentioning their mission in communications with loved ones back home, so there's no documentary evidence to confirm the exact date of some of the episodes recounted here. The soldiers were, however, later interviewed by Army historians as part of the Army's oral history program. I was provided these interviews by Michael Gordon in 2010 as I assisted him with research for his book *The Endgame: The Inside Story of the Struggle for Iraq, from George W. Bush to Barack Obama.* Consequently, in constructing this book's chronology, I began with the recollections the soldiers shared in these oral histories before conducting nearly sixty hours of my own interviews with some of the soldiers. (Those interviews are among the nearly one hundred I conducted with government officials—both U.S. and Arab—as well as scholars, spies, lawyers, and others with unique insights.)

If a passage is enclosed in quotation marks, it means that I obtained it from an interview or material published elsewhere.

Much of the dialogue in this book wasn't recorded as it happened, and in these instances the speaker's words aren't in quotation marks. The remarks do, however, faithfully represent the recollections of people involved in the conversations and, in the case of Saddam's interrogation, declassified FBI accounts.

Throughout the book, in referencing source material, I've made some grammatical changes for the sake of clarity and minor edits for brevity.

Though this book is a work of nonfiction, I have taken certain storytelling liberties, particularly having to do with the order and arrangement of scenes. In so doing, I'm confident that I've accurately captured the essence of what happened.

I researched and wrote about the events recounted in this book as a journalist. Though I was serving as an infantry officer in Anbar Province, Iraq, when Saddam was executed, I did not participate in or have firsthand knowledge of the events in this account. Furthermore, none of the material in this book was derived from my subsequent time working as a civilian in the Department of Defense.

One last thing: All the characters in this book are real. To protect privacy in certain cases, though, I *have* used the following pseudonyms: Andre Jackson, Luke Quarles, Tom Flanagan, Chris Battaglia, Art Perkins, Jeff Price, James Martin, Tucker Dawson, Joseph, Amanda.

CHARACTERS

The Super Twelve

First Lieutenant Andre Jackson
Staff Sergeant Luke Quarles
Sergeant Chris Battaglia
Sergeant Tom Flanagan
Specialist Steve "Hutch" Hutchinson
Specialist Art "Old Man" Perkins
Specialist Adam Rogerson
Specialist Chris Tasker
Private First Class Tucker Dawson
Private First Class James Martin
Private First Class Jeff Price
Private First Class Paul Sphar

Other Key Players

Ramsey Clark—Former U.S. attorney general who assisted with Saddam's defense
Robert "Doc" Ellis—Master sergeant who provided medical care to Saddam
Raghad Hussein—Saddam's eldest daughter
Rod Middleton—FBI agent who interrogated Saddam
Jaafar al-Moussawi—Chief prosecutor in the trial

CHARACTERS

Dr. Najeeb al-Nuaimi—Former Qatari minister of justice brought onto Saddam's defense team by the dictator's daughter

Rauf Abd al-Rahman—Took over as judge in Saddam's trial and saw the proceedings to a verdict

TIMELINE

April 28, 1937: Saddam is born in Awja, Iraq.

October 7, 1959: Twenty-two-year-old Saddam participates in a failed assassination attempt on then Iraqi prime minister Abd al-Karim Qasim.

July 17, 1968: The Baath Party seizes power in a bloodless coup led by Ahmed Hassan al-Bakr, who assumes the presidency with Saddam serving as a deputy.

July 16, 1979: Saddam forces Bakr's resignation and officially seizes the presidency.

August 2, 1990: Iraq occupies Kuwait.

August 2, 1990–February 28, 1991: The United States leads a coalition of thirty-four countries against Iraq.

September 11, 2001: Al Qaeda attacks the World Trade Center and the Pentagon, inspiring many of the Super Twelve to join the military.

March 20, 2003: The United States initiates a bombing campaign that begins the Iraq War.

December 13, 2003: Saddam is captured by U.S. forces.

December 2003–June 2004: Saddam is interrogated.

October 19, 2005: The trial of Saddam for crimes against humanity begins.

August 2006: The Super Twelve begin their deployment.

November 5, 2006: Saddam is found guilty by the Iraqi High Tribunal and sentenced to death by hanging.

December 30, 2006: Saddam is executed.

INTRODUCTION

Baghdad, Iraq—December 30, 2006

It was time.

The old man slipped into his black peacoat, then deliberately placed a dark fur hat on his head to protect against the predawn chill.

This December night was one of the coldest the American soldiers had experienced in Iraq. Six of them stood outside the bombed-out palace that had been converted to hold the prisoner. They could see their breath in the night air. They were dressed in "full battle rattle," clunky in their Kevlar vests and helmets with mounted night-vision goggles. They each carried a full combat load of hundreds of rounds of ammunition. As they scanned their surroundings for anything out of the ordinary, six more soldiers led the prisoner outside into an idling Humvee for the short ride to the landing zone.

The silver-bearded old man moved deliberately, almost proudly, working to maintain an upright posture despite the bad back he often complained of. His arms swung freely at his sides. Nearby, two Black Hawks waited, rotors already a blur, violently kicking up clouds of loose sand and gravel. The greenish glow of the soldiers' night-vision goggles added to the disorienting maelstrom of sound, temperature, and light. It was always a shock for the young men to emerge from the cocoon-like warmth of the cell area and approach a waiting helicopter, its furious power ready to provide vertical lift and whisk away the man they'd come for.

The six MPs who clustered around the old man led him into one of the Black Hawks, ducking under the swirling rotors and gingerly climbing aboard so as not to trip—their night-vision goggles impaired depth perception. One of the soldiers was especially vigilant, having been instructed to keep a close watch on the prisoner for "anything froggy." The soldiers were joined by two medics and an interpreter, who lent welcome body heat to the cramped fuselage. Once the first group had piled on board, the other six soldiers quickly filed onto the second Black Hawk.

The choppers lurched skyward, beginning their short flight to an Iraqi installation in Baghdad's Shiite Kadhimiya district. A brief look of fear flashed across the old man's face when the chopper bounced a bit in some rough air. He'd always been a nervous flier. Otherwise he was silent and stoic.

As soon as the choppers landed, the soldiers ushered him to a waiting "Rhino," a massive armored bus. The American soldiers piled in alongside, as did the Lebanese-American interpreter, who always had a tough time wedging his large frame into the vehicle.

It was eerily quiet as the thirteen-ton Rhino began rumbling across the compound in the chilly predawn hours. There was none of the casual banter that usually accompanied missions; none of the familiar jokes volleyed between buddies who'd grown to know each other's idiosyncrasies. Just silence.

After a short ride, it was time to turn the man over. He rose from his seat near the back of the Rhino and carefully straightened his black peacoat, making sure it wasn't rumpled from the brief ride. One of the soldiers had carefully applied a lint roller to it before they'd left his cell. The man then began to walk slowly from his seat near the back toward the front door. As he made his way to the front of the dimly lit armored vehicle, he stopped to grasp each of the twelve young Americans and, in a few cases, to whisper final private words.

Some of the soldiers now had tears in their eyes.

When the old man reached the front, he turned to them one last time and said, "May God be with you." With that, he bowed slightly, and turned toward the door.

PART I

THE SUPER TWELVE

Is evil something you are? Or is it something you do?
—Bret Easton Ellis, *American Psycho*

CHAPTER 1

Ocala, Florida—September 11, 2001

The phone rang, waking Steve Hutchinson from an uncomfortable sleep. His head was pounding, his mouth sandpaper. He was staying at his cousin's house, and his large frame was draped across the couch. It felt like it had only been a few hours since he'd passed out there after getting home from a long night working security at the Midnight Rodeo, a rough honky-tonk bar in the central Florida town of Ocala. He blamed the nasty headache on the beers he'd torn through after his shift ended around 4:00 a.m. Though he tried to ignore it, his phone kept ringing, each series of tones sending searing pain through his hungover skull. Too sapped of energy to hold the phone to his ear, he put it on speaker and clumsily dropped it to the floor.

"Turn on the TV," a voice urged. It was his cousin's wife, calling from work, and she sounded panicked.

"Which channel?" he asked.

"Any of them," she replied.

It was just after 9:00 a.m. on September 11, 2001. Hutchinson turned on the television just in time to see United Airlines Flight 175 strike the South Tower of the World Trade Center, not quite twenty minutes after American Airlines Flight 11 had slammed into the North Tower.

Until that morning he'd been on an uncertain career path. A muscular former Georgia high school football and baseball stand-

5

out, he'd been working for the county road department during the day and doing some bouncing at the Rodeo at night, but the images of a smoldering lower Manhattan decided something in him. "I wasn't getting over there fast enough," he'd later say, referring to his decision to join the Army and go overseas.

Baghdad, Iraq—August 2006

Five years later, Steve Hutchinson, known as Hutch to his buddies, was doing the "duffel bag drag" across the steamy tarmac of Baghdad International Airport, often referred to as BIAP. He'd arrived as part of the 551st Military Police Company based out of Fort Campbell, Kentucky, and he knew the drill. Like many who joined the military in the wake of the September 11 attacks, he'd found himself thrust into an exhausting operational tempo. By 2006, he'd already spent a year deployed to Iraq during the initial invasion in 2003, and another in Afghanistan. He was one of the more tenured members of his squad of eleven other American military policemen, mostly in their twenties, who'd just arrived "downrange." The youngest, Private Tucker Dawson, wasn't yet twenty-one; the oldest, Specialist Art Perkins, was in his mid-thirties. With the "War on Terror" already nearly five years old, about half had deployed previously while the other half had spilled from the Air Force C-130 into a combat zone for the first time. The lieutenant to whom they reported, Andre Jackson, was a recent ROTC graduate. The junior enlisted soldiers and noncommissioned officers (NCOs) under his command came from all over the United States, though a disproportionate number hailed from working-class communities scattered across the Rust Belt.

They didn't know it yet, but in a few months they'd be playing a pivotal role in a historical drama they couldn't have imagined.

The men—there were no women in the squad—had grown reasonably tight in the months preceding deployment. They'd performed countless training missions back at Fort Campbell to prepare for deployment, which they expected would be spent carrying out assignments common for military policemen—for example, guarding detainees and providing convoy security. And during the training lulls those who were single grabbed some downtime at Kickers bar or the Lodge in nearby Clarksville, Tennessee, while the married among them stuck with more domesticated routines, such as taking turns babysitting each other's kids so that they could enjoy dinner with their wives at the popular Yamato's Japanese steakhouse off post.

Those who'd deployed before, like Hutchinson, Art Perkins, Tom Flanagan, and Chris Tasker, were familiar with the routine. Less so Tucker Dawson, Adam Rogerson, and Paul Sphar, for whom this was an altogether new adventure. Sphar had barely been allowed to deploy at all, due to his persistent weight problems. In the months leading up to their leaving for Iraq, Sergeant Chris Battaglia had "run the dogshit" out of Sphar to trim his ample midsection. The young private stood out from the others for reasons other than his weight, though. The fact was, he seemed a better match for a skate park or mosh pit than a military parade ground. He was covered in tattoos, proud to have almost a "full shirt" of them.

The soldiers had arrived in Iraq after a marathon journey that took them from Fort Campbell to Maine to Germany to Kuwait to—at last—BIAP's floodlit tarmac. The temperatures had continued to linger in the nineties even after the sun had set, and before the men had even finished unloading their bags, their clothes were drenched in sweat. It was a not-so-subtle reminder that they were far from home, and that this was for real.

CHAPTER 2

Baghdad, Iraq—August 2006

Upon arrival at Baghdad International Airport, each soldier in the twelve-man squad was issued an initial magazine containing thirty rounds of 5.56 ammunition. As the men were shuttled by local "hajji buses"—run-down vehicles that wouldn't be out of place in communist Havana—to Freedom Village, the collection of containerized housing units, or CHUs, that would serve as their new homes, they took notice of the ubiquitous Hesco barriers and concrete walls designed to provide cover from the incoming mortar and rocket fire.

That the fortifications suggested potential danger was both sobering and exciting. Unbeknownst to the new arrivals, they were in fact stepping into a cauldron of violence whose temperature had been steadily rising since the initial invasion had unseated Saddam Hussein in 2003. It was now the summer of 2006, and U.S. commanders were so alarmed by the escalating Sunni versus Shia violence in Baghdad that twelve thousand additional troops were being rushed in. Just days before Hutch and the others had arrived in Iraq, a Sunni suicide bomber had detonated himself outside one of Shia Islam's holiest places, the Imam Ali Mosque in Najaf, killing 35 and injuring 122. Volunteers would scramble for hours afterward to mop up the blood and collect body parts.

Confronting the deteriorating security situation would be the work of another day, though. For now, giddy excitement gripped those who were experiencing a war zone for the first time, and everyone—not just the greenhorns—rushed to lay claim to creature comforts that would have been unimaginable in previous conflicts. In a peculiar way, this ritual of appropriation reminded Specialist Adam Rogerson of scenes from the MTV show *The Real World*, in which new roommates arrive at their group house and madly scramble to claim the most desirable living spaces. In the case of Rogerson and his squad mates, the hunt was on for fridges and televisions sold cheap by the National Guard unit they'd be replacing. Though the conditions were hardly luxurious by standards back home, those who'd deployed before into more austere circumstances recognized that they now had it pretty good.

The squad would spend its first week shadowing the outgoing National Guard unit. These transitions were always a little awkward, because the soon-to-be departing soldiers were fatigued, somewhat jaded, and itching to get home, while the incoming units brimmed with enthusiasm—especially the younger soldiers eager to put their training to use.

The soldiers from Campbell were initially assigned a grab bag of missions, some resembling those they'd trained for, and others falling into their laps by default, since they were a well-trained combat support unit that was part of the Army's storied 101st Airborne Division. The twenty-first-century American Army was still in many ways a tribal institution, and within its various hierarchies, the 101st was regarded as "squared away"—Army parlance for "competent and professional."

"Our squad was good at what we did," Adam Rogerson would later say with pride. "We trained hard, learned how to call in nine-line medevacs, stick IVs in each other, and went on lots of twelve-mile ruck marches." These things mattered to Rogerson, and indeed to most of the squad, which exhibited a pride bordering on cockiness that is common in hard-charging units.

CHAPTER 3

Baghdad, Iraq—summer of 2006

The twelve MPs were tasked with overseeing security at a hospital staffed by American medical personnel who were responsible for treating both coalition service members and Iraqi insurgents wounded in combat operations. Located just inside Baghdad's Green Zone, the facility was a grim, nasty place. The doctors were buffeted by relentless waves of trauma injuries, and they labored long hours to save lives in a dilapidated building in which blood would sometimes pool on the floor and flies were a persistent menace. Some of the suspected insurgents had to be handcuffed to their beds as they were treated. Chris Tasker, who, like Hutchinson, had been "hell-bent" on enlisting after the attacks of September 11, once had to pin down a suspected insurgent who'd been shot in the neck and was flailing around on his gurney. Not caring about the man's allegiances, the doctors struggled intently to peel back his torn flesh and treat his hemorrhaging wound.

Some days the squad never left the hospital. They made themselves useful by helping the nurses replace dressings on the same insurgents they thought they'd come to this country to capture and kill. Many of the squad members were frustrated to be essentially "babysitting bad guys," some of whom were only in their early teens but already spitting on the Americans who were laboring to take care of them. Looking back later on the experience,

Rogerson said, "They didn't like us, and we didn't like them, but they had to see us every day, and we had to see them."

The squad was also assigned periodic convoy escort missions, which at least got them out of the hospital, and more closely resembled what they'd imagined doing in Iraq. Every trip "outside the wire," as soldiers referred to patrols beyond the secure perimeter of their operating bases, entailed a degree of risk, which was actually welcomed by some of the less experienced and more eager troops. Specialist Art Perkins wasn't one of them. Already in his mid-thirties, Perkins had left the Army and married a woman he'd met while stationed in Germany. But then he reenlisted years later. Bespectacled and knowledgeable on a diverse array of topics, Perkins reminded Rogerson of the comedic actor–turned–pundit Ben Stein. Perkins exhibited Stein's dry wit and curmudgeonly manner. Some soldiers took to calling Perkins "Snapple," after the trivia questions inside the tops of the juice bottles, since he would volunteer so many random facts. To Hutch, "Old Man Perkins" seemed like "an unsuccessful tweedy professor who had all this random knowledge," and whose attitude was the antithesis of the "hooah" brand of enthusiasm that the Army inculcated in young recruits.

One day the squad was tasked with providing security for a convoy bound for the U.S. Embassy, a mission that most welcomed, since it might provide an opportunity to enjoy the State Department cafeteria. As they snaked their way through Baghdad's often chaotic streets, Rogerson stood in the Humvee's turret manning the .240 machine gun, doing the best he could to remain vigilant, scanning for potential roadside bombs, waving Iraqi traffic to the side, and, unavoidably, baking in the overpowering sun. He looked forward to the relief that would come when they finally reached the embassy and he could strip off his body armor. He imagined his inflamed back muscles relaxing after hours of forced tension. Upon arriving at the embassy, shirts soaked in sweat, looking like they'd just dragged themselves from a swimming pool, the soldiers dismounted from their Humvees and quickly stripped off the suffocating protective gear they were required to wear outside the wire. Everyone's mouth watered as the men envisioned the spread of food and cold Gatorades that awaited. All but *one*, that is. Perkins refused to leave his vehicle. He was volunteering to stay behind, which was unnecessary, since they were already in the secure Green Zone. The soldiers were confused and asked Perkins why he wasn't joining them. Then Rogerson noticed that not only was Perkins's uniform top soaked, as were most of theirs, but so, too, was a large area around his crotch. He'd peed himself.

Accounts differ as to what had triggered the unfortunate release. Some contended that Perkins simply couldn't hold it anymore, while others suggested that a distant explosion or outbreak of small arms fire had spooked the Old Man, causing him to lose control of his bladder. Whichever theory was correct, Perkins would be mercilessly reminded of it for weeks. Specialist Rogerson and Private Dawson were the chief teasers. They constantly referenced the Will Ferrell comedy *Talladega Nights*, in which a young boy says, "And I never did change my pee pants all day—I'm still sitting in my dirty pee pants." Dawson, a fresh-faced twenty-year-old who looked like he'd just stepped out of an Abercrombie & Fitch catalog, reminded the more awkward and less photogenic Paul Sphar of the "new kid in school who's trying hard to impress the cool people right off the bat." Rogerson, the popular jock who wasn't many years removed from roaming the hallways of North Ridgeville High School outside Cleveland clad in his Rangers football jersey, was the perfect ally, and to Perkins's continuing dismay, he was their perfect foil.

After one especially long and hot patrol, Rogerson began wrestling with his .240 machine gun while the rest of the squad knocked out their usual post-mission tasks. Old Man Perkins happened to be pontificating—or so Rogerson considered it—and the grimy, sweaty Ohioan tackled the smaller, somewhat chubby Perkins. Rogerson pinned Perkins on the ground and wrapped him up in the strap of his machine gun. Later admitting to a tinge of guilt for his overheated outburst, Rogerson explained, "He was my roommate, and I liked him, but I'd just had enough."

Meanwhile, the rhythm of life in Iraq—the loading up of the gun trucks, going out on convoys, and returning to base to steal some time for relaxation—continued. In this, the squad of MPs was not unique. U.S. soldiers across Iraq were embarking on hundreds of patrols, largely indistinguishable from theirs, every day.

Hutchinson remembers the moment when everything changed.

Their transition from an ordinary squad of military policemen to the Super Twelve, as they'd take to calling themselves, began one night as Hutch returned from a mission and looked forward to some downtime to relax. He was the father of two young daughters and one son, and tried to visit the Morale, Welfare, and Recreation (MWR) tent as often as possible to call home and hear his kids' "crazy little stories." It was a routine he'd grown familiar with over the past five years, since he'd spent more of that time deployed than at home. The MWR tents were charmless yet treasured. They included a bank of phones and some Internet terminals, separated by plywood partitions, at which soldiers would queue up to briefly tap into the currents of life back home. On this night, though, Hutch wouldn't get the opportunity to talk to his wife, as he was summoned to a meeting with his squad leader, Sergeant Luke Quarles.

Quarles, who hoped to qualify for the Army's Special Forces when he got back to the States and had been spending his downtime in Iraq pursuing an exhausting fitness regimen to improve his chances, told his assembled team, We have a mission change, boys. No more convoy escorts. No more watching low-level hajjis. You may not like it, you may like it, but bottom line is, we're gonna do it. We've been assigned a high-value detainee.

This news, while intriguing, didn't come as a shock, since "detainee ops" were a common assignment for military policemen. What came next, however, was anything but common.

The detainee was Saddam Hussein.

For an instant, there was a collective intake of breath, then the smart remarks started. "We should kill him!" someone half-jokingly exclaimed. *Fuck him, let him burn*, thought Hutch.

Chris Tasker was dejected when he learned the news. "I was bummed, since I wanted to be on patrols outside the wire, not guarding people."

As anyone who has ever joined the Army knows, "closing with and killing the enemy" is a core objective that the institution continually reinforces. This ethic is ingrained in any number of ways, from having soldiers achieve marksmanship proficiency by shooting hundreds of rounds at life-sized silhouettes to conducting bayonet drills while chanting, "What makes the green grass grow? Blood, blood, blood!" It's all designed to erode a person's natural aversion to taking a human life, so that if the time comes in battle, a soldier won't hesitate to pull the trigger.

Now, though, after having spent months stoking these soldiers' enthusiasm for mixing it up with the "bad guys" outside the wire, the Army was assigning them the task of standing watch over a prisoner in his jail cell.

Sensing the frustration of Tasker and some of the others in the squad, Sergeant Chris Battaglia tried to boost morale, explaining: Dudes, you're going to be guarding Saddam Hussein, that's pretty cool.

Yeah, I guess you're right, it's not that bad, Tasker responded. Still, he wasn't convinced he'd get much out of the mission. His knowledge of Saddam was limited to the basics; he was aware of Iraq's wars against Iran and Kuwait, for example, and, more generally, that Saddam had been "a vicious dude killing his own people."

Hutch also had reservations about the new mission. "At first I was really hesitant about it," he later recalled. "Nobody wakes up one day and wants to spend time with a guy who's been accused of all the things Saddam was accused of." Hutch considered asking for a transfer before concluding that he'd never backed down from anything and wasn't going to start now.

The squad's youngest member, Tucker Dawson, quietly marveled, *Out of all the people in the Army, how did I get chosen to do this?*

CHAPTER 4

Baghdad, Iraq—summer of 2006

Steve Hutchinson was working nights again. But he was a world away from listening to country music and peeling drunken brawlers off each other's back at the Midnight Rodeo in central Florida. His first shift guarding Saddam began at midnight.

Hutch found himself in the bowels of the Iraqi High Tribunal (IHT), the courthouse that had been constructed to try Saddam and his seven codefendants for crimes against humanity. Beneath the courtroom was a collection of subterranean cells—essentially glass cages—in which Saddam and his codefendants would be held on the days when they were in court. When the proceedings were in session, the defendants would bunk there for up to a week at a time.

The IHT was housed in a former Baath Party headquarters building, a hulking, pillared structure that bore a resemblance to many of Saddam's palaces. The IHT had been established by the Americans and modeled on UN war crimes tribunals. The court had chosen to try Saddam for the reported killing of 148 Shiite residents of the Iraqi town of Dujail, in response to a failed assassination attempt that had taken place when Saddam had visited the town in the early 1980s. The Dujail crackdown was an odd choice as the first crime to prosecute Saddam for, given the other, more well-known killings for which he was thought to be responsible, most notably the chemical gas attacks directed at Iraqi Kurds during the Iran-Iraq War.

The previous days had been an exhausting blur for Hutch. He and the rest of the Super Twelve had been forbidden from telling anyone about their new mission. Not only would they *not* be allowed to tell their loved ones what they were doing, but they wouldn't even be permitted to keep a journal of their experiences. They were told that their email correspondence would be monitored, and that they'd be subject to random searches to make sure that they weren't taking notes about what they were observing.

With those warnings still echoing in his head, Hutch took a seat on an old metal chair outside Saddam Hussein's shatterproof Plexiglas cell. The dictator appeared to be sleeping comfortably. His temporary home was at the end of the hallway, the last of four cells. The man whose palaces dotted the landscape above was now locked up in a subterranean hallway that had all the charm of a boiler room. It was dreary and claustrophobic. The cell itself looked a bit like a hospital nursery for newborns. A concrete wall was topped by Plexiglas starting around waist level so that the prisoner could be observed from the outside.

The Super Twelve would eventually take to calling their temporary lodging beneath the IHT courtroom "the Crypt," since their quarters, just down the hall from the detainees, was dark twenty-four hours a day to accommodate the fact that, at any given time, some of them would be sleeping. Life in the IHT was divided into eight-hour shifts, but it was the night shift Hutch was now settling into that was devoid of any noise whatsoever. "It was so deafeningly quiet that the silence was loud," Hutch would later say.

He'd been a "screamer" on previous deployments at detention facilities. The job of the screamer was to let detainees know on their arrival that no guff from them would be tolerated. As Hutch explained it: "You give them that initial shock, where you stand in front of 'em, probably about an inch from their face, and scream out the rules and regulations of the camp. . . . Your job is to establish that the guard has ultimate control of the guard-detainee relationship."

Though Hutch had vowed to treat this as just another mission, as he sat observing Saddam late that night he felt smaller than he ever remembered feeling. He wondered if he was the right person for this unique duty. His mind wandered back to the first Gulf War, when as a young kid he'd written to soldiers deployed to Iraq and sometimes received notes back that included Iraqi dinar—Saddam's face staring from them—as a souvenir. The man he'd always imagined as a larger-than-life demon was now snoring in front of him.

The soldiers had been instructed to maintain visual contact with Saddam at all times to ensure he wasn't able to harm himself, or be hurt by others. In the wake of the Abu Ghraib prisoner abuse scandal, the United States was acutely aware of the public relations disaster that would result from allegations of mistreatment. Hutch was joined during this eight-hour overnight shift by two additional guards. An NCO was assigned to observe Saddam remotely via a closed-circuit TV camera, while a "roving" guard patrolled the area and was on call for any additional tasks that might pop up. Not long ago, the assignment would have been unimaginable to some of the younger soldiers who at basic training had performed similar roving guard duty armed with fake "rubber duck" rifles.

The IHT was a massive facility consisting of several floors that included the courtroom and an "amphitheater-like" room resembling "mission control in Houston" in which security personnel monitored a large bank of TV screens showing the underground cells.

"You could sit in mission control and watch the prisoners taking a dump if you were so inclined," wryly recalls William Wiley, a Canadian lawyer who was assigned to assist with Saddam's defense.

Having settled into his uncomfortable chair just outside Saddam's cell, Hutch began anxiously leafing through a graphic novel, *Resident Evil: Code: Veronica*, to pass the time. Over the course of this deployment he'd eventually work his way completely through the Harry Potter books and the *Hunger Games* series, ostensibly so that he had something to discuss with his daughter when he called home.

Suddenly, the silence was shattered. "Chemical" Ali Hassan al-Majid, one of Saddam's top lieutenants, had begun praying in a nearby cell. Ali was accused of having helped mastermind a genocidal campaign that used both chemical and conventional weapons to try to exterminate Iraqi Kurds, who were considered a threat to Saddam's rule. According to Baath Party records, the man who'd suddenly risen from his cot to pray aloud had once signed orders instructing the Iraqi military to "carry out random bombardments using artillery, helicopters, and aircraft at all times of day or night to kill the largest number of persons present in those prohibited zones." The orders instructed northern field commanders that "all persons captured in those villages shall be detained and interrogated by the security services and those between the ages of fifteen and seventy shall be executed after any useful information has been obtained from them."

All told, Ali Hassan al-Majid may have been responsible for the deaths of more than a hundred thousand human beings.

Saddam, who'd been snoring, was abruptly awakened by Ali's prayers, and began to tiredly mumble prayers of his own, all the while remaining prone in bed. He seemed to be going through the motions, without much feeling, as if he were trying to get it over with as quickly as possible. Though the Baath Party that Saddam had led was in theory secular, he'd launched a "faith campaign" in the 1990s designed to push Iraq in a more devout direction. He'd even donated blood at regular intervals so that a copy of the Koran could be written entirely in the dark red liquid. The extent to which Saddam's religious faith was sincere was a much debated topic. Hutch, though, wasn't expending mental energy wondering if Saddam's halfhearted prayer was genuine or not. Instead, his mind was troubled by thoughts that only a week prior would have seemed far-fetched, such as that Sunni insurgents might somehow break into the heavily fortified Green Zone in an effort to free their deposed leader.

Hutch chided himself for letting his imagination run wild. Still, there was something spooky about being down in these shadowy underground corridors late at night, surrounded by men with so much blood on their hands. The man who'd been sleeping just a few feet away had, after all, once said, "I wish America would bring its Army and occupy Iraq. I wish they would do it so we can kill all Americans. We will roast them and eat them." Hutch couldn't help but equate Saddam with Hannibal Lecter, the iconic serial killer in *The Silence of the Lambs*: diabolically manipulative, "the greatest devil on the planet—someone who could kill you instantly."

More nervous than he'd expected to be, Hutch resolved to remain vigilant and not let down his guard in Saddam's presence. In addition to the possibility that insurgents would somehow launch a mission to free Saddam, he'd also been cautioned to watch out for an unbalanced soldier trying to harm the former president, either as an act of vigilante justice or to become famous.

It was then that he heard a noise coming from the shadows down the hall. While he didn't want to leave his post, he needed to determine what it was, so he crept forward in the direction of the sound, heart racing. *It would be just my luck that something crazy happens on my first night*, he thought. Inching closer to the source of the commotion, fearing the worst, he was startled by a cat that suddenly leapt out of the shadows and darted past him. *You've got to be fucking kidding me*, thought Hutch. Relief quickly turned to embarrassment as he recognized his own jitteriness.

The rest of the night passed without event. Saddam fell back asleep, and from that point forward offered only an occasional snore to break the silence. Hutch returned to his graphic novel, finally able to throttle his imagination down to a manageable level.

Private Sphar, who pulled similar nighttime shifts, later reflected that during times like these when Saddam slumbered he was like a lion at the zoo. "He looked majestic and peaceful, but if you removed the glass, you'd see a different animal." Over the many days and nights that the Super Twelve would interact with the former Iraqi ruler and see his different sides, many would wonder about his origins. Dr. Jerrold Post, founder of the CIA's psychological profiling unit, simply referred to him as "the most traumatized leader I have ever studied."

CHAPTER 5

Al-Awja, Iraq—late 1930s

Awja means "the turning," and the town is named after a sharp bend in the Tigris River, on which it sits. Elites in Baghdad sometimes refer to the region as a Hamptons socialite might describe a blue-collar bumpkin from a rural hamlet in West Virginia. Awja was, by all accounts, a frightening backwater, a place that achieved notoriety for its violence even within a larger society in which bloody feuds were common. It was rife with bandits who found its location ideal; passing barges, en route from Mosul to Baghdad, proved especially vulnerable to low-level piracy, as they had to slow down to carefully navigate the twist in the Tigris as they floated past.

Awja was desperately poor, a sinister place inhabited by locals who spoke in a rough unrefined dialect and were famously prone to resolve disputes with violence. Even the natives of Tikrit, just a few miles upriver on the Tigris, reportedly shuttered their market stalls when rough men from Awja strode into town, too aware of the potential for thievery and violent confrontation. The region resembled "the badlands in a western movie," and the local Albu Nasir tribe was known as "a difficult lot of people, cunning and secretive."

A Middle East scholar, Amatzia Baram, tells the story of a Jewish family in the 1930s—the Vilkhas, from Tikrit. Merchants, the Vilkhas were well-to-do by local standards, and had gotten to know a pregnant woman named Subha from nearby Awja. The Vilkhas had heard that Subha's twelve-year-old son was extremely sick with headaches and vomiting. Recognizing that mother and son needed to get to the hospital in Baghdad, the Jewish family offered to deliver them there in their black sedan, since the Vilkhas had a sister in Baghdad who lived across the street from the hospital.

They rushed to the hospital, where they leveraged family connections to make sure Subha's son was quickly seen by a doctor. But it was too late. The boy died on the operating table, perhaps of a brain tumor, and Subha fell into hysterics. She'd always been an odd one, Subha, different from the other villagers—she fancied herself as something of a clairvoyant—and her son's death seems to have magnified her eccentricities and instability. Despairing that she no longer had a husband—he'd disappeared months before—and that her son had died, she supposedly tried to smash her pregnant stomach against the door on the way out of the hospital, hoping to crush the life out of her eight-month-old fetus. She then tried to launch herself under a bus.

The Vilkhas returned the distraught Subha back to her home in Awja, where one of the Vilkha women alleged that Subha would scream, "I'm carrying Satan in my belly—this fetus has already killed his father and his brother and wants to be the only man in the family." Despite Subha's mental instability, she eventually gave birth to "a beautiful, intelligent, sweet, somewhat naughty and mischievous young boy." She named him Saddam, meaning "one who confronts."

Saddam likely grew up in a cramped one-room mudbrick dwelling without electricity or running water, and with only a dirt floor to sleep on. He was subjected to cruel taunts from the village boys for not having a father, who was rumored to have been killed in an act of banditry, and he was bereft of his older brother, who might have helped shield him from abuse. Forced to navigate the dusty alleyways of the desolate riverside town alone, he reportedly took to wielding an iron bar to fend off attacks. He quickly learned what it took to survive in this predatory world, becoming what Arabs called a "son of the alleys."

Saddam hardly had a childhood. As a young boy he'd cower as his stepfather, a brutish man known locally as "Hassan the Liar," lunged toward him with a large pipe, soaked in boiling tar, swinging wildly. The man cursed at the boy, calling him the "son of a dog," and laughed menacingly as he tried to duck the blows. A former CIA analyst began a story about him by saying, "When Saddam was a child," before catching herself. She continued, "If he ever *was* a child." Saddam was forced to survive on his wits and strength from the very beginning.

Awja was and is a deeply patriarchal society. Tribal codes in Iraq are more dominant in rural towns like Awja than in more diverse cities. Local strongmen—sheikhs—dominate their fiefdoms like mafia dons, employing both carrot and stick to remain on top and ensure that their tribe remains strong relative to rivals.

Observing early in life the brutal and unforgiving Awja brand of governance, Saddam would go on to become one of its most skilled practitioners.

CHAPTER 6

The forbidding backwater that spawned Saddam Hussein couldn't have been more different from the idyllic backyards of Amherst, Ohio, where young Chris Tasker and his childhood friends reenacted Civil War battles, clutching toy muskets and pretending to be the officers and generals they'd read about in history books. The boys would converge after school, eagerly don mismatched scraps of Civil War–era regalia—Tasker's family didn't have enough money to buy him a proper uniform—and practice military formations. His buddy even located a recipe for hardtack, a dietary staple of Civil War infantrymen, and would cook it up for them to snack on as they pretended to set up camp.

Amherst hadn't changed much since those childhood days. The big difference was that when Tasker was home between deployments, instead of marching around in an ill-fitting Union or Confederate uniform, he and his grown-up friends spent their free time bar crawling, visiting the Captain's Club, Pour House, and Ziggy's on downtown's Park Avenue. It was a city of slightly more than twelve thousand where Lenten fish fries at the local VFW Post 1662 were still popular on Friday nights in the spring—an overtly patriotic spot on the Ohio map that was often draped in American flags, the kind of place celebrated in Bruce Springsteen's elegies for the Rust Belt working class.

While hitting the bars back home prior to his deployment to Iraq, Tasker always kept pretty quiet about his time in Afghanistan. He'd politely answer questions if asked, but he didn't go overboard volunteering stories. He didn't want to be one of those guys who get ridiculed as "hometown heroes"; the type who serve as supply clerks while deployed, but return with stories that are full of blood and guts.

Tasker also tried to savor every moment with his girlfriend, Amanda, since he knew from experience what it would be like to go for a year without female companionship. She was the sister of a childhood friend and Tasker had always known her, but it wasn't until he went to a birthday party for her while on leave from basic training that he began falling for her. During his subsequent deployment to Afghanistan, their virtual relationship picked up steam.

When he got back to the States, their relationship was still long-distance, but not *so* long: she was at Ohio State and he at Fort Campbell. He tried to make the six-hour drive up to visit her as often as he could. Sometimes, when he prowled the campus with Amanda and her friends, it occurred to him how exotic he must seem, having done things in Afghanistan that were beyond the comprehension of most students whose lives were defined by Buckeye football and fraternity parties. In those moments, he felt both proud and a little wistful. It must be nice for your chief worry to be the next big paper that's due.

Now stationed in Iraq, Tasker did his best to keep in touch with his family in Ohio. He remembered how much his mother had worried about him when he'd been in Afghanistan, and he knew it was important to reassure her he was okay. For American troops, the ability to remain in such close contact with home was one of the unique features of twenty-first-century war. The ease of communication was generally considered a good thing—though, of course, there was always the chance that being just an email away might thrust a soldier back into a festering problem.

As Tasker logged on to one of the shared computers that the Super Twelve used to contact friends and family, he was careful not to repeat a recent mistake. In emailing his dad to tell him that his convoy had been hit by an IED, he'd begun with the words

"Don't tell Mom." He hadn't realized that his parents shared their email passwords, and that his mom had read the message first, with a predictable effect on her anxiety level. In truth, her worries weren't without cause. At this point in 2006, America's cable news networks were busy beaming grisly footage of Baghdad's violent streets and reporting on the nearly one hundred Iraqis who were losing their lives every day.

When Tasker opened his email inbox he found a message from his mom. She'd written to let him know that he'd received a letter from the Ohio Public Safety Department. He needed to pay a two-hundred-dollar fine for a speeding ticket. After finishing the email, Tasker exhaled. He was relieved that it wasn't worse.

Shortly before his most recent deployment he and his buddy Adam Rogerson had done something stupid. Like most things young men do, it didn't seem stupid *at the time*—or, at least, as fully stupid as it obviously was.

Seat-belted in Tasker's powerful silver Mustang, the two soldiers had hoped to make the nine-hour drive between Fort Campbell, on the Tennessee-Kentucky border, and Tasker's hometown of Amherst, Ohio, in seven or eight hours. The two MPs lived only a few exits apart, and they were looking forward to making the most of one of their last weekends of freedom. They were still in uniform, which was technically against the rules, but they'd wanted to hit the road as soon as they got off duty. The top was down, and the heat of the long southern day slowly gave way to a cooler night. There was nothing in either direction, and, after a long week of being barked at by NCOs and uptight officers, the young men reveled in the freedom of the open road. Rapidly, the needle on their speedometer crept up.

Suddenly they saw the blur of a police car passing in the opposite direction. A few long seconds elapsed as they held their breath, hoping its siren wouldn't soon shatter the soft Kentucky twilight. Then they saw the police car's brake lights flash.

Shit, he must be turning around to bust us, was their simultaneous thought.

"Gun it," said Rogerson, who, ironically, had wanted to be a cop when he got out of the Army; "we can take him." Thinking back on it later, he'd say, "I don't know what we were thinking. Two young MPs looking for that last thrill, I guess."

The Mustang responded to Tasker's foot, thundering down the highway, the speedometer rocketing well past 100 miles per hour before they saw blue lights flashing in their rearview mirror. With no real options, Tasker reluctantly decelerated and brought the Mustang to a stop on the shoulder.

As the Kentucky state trooper approached, it dawned on both soldiers how ridiculous they must have appeared. Large Military Police brassards visible on their arms, and laying rubber on the road like they were in a scene from that old car chase movie *Smokey and the Bandit*. The cop eyed them quizzically.

"You're lucky you're wearing this uniform or you'd be facedown on the cement and on your way to jail," he said.

"Well, I'm glad I'm wearing this uniform, too, then," Tasker replied coolly, despite the adrenaline coursing through his body.

By now another cop had pulled up and exited his car—more blue lights lighting up the Kentucky dusk. "Good thing you pulled over," the second cop said. "I was sitting at the next exit with a spike strip across the road. We also had a helicopter en route," he said.

Tasker was sent on his way with a hefty ticket and a summons to appear in court on the same day that they were scheduled to deploy. Beneath the bravado that Tasker and Rogerson affected as they continued on their trip, both realized that they had some growing up to do.

In Iraq in 2006, they'd grow up fast.

CHAPTER 7

Baghdad, Iraq—summer of 2006

Memories of pre-deployment hijinks rapidly fading, the Super Twelve found themselves thoroughly immersed in the task of guarding the man whom most people back home regarded as the face of the "Axis of Evil." When Saddam wasn't awaiting trial appearances in the Crypt underneath the Iraqi High Tribunal, the twelve MPs guarded him in a bombed-out former palace that was rumored to have belonged to Saddam's son Uday. It was located on a small island accessible only by crossing a drawbridge. Saddam had been moved here during the summer following his capture and subsequent interrogation at Baghdad's Camp Cropper. His relocation to the high-security island, tucked away on the U.S. military's larger Camp Victory, was a closely held secret.

The Super Twelve nicknamed the island palace-turned-prison "the Rock," after the movie about Alcatraz. It was almost as if the dictator were being hidden in plain sight, since he was the only prisoner there and confined inside a single cell that had been specially outfitted with state-of-the-art surveillance equipment. From a distance, an observer wouldn't have regarded the building as anything more than a crumbling palace. Though those holding Saddam had tried to prevent him from figuring out his location, going so far as to use blankets to cover the windows of vehicles as they moved him for court appearances, he soon deduced exactly where he was. He'd helped to design some of the buildings, after all, and in many of them his initials were carved into columns and ceilings.

The Rock was near Saddam's Al-Faw Palace, located within what had been a luxurious private retreat for Saddam's family and Baath Party dignitaries about ten kilometers from Baghdad's Green Zone, the former seat of the Iraqi government and current headquarters of the American occupation. The building they called the Rock was one of a sprawling collection of mansions and villas previously enjoyed by the party elite. The complex's strategic location near the international airport was one of the reasons it had been selected by the Americans as a major logistics hub housing thousands of troops.

Though years before in this location Saddam and his favored ministers had enjoyed hunting outings followed by extravagant dinners, and his son Uday had indulged in sadistic alcohol- and drug-fueled orgies, Camp Victory was now like a mini-America. It included a Burger King and a Subway, and it hosted a wide array of entertainers, from country singer Toby Keith to professional wrestling stars. The scantily clad WWE Divas were especially popular.

The Super Twelve had been instructed to avoid interacting with the deposed leader, while doing whatever they could to keep him safe and happy as he stood trial. U.S. leadership could ill afford even the faintest suggestion that he'd been mistreated, and they figured that the more content Saddam was, the more smoothly his trial would progress. At first, the MPs were careful not to engage him in conversation, limiting their interaction to chilly "yes, sirs" and "no, sirs." But the soldiers spent twenty-four hours a day with him, broken into three eight-hour shifts, and some thawing on both sides was inevitable.

Every once in a while Saddam would relay requests to them through his interpreter, Joseph, a burly Lebanese-American who'd been paired with the imprisoned dictator a year prior. Saddam would have the MPs adjust the thermostat or fetch some tea. It was like that for a while—awkward interactions mostly. Months later, Tucker Dawson, the youngest of the Twelve, would remember engaging in a playful—borderline childish, really—cat-and-mouse game in which Saddam would try to catch Dawson staring at him. "I was like a little kid. I'd seen him on TV, waving AKs up in the air and stuff. And now he's in a cell. And I just looked at him. Then he'd look up at me, and I'd look away real quick . . . and then he'd look at me real fast. He was messing with me. He finally looked up at me real fast and he said, 'I got you!' Then he started laughing. And I was like, 'Yes, sir.' And he was like, 'You new?' And I said, 'Yes, sir.' And he laughed, 'Huh huh huh huh.' That's how he laughed. He had a crazy little laugh."

Hutch, veteran of numerous deployments as a military police-man and aware of the pitfalls associated with growing too close to detainees, was intent on treating the mission as no different from any other. He resolved to approach his new dictator-guarding responsi-bility as "no more, no less than burning shit in barrels," one of the less enviable duties sometimes assigned to junior-ranking soldiers in Afghanistan and Iraq. He was okay with the fact that at first, "I didn't exist in Saddam's eyes." He remained wary around the pris-oner, always reminding himself that the former president was gen-erally regarded "as one of the most violent people in the world."

For the Super Twelve, then, the first few weeks of monitoring Saddam were a mix of fright, nervous vigilance, and boredom. For these young men, it was like visiting the zoo and being forced to watch a creature who, though deadly, rarely does anything but sit, only occasionally deigning to walk across the cage to thrill the assembled spectators.

Slowly, things began to change, though. One late-summer eve-ning, a few weeks into their mission, Hutch and Paul Sphar found themselves sitting across from the former dictator in the open-air outdoor rec area near his cell on the Rock. The space was about fifteen feet long and seven feet wide, enclosed by tall concrete walls that were topped with barbed wire. Though nondescript and shabby, it did offer something of value to a prisoner who spent most of his time in a windowless cell: a daytime view of Baghdad's gener-ally blue skies and a nighttime view of its generally clear evenings.

Joseph, the interpreter, sat next to the former president, creating a bizarre foursome. There was Hutch, the former bouncer; Sphar, the rotund, tattooed former grocery store clerk; Joseph, the Lebanese-American who possessed a mysterious gravitas; and, finally, seated on a wobbly piece of patio furniture, the man who seemed fated to be judged one of history's all-time villains.

Back home at Fort Campbell, it would have been rare enough for junior-ranking soldiers like Hutch and Sphar to cross paths with someone as lofty as an Army colonel, and on the occasions when they might, such as at a brigade ball, bridging the rank gap could be terribly awkward. Yet, here the two MPs were, sitting a few feet from a former head of state—an accused war criminal on trial for crimes against humanity.

Sphar, in particular, felt cognitive dissonance. He'd been raised in a broken home in the small farming community of Orland, California, where he hung out with the "rowdy kids" growing up. He and his friends had spent their time searching for harmless mischief like sneaking into construction sites and abandoned buildings. As in most small towns, everyone in Orland seemed to know everyone else. In reflecting back on his upbringing, Sphar would later say, "It never entered my mind to do college." Partly inspired by his grandfather who'd lied about his age to serve in World War II, he joined the Army out of patriotism—but he also didn't want to spend the rest of his life working at the grocery store checkout counter and racking shopping carts.

Now he was facing Saddam Hussein, who sat on a red plastic chair fitted with arms that had been taped with rubber pads to make it easier on the old man's back. Safely within "lunging distance," he and Hutch sat on flimsy plastic chairs of their own and regarded Saddam across a small plastic table. At the far end of the rec area, opposite the door that opened out to it, was a plot of dirt, from which some weeds had sprouted. Saddam had already established a routine of watering them, treating them more like beautiful flowers than the ugly growths they were.

Saddam and Joseph puffed on Cohiba cigars as they chatted animatedly, like two retirees meeting at the local diner to catch up on current events. Hutch and Sphar couldn't decipher their Arabic words. Looking up at the starry night, the two soldiers, trying to be quiet and not disturb the former president, would sometimes find themselves thinking back to late-night training exercises back home in the Tennessee wilderness, and fantasizing about the porterhouses they'd devour at Outback Steakhouse as soon as they got home.

On nights like these Saddam appeared to derive immense satisfaction from simple pleasures, like smoking his cigars. He would carefully—almost theatrically—pull a Cohiba from the empty wet wipe box that he used to carry them in. Then he'd light the cigar, savoring every inhalation before exhaling. The soldiers were puzzled as to where he got this seemingly limitless supply of cigars.

Suddenly, Joseph looked up from his conversation with Saddam and spoke to Hutch: He wants to know where you're from, your nationality.

Hutch was momentarily taken aback. Up to this point, the dictator hadn't seemed to regard him as anything but an additional piece of the patio furniture. Now he wanted to know something about him. Tell him America, replied Hutch.

No, no, before that, Joseph clarified.

Well, I guess from Europe, Hutch replied.

No, no, there is more, Saddam said, breaking into the conversation directly, showing that he'd been following the entire exchange between Joseph and Hutch in English. This was one of the first indications of how surprisingly good Saddam's English was. As the Super Twelve would learn, the prisoner only employed it strategically to engage with people he wanted to talk to.

Hutch was unsure where Saddam was headed. What's he talking about? Hutch asked Joseph. What does he want from me?

He just wants to know your heritage, Joseph said.

Hmm, well, I am also part Native American.

Perhaps Saddam had wondered about Hutch's ethnicity, as his complexion had darkened considerably from exposure to the relentless Iraq sun. Suddenly, the deposed president put one hand up like a feather behind his head, and another in front of his mouth, mimicking an Indian war cry, at which point he and Hutch burst into laughter.

Saddam's primitive radio played quietly in the background. Though he'd been offered access to more modern entertainment like a portable DVD player, he preferred the old radio with its antennas grasping for signals in the desert sky. He'd sometimes switch channels between Arabic and American pop music. Curiously, he'd always stop tuning if he stumbled across a Mary J. Blige song.

Sphar ducked inside to prepare some hot tea—Lipton. Saddam drank it constantly, enjoying it with honey and sugar. If the water wasn't boiling, he'd have the guards reboil it. When Sphar returned with the tea, Saddam beckoned for him and Hutch to come closer. This had never happened before. They approached the former president with trepidation, as they would a wild bear who'd suddenly lumbered onto a path they'd been walking down.

Saddam opened a book that had been resting on the plastic table. He flipped through it as the two soldiers looked over his shoulder. He studied it carefully through his reading glasses, occasionally pausing when a picture seemed to trigger a particular memory.

Finally, he pointed to a picture of himself as a young schoolboy. The fact that he'd even been able to attend school was the stuff of Baath Party mythmaking. A young Saddam, the story went, ambitious and desperate to escape his stepfather's abuse as well as a dismal future as a subsistence farmer in the dusty backwater of Awja, snuck out of his mother's mud hut in the dead of night and made his away alone along desolate, bandit-infested trails to his uncle Khairallah Tulfah's house in Tikrit. Khairallah was a former Army officer and Iraqi nationalist who'd spent time in prison for participating in a rebellion against the British.

Headmaster expelled me when I was young! Saddam exclaimed to Hutch and Sphar in English, still squinting closely at the figures on the page.

Saddam, who had a twinkle in his eye as he enjoyed the attention of his eager audience, told the two soldiers how the headmaster had enraged his uncle by kicking the young Saddam out of school. His uncle viewed this as an affront to the entire family.

Headmaster paid for this insult, Saddam said. When my uncle heard, he gave me a gun, told me to make sure they let me come back!

Pausing to sip his tea and take a puff on his cigar, Saddam concluded the night's story by sitting back and smiling, leaving the unfortunate headmaster's fate to the soldiers' imaginations.

Hutch would begin to notice a difference in Saddam's demeanor depending on who was on guard duty. In a weird way, it was a thrill to be one of the soldiers whose company Saddam approved of and enjoyed. This sensation wasn't unique to the Super Twelve. An Iraqi woman whose family was part of Saddam's inner circle for a portion of her childhood describes Saddam's uncanny ability to motivate people to please him, explaining, "When you did something to cause Uncle Amo's [Saddam's] admiration, he would shine his eyes on you. We all knew that shining eye look and sought it out. It was the prize, the deposit you put in the bank against a dry spell."

Saddam's deputies had felt the same way when he'd been in power, only then the consequences of falling out of favor could be deadly.

CHAPTER 8

Al-Khuld Conference Center, Baghdad, Iraq—July 22, 1979

Saddam Hussein was seated on an elevated podium in the Al-Khuld Conference Center, clad in a well-tailored suit and occasionally taking deep puffs from a large cigar. Assembled before him in the hot auditorium were almost one thousand senior Baath Party leaders, fidgeting in their seats and fanning themselves from the heat. Saddam appeared totally relaxed, almost disinterested at times. He was now, at age forty-two, president of Iraq, having won the position by virtue of his ferocity, cunning, and unmatched tactical brilliance in internal party machinations.

The session began with Taha Yassin Ramadan, a longtime deputy of Saddam's, solemnly announcing the discovery of a "painful and atrocious plot." Ramadan revealed that the plotters were in the audience, and would soon be publicly identified.

The Baath Party's secretary-general, Muhie Abdul Hussein Mashadi, was then ushered onto the stage. Mashadi had made the mistake of publicly objecting to the mysterious resignation of Saddam's predecessor, Ahmed Hassan al-Bakr, a leave-taking that had propelled Saddam into the presidency. Mashadi was reportedly given a choice: either publicly confess to participation in a plot involving twenty-two other party members suspected of sharing his objection, or know that the last sight of his life would be watching his wife and daughters raped in front of him before he was killed. Mashadi chose the first option, likely with some sliver of hope that it would spare his life.

Mashadi was visibly shaking as he began speaking, his voice unsteady and raspy. Saddam occasionally interrupted with leading questions, simultaneously making the process appear less rehearsed while ensuring that Mashadi spit out the story in all its contrived detail. Mashadi had been reduced to a pathetic actor, desperately hoping that a convincing performance might save him. Wanting Mashadi's words to pour out so that the proper people would be implicated, Saddam went so far as to get up from his chair on the podium and invite Mashadi to sit in it, so that he could be more comfortable while elaborating.

Returning to the podium, Saddam theatrically produced a list of the alleged coconspirators. Emotionless, he said, "Everyone I will name should stand up, repeat the party oath, and follow his comrades out of the hall." Saddam then slowly began reading the names. As each name was called, a man would rise to be ushered from the hall to confront his fate. Some were led out by security, while others quietly removed themselves when their names were announced, careful not to step on the toes of others as they exited. One man, in a virtual panic, rose and haltingly asked, "Did you mention my name, sir?" Saddam paused, repeated the name, and the fellow then excused himself, obediently walking to what he must have known could be his death. Sixty-six conspirators were named in all.

As if to ward off any possibility that their names would appear as an afterthought on their leader's list, some of the more shameless leapt to their feet and shouted, "Long live Saddam." They clapped violently, bringing to mind tales—perhaps apocryphal—of Stalin's audiences standing and clapping until they began to pass out, terrified to be the first to stop and thereby risk being labeled an enemy of the state. Others wept, likely out of relief at having dodged possible torture and death. In fact, Saddam was a devoted student of Stalin. He reportedly maintained a personal library that was stocked with studies of the paradigmatic tyrant.

Saddam even managed to produce a few tears of his own, dabbing them away with a handkerchief, as if he, too, were overcome by the emotion of such a painful betrayal.

As he gazed down at the terrified functionaries, a trace of disgust crossing his face, the audience cried for blood, their denunciations of the conspirators approaching a crescendo. One sycophant shouted, "We demand the execution of the traitors." Saddam played off of the crowd's contrived bloodlust, rhetorically asking, "How do we treat the traitors? You know how we will treat them—with nothing but the sword."

The executions were videotaped by Saddam's security service. The condemned men were blindfolded and forced to their knees, their hands tied behind their backs. Saddam reportedly led the way as the camera zoomed in to show a brutal succession of guns placed to the heads of the "conspirators," triggers pulled, rounds exploding into brains, bodies collapsing onto the ground, last heartbeats pumping spurts of life into the dirt. The tape was then distributed to party and military leadership.

Not even Saddam's close personal friends and associates were immune from the purge. The condemned included a deputy who'd often joined Saddam and his wife, Sajida, for dinner over the years. The man's wife was supposedly on a shopping trip to Paris with Sajida when he was executed.

The young boy who'd grown up in the rough-and-tumble town of Awja and who'd had to repeatedly learn how to master fear had himself become expert in strategically using it. He'd finally eliminated any possibility that potential rivals would oppose him. Like herds of animals startled into flight, they were driven by an instinct for self-preservation.

CHAPTER 9

Baghdad, Iraq—summer of 2006

Chris Tasker sat watching as the former president of Iraq set down a breakfast tray on his bedside table and gingerly lowered himself to the edge of his bunk. Carefully, Saddam took up knife and fork and prepared to dig into his breakfast: a vegetable omelet, accompanied by some muffins and freshly cut fruit. Tasker observed from just outside the former president's cell on the Rock, manning the small desk that had been placed there for the guards to use. Though Tasker had an abstract understanding of the violence of which Saddam was capable, he'd never really be able to feel—at that deep, visceral, fight-or-flight level—what it was like for those Baath Party officials summoned to the Al-Khuld Conference Center on that hot July day in 1979. Iraqis under Saddam possessed an intuitive understanding of the physiology of terror. It bound them together in a shared understanding that the American guards could never fully appreciate, no matter how many hours they spent with the deposed ruler.

As Tasker reflected on his new assignment, he still sometimes couldn't believe that it had only been a few years ago when he and his fellow recruits had been pulled aside during basic training for an important announcement.

Tasker had been just days away from graduating basic when his drill sergeant called the recruits into a break room at Fort Leonard Wood. Snow blanketed the sprawling base, spreading a layer of

37

gauze over Missouri's rolling hills and spurring thoughts of Christmas, which was only a couple of weeks away. The early Christmas present they received, though, was wholly different from anything anticipated. The news announcer on the break room's TV seemed chirpier than usual: Saddam Hussein had been captured. It was December 13, 2003.

Tasker and the other recruits had let out a loud cheer. Tasker felt goose bumps ripple across his body. *Shit, we got him*, he thought. Along with some of the other recruits, he feared that the war would be over before they even had a chance to deploy and put their training to use. Still fueled by the powerful motivation to serve that had led him to enlist after 9/11, he didn't want to be stuck on the sidelines back in the States when it looked like the action might come to a quick and decisive conclusion in Iraq. Was there a chance of that happening? U.S. secretary of defense Donald Rumsfeld had confidently predicted that the war might take "five days or five weeks or five months, but it certainly isn't going to last any longer than that."

The expected quick resolution hadn't materialized, and now, nearly three years later, Tasker was one of about 140,000 troops still deployed to Iraq. He sat watching as Saddam carefully began to eat his breakfast in sections, beginning with the omelet (which he'd reject and send back for a new one if it was "torn" in any way) before moving on to a sugary muffin and finishing up with fresh fruit.

Tasker noticed that Saddam had a sweet tooth. The young soldier had begun to pick up on the former president's human idiosyncrasies—some trivial, some more revealing—and he wasn't quite sure what to make of them. He supposed it made Saddam less intimidating, that he could yield to the siren call of a sugary muffin the way anyone else might.

Saddam then lit a cigar. The cigar tastes better after the fruit, he announced.

After enjoying a hearty breakfast, Saddam oriented himself toward a small mark the soldiers had placed on his cell wall to indicate the direction of Mecca, and began his morning prayers. He seemed remarkably content, perhaps because for the first time in decades he was able to rest comfortably without fearing, as one of the Super Twelve put it, that "someone in his security detail would cut his head off in the middle of the night."

Chris's quiet observation of Saddam was interrupted by the arrival of the medic, making his morning rounds. Tasker watched as Saddam, finishing his prayers and clad in his dishdasha—or "man dress," as the soldiers called it—walked over to his rickety exercise bike.

Time to ride my pony, he said spiritedly.

His pony was in fact little more than "a shitty old bike like you'd find at Goodwill," Paul Sphar recalled.

Saddam fixed his gaze on Tasker and flashed his devilish grin.

What now? wondered Tasker.

Saddam patted one leg, said, "This leg gazelle," and then patted the other one, saying, "This leg not gazelle." He paused briefly, still smiling, and concluded, "Once I get stronger, and am a full gazelle, I am going to jump that fence outside and escape." He then burst out in his trademark deep-throated laugh that reminded Tasker of "that Dracula dude from *Sesame Street*," mounted the bike, and began pedaling.

Saddam rode the bike for about ten minutes so that the medic could check his blood pressure after the moderate exertion. Following the check of his vitals, the former president then retreated to the stack of books and papers on his desk. Though papers were strewn about everywhere, he always seemed to know exactly where everything was.

Another member of the Super Twelve, Tucker Dawson, would later recall how, following one of these morning rides, Saddam had beckoned to him. Come here, he asked.

Saddam's interest was something new. At first Saddam had barely acknowledged the soldiers, though he would occasionally appear to be studying them, almost as if sizing them up. *Better be careful*, Dawson thought.

Come here, friend, Saddam repeated, gesturing to the young American.

I escape from jail before, you know, he said in his broken English, suggesting by his tone that the potential was there for him to do it again. After I try to kill Qasim, I was shot in the leg. He grew more animated as he recalled his failed 1959 assassination attempt on Iraq's then prime minister, Abd al-Karim Qasim.

So I got a horse, and ride across desert, but then I need to switch horse for a donkey, so no one knows it was me. Then I swim across river and escape all the way to Syria, he concluded.

According to former CIA officer Charles Duelfer, the notion that there is a nobility to be found in valiant struggle—even a potentially futile one—resonated with Saddam. He'd enjoyed Hemingway's *The Old Man and the Sea* when he was younger while serving time in prison for conspiring against the government. In the book Santiago, an old fisherman, risks everything to bring home a record marlin, stubbornly persisting in his effort to haul it to shore. Perhaps that doomed quest reminded Saddam of his own fearsome struggles, all of which he'd been able to endure long enough to stave off defeat.

One of Iraq's most decorated generals, Ra'ad al-Hamdani, recalls how, following some of the many occasions on which Saddam escaped brushes with death, the president would retreat to his palace in Tikrit, on the banks of the Tigris, don his bathing trunks, and reenact his swim across the river as a young fugitive on the run, desperate to evade authorities after his failed assassination attempt on Prime Minister Qasim. Indeed, the peculiar tradition would become something of a good-luck ritual for the superstitious Saddam. Unsurprisingly, when Saddam needed to escape Baghdad after the U.S. invasion, the "boy of the alleys" would once again flee to the hardscrabble villages along the Tigris that he always considered home.

PART II

THE ACE OF SPADES

He never sleeps, the judge. He is dancing, dancing.
He says that he will never die.
—Cormac McCarthy, *Blood Meridian*

CHAPTER 10

Ad Dawr and Tikrit, Iraq—December 13, 2003

"My name is Saddam Hussein, I am the president of Iraq, and I am willing to negotiate."

It was December 13, 2003, just after 8:00 p.m., when special operators from the Army's Delta Force dragged the former president from his infamous "spider hole," a coffin-like hiding place that was roughly five feet deep and just wide enough to lie down in. He was armed with a pistol but put his hands up in surrender. Less than a year before, his power extended over 170,000 square miles. That domain was now reduced to a dirt hole near the village of Ad Dawr, less than ten miles to the southeast of the mud hut in which he'd grown up.

He looked frail and dirty, clad in a raggedy black dishdasha. Always one to cultivate a stylish, debonair persona, he would have been horrified by the images of himself, which showed a man bedraggled and confused. He'd briefly resisted before the elite soldiers quickly overpowered him, resulting in a split lip. He hadn't been physically dominated in decades, and he appeared to lapse into a state of shocked bewilderment in the immediate aftermath of his apprehension. His cowed state wouldn't last long, though.

U.S. forces had been hunting for him since the spring. But even before that, for years, he'd inhabited a world populated by enemies, real and imagined. He'd survived numerous assassination attempts, waged three wars, and rarely slept in the same place for more than a few nights. Fleeing Iraq was out of the question. "Saddam would never leave Iraq; in his mind he *was* Iraq," says Judith Yaphe, a former Middle East analyst with the CIA. Rumors had abounded as to where he was hiding. There'd been reports of him hiding in plain sight near Tikrit, posing as everything from a taxi driver to a shepherd. "He was everywhere, yet nowhere," said Lieutenant Colonel Steve Russell, whose 1st Battalion, 22nd Infantry Regiment, was responsible for the area. Russell's unit called them Elvis sightings.

"He's probably pumping gas in Awja," they joked.

Saddam had made his way home to Ad Dawr. His tribal roots there ran deep, and the local population was as fiercely loyal to him as any in Iraq. It remained a poor place, a slice of lush riverfront terrain quickly giving way to arid scrubland, just as removed from Baghdad's corridors of power as it had been when he fled there more than forty years prior following the failed assassination attempt of then prime minister Qasim.

The Delta operators were recognizable from their lack of identification—name tags and rank are often missing from their uniforms—and from their beards and cutting-edge communications equipment and weaponry. They loaded Saddam into a waiting helicopter and spirited him to his Tikrit palace complex, which was only a few minutes away and had been converted into a U.S. outpost.

The palace complex, which consisted of more than ninety buildings occupying two miles of riverfront property, looked like a massive, but defunct, desert resort. It was built into the hills overlooking the Tigris and surrounded by limp palm trees that encircled a man-made lake. This had been Saddam's favorite home, a sanctuary to which he'd often escape from the stresses of Baghdad. Where he once swam and fished with his family and associates, American soldiers now sometimes water-skied.

The 4th Infantry Division occupied many of the structures, leaving a once ornate guesthouse as the base of operations for

Delta. As the burly special operators led Saddam to a spare room for temporary holding, they passed the gold trim, grandiose foyers, and plush seating that the former president had once proudly showed off to guests. Saddam spent the next two hours locked in the stark overflow room that had once served as a closet or pantry, likely touched only by Saddam's servants in years past. A medic was assigned to observe him during this span, at one point escorting him down the hall to the bathroom. Saddam was home. It was odd and dreamlike.

Soon the Delta operators were ready to deliver him to a more secure holding area in Baghdad. As they led him from his palace, Saddam halted at the top step, looking out at the city lights of Tikrit. It was the birthplace of his idol, the legendary warrior Saladin, and had been the center of his universe. Saddam slowly looked right, then left, and took a deep breath, making what appeared to be a conscious effort to soak it all in. It was as if he was taking a mental snapshot to carry with him into the unknown.

Having finally begun to descend the palace steps, Saddam suddenly stopped again. He objected to the raggedy black dishdasha in which he'd been captured. Look at me, he said. I am Saddam Hussein, president of Iraq. Do you want the world to think that this is how the United States treats heads of state?

One of the operators ran inside for some other clothes. "We'll make you look like a rock star," he said reassuringly.

As the special operations team loaded Saddam onto a helicopter, they put a mask over his head so that he wouldn't be able to observe the top-secret technological gear inside the cockpit and fuselage. A number of Delta operators piled in alongside Saddam for the ride. Tex, a burly southerner, wedged his muscular body in next to Saddam. As the chopper made its way south toward Baghdad above the Tigris River valley, Tex felt Saddam gently patting his leg.

For the wily dictator there was always one more game to play.

CHAPTER 11

Omaha, Nebraska—January 10, 2004

Rod Middleton, a veteran FBI agent, was at home on a freezing Saturday afternoon a little more than a month after Saddam Hussein's capture. The temperature outside was dipping into the low twenties, and Middleton was thankful to be warm inside, painting the bedroom of his family's new house yellow—his wife Barbara's favorite color. After the absurdly expensive cost of living in Washington, DC, where Middleton had been assigned to FBI Headquarters, they were thrilled to now be able to afford a nice house on a golf course. Middleton had spent his first summer in Omaha supervising a Joint Terrorism Task Force, as well as enjoying more free time with his family. He'd even managed to get his golf handicap down to a respectable 12.

The phone rang, interrupting his painting. It was FBI Headquarters calling with a simple question. Would you like to participate in the interrogation of Saddam Hussein?

It took Middleton a moment to digest what he'd been asked. He was a marathoner with a competitive streak, and his curiosity was definitely sparked, but he explained that he'd first need to check with his wife. After more than twenty years with the Bureau, including considerable time hopscotching across the globe conducting terrorism investigations, he'd been looking forward to a change of pace with his quieter assignment in Omaha. And his wife had been looking forward to it even more.

46

Nonetheless, Barbara Middleton said yes and two weeks later, having read everything he could find on Iraq and Saddam, Middleton found himself on a C-5 headed to Baghdad. He was traveling with George Piro, a Lebanese-American Arabic-speaking agent who would lead the FBI's interrogation; Tom Neer, an FBI behavioral profiler; two intelligence analysts; and an Arabic linguist.

Baghdad, Iraq—first few months of 2004

On the sprawling U.S. base at Baghdad International Airport, Middleton, Piro, and the rest of the interrogation team set up shop in a seagoing cargo container that had been outfitted with secure communications equipment, enabling them to remain in constant contact with their headquarters in DC, as well as other intelligence and law enforcement community personnel stationed around the world.

After they began settling in, the FBI team was updated on the progress of Saddam's interrogations thus far. It had been a little over a month since the Iraqi leader had been captured, and by now he'd been questioned by the CIA around twenty-five times. The Agency's primary focus had been to determine the status of Iraq's WMD (weapons of mass destruction) program, since U.S. forces had turned up nothing after nearly a year of searching, and leaders in Washington were growing impatient. The interrogators were also interested in gathering sensitive, "real-time" intelligence to assist in capturing high-level former regime figures and to contain an insurgency that seemed to be gaining momentum. In the prior month, forty-eight American soldiers deployed to Iraq had been killed.

The CIA team had found Saddam to be a frustratingly elusive interrogation subject, though, and the decision was made in Washington to turn the questioning over to the FBI, since they'd be more capable of building a case against Saddam that could eventually be presented before an international or Iraqi tribunal. A decision had *not* yet been made on how the former Iraqi president would be brought to justice for alleged crimes against humanity.

The FBI team agreed that George Piro would be the lead interrogator, in part due to his proficiency in Arabic. It was a remarkable opportunity for the young FBI agent, who at that time had only been with the Bureau for five years. Joining Piro in questioning Saddam would be Middleton. Despite the fact that both men spoke Arabic, they'd still be accompanied by an FBI linguist who would function as translator. Tom Neer, the FBI's behavioral analyst, set about developing a strategy to extract information from Saddam based on his psychological profile, which had years before been described by the CIA's Jerrold Post as that of a "malignant narcissist" with certain psychopathic attributes. The FBI team prepared themselves for someone who would exhibit a combination of extreme grandiosity and paranoia, no constraints of conscience, a lack of empathy, and zero respect for the truth.

In short, they didn't expect their job to be easy.

The interrogation room featured white cinder-block walls and an overhead fluorescent light. It was simple and bare, containing only four folding chairs for Saddam, his two FBI interlocutors, and the linguist. Each day, Saddam would don his dishdasha, sometimes adding his warmer dark jacket if it was cold, pray in his small cell with the Koran he was provided, and meet with his interrogators. His back would be to the far wall, with the interrogators between him and the door.

As the sessions began, Saddam took a seat and crossed his legs, seemingly perfectly at ease.

The interrogators' first challenge was determining how to address him.

Saddam had been insistent that he remained the lawful president of Iraq, and, sure enough, he introduced himself as such at their first meeting. The men grudgingly went along with it in the belief that immediately challenging him would just trigger a narcissistic rage and be counterproductive. Said one team member: "If we'd instantly created an adversarial situation, we wouldn't have gotten a conversation at all."

The team believed that by establishing a rapport with Saddam they could get him talking, which might eventually result in his volunteering more information than he might have otherwise. Indeed, at one point in the CIA's sessions Saddam began coughing and was hacking up phlegm. His interrogators provided him with cups of tea.

The FBI's behavioral profiler didn't even like to refer to the sessions as an interrogation, preferring the more innocuous term "a conversation with a purpose." The men found Saddam to be an eager talker in response to softball questions that allowed him to embellish his accomplishments. He would point out to Piro and Middleton that it wasn't important what people thought of him now, but rather what they'd think in five hundred or a thousand years.

People will love me more after I'm gone than they do now, he said, steepling his hands together. He assiduously maintained an upright posture, never slouching.

Though never betraying angst, he was always wary. If presented with a string of three or four easy questions followed by one that probed a thornier topic, he never took the bait. He either clammed up, changed the subject, or grew defiant. In response to a question about his use of chemical weapons in the Iran-Iraq War, he responded, "I will discuss everything unless it hurts my people, my friends, or the Army," thereby, with one declaratory sentence, establishing as off-limits just about everything that would be of value to the Americans.

At one point he expressed his displeasure at a line of questions by saying, "I thought this was a historical discussion and not an interrogation."

"He really was a genius in an interpersonal setting," says Jeff Green, one of the agents who worked on the interrogation. He explained that Saddam "was in complete control of himself and always maneuvering—little micro-maneuvers—to remain in control of the situation."

Saddam was in no way constrained by the truth. He'd deny complicity in alleged war crimes during the Iraqi invasion of Kuwait, despite the existence of Baath Party archival footage showing him threatening his deputies with firing if they didn't brutally crush Kuwaiti resistance. In one recorded Revolutionary Command Council meeting, Saddam growls in his guttural Tikriti dialect, "If I hear that you did not cut the tongue of talking there in Kuwait deep from the esophagus, I will replace you all, including the Republican Guard Commander. You tell the Kuwaitis, 'You are Iraqi now,' and if anyone opens his mouth, you need to empty all your bullets in his throat."

At no point did Saddam express any remorse or regret. With Middleton's concurrence, Piro decided to show Saddam excerpts from a BBC documentary that highlighted the human cost of his decision to drain the marshes south of Baghdad, which he thought was a sanctuary for Shia rebels. The decision essentially exterminated a way of life for hundreds of thousands of Iraqi "Marsh Arabs" who were driven from their homeland. Piro and Middleton were curious to gauge the deposed president's reaction to the displays of human suffering that directly resulted from his policies.

Wait, this is not a neutral film, interrupted Saddam as the film began to play. It was prepared in the West and aired in America, he said, as if that fact alone proved it to be hopelessly biased.

Piro and Middleton let it play on. Scene after scene of Marsh Arab suffering unfolded. One clip showed footage of Marsh Arabs fleeing north in rags, left with nothing more from their previous lives than what they could carry. Saddam watched intently, before observing, "They do not look scared, they look happy."

Twenty-three minutes into the film, Saddam had had enough. It is exercise and prayer time, he announced.

We can postpone that, said Piro, trying to exert his authority over the prisoner.

No, I think this has been enough, said Saddam, adding breezily, we can watch it another day, why rush?

CHAPTER 12

Baghdad, Iraq—first few months of 2004

Two years before the Super Twelve would meet him, the American who most often saw the former president at his least guarded and most candid—other than his interpreter—was medic Robert "Doc" Ellis.

"Act confident, don't be afraid," Ellis was told the first day he approached the dictator's cell. "This guy is good at picking up nonverbal cues." Ellis's assignment was to examine Saddam daily while he was being interrogated at Camp Cropper. Leaving no doubt as to Ellis's mission, a colonel had pulled the medic aside and emphatically explained, "Saddam Hussein cannot die in U.S. custody. That would be a huge embarrassment to the president and the United States of America. Do whatever you have to do to keep him alive."

Ellis, an African-American master sergeant in his early fifties, with a medium build, round face, and mustache, had grown up "around thieves, robbers, and murderers" in the notorious Pruitt-Igoe projects in St. Louis, one of the closest American approximations to the violent village from which Saddam came. According to Ellis, "I had to fight all the time. I was robbed and beat up more than once, shot at, and saw people being killed." So right away there was the possibility of a special rapport between the medic and the now infamous "son of the alleys."

"He was once a street fighter like I was when I was a kid," Ellis later recalled. "I was fighting thugs and bullies in the projects, he was fighting gangs in Tikrit."

When the two men met, Saddam was always clad in one of his two dishdashas (one white, one gray, which he carefully hand-cleaned and let air dry under the Baghdad sun in his outdoor rec area each day) and usually finishing a vegetable omelet for break-fast, which he enjoyed with mushrooms, onions, and tomatoes. Occasionally, he'd already finished eating, and Ellis would stand by patiently as he said his morning prayers.

Like many of the Americans who dealt with the imprisoned Saddam, Ellis was initially struck by how, despite being "locked up and in isolation," he nonetheless "carried on like a man in charge." Saddam would refer to Ellis as "Doc," echoing the respectful hon-orific that U.S. troops have long assigned to combat medics. Ellis elected to address the aging prisoner simply as Saddam, as opposed to the more formal "Mr. President." He asked Saddam how he felt, before going on to check his blood pressure and body tempera-ture. Aside from high blood pressure, Saddam seemed reasonably healthy.

In the evenings, Ellis would usually make the trek over to Sad-dam's cell alone. He didn't need an interpreter, as he recognized that Saddam's English was better than he let on. When Ellis arrived, the cell sometimes smelled of Lysol, which Saddam often used to clean up in the afternoon. The former president was always well groomed and made sure that his cell—while cluttered with books and papers—was free of dirt and dust. It would gradually become clear that Saddam had begun to see these daily medical checks as more than a simple formality to which he needed to submit. One night, Ellis had retrieved Saddam's daily blood pressure med-ication and was about to hand it to the former president when Saddam suddenly interrupted, saying "No" and waving the med-ication away. Saddam was sitting at his desk writing on a yellow legal pad—something that he seemed to spend a lot of time doing.

Looking up from his composition, Saddam said, "I know you can't understand, but I like to read this to you." He picked up the pad and began reading what he'd written in Arabic. The rhythm and cadence suggested it was a poem. After a few minutes, Saddam finished, looking up from his creation with satisfaction, and said, "Now, we do medicine."

That, Ellis later observed, "was the beginning of our relationship."

The same scenario would be repeated in the weeks and months to come. Ellis recalls, "Saddam would read and I'd sit and listen, and then he'd try to explain to me. Basically, he wanted to socialize, and we did." Ellis viewed this social interaction as part of "treating the whole person, and not just their aches and pains." In his mind he was carrying out the colonel's broadly defined order to make sure Saddam remained healthy under his watch.

On a few occasions Saddam tried to convince Ellis that cigars and coffee helped with blood pressure. Ellis knew that argument didn't hold much water, but he figured, if it helps Saddam relax it may be worth a shot. Thus it was that Ellis found himself in the peculiar position of helping to requisition some of Saddam's favored Cohiba cigars. Saddam would be visibly thrilled when Ellis, sometimes accompanied by the camp doctor, arrived, modest gift in hand. He stood to greet them, exclaiming, "My friends, three Cohibas," waving the men from his small cell down the hall and outside to an open-air rec area. He moved a few of the plastic chairs out there, inviting them to sit and join him for a cigar in the Baghdad twilight. In contrast to his vigilant and cautious comportment in the interrogation cell, Saddam appeared enlivened by these encounters.

As they sat outside, the conversation could often be mistaken for the sort of happy-hour barroom banter that men around the world—who may not know each other particularly well but are feeling relaxed and in the mood to socialize—might engage in to pass the time. Saddam's interrogators had adopted a remarkably convivial approach, and with his trial still in the distant horizon, the former president appeared untroubled and relaxed.

Predictably, during these evening cigar sessions, the conversation would sometimes turn to women (though there were few around to receive any of the men's attention). When it did, Saddam would alternate back and forth between the persona of a somewhat lecherous older man and that of a more caring and devoted husband. Though the Americans were sometimes confused as to which of his multiple wives he was referring, it was generally believed that he harbored the most affection for his second wife, Samira.

As the men sat and enjoyed their cigars under Baghdad's clear skies, Saddam sometimes tried his hand at a ribald joke. He particularly liked the story of how "one man from our village had a wife without much passion, so he went to his tribal elder, who found him a younger wife who had enough passion for an entire tribe." At that point he let out one of his deep "a ha ha ha" laughs.

Saddam's lustier side was evidenced on another occasion when he visited a clinic for a minor medical procedure and was treated by an attractive female Army nurse. When the nurse asked Saddam if she could roll up his sleeve to take a blood sample, he replied in Arabic, "You may begin with the sleeves and continue as far as you want." Saddam poured on what he regarded as his charm, relishing her attention. The story goes that after the visit, Saddam, still bewitched by the nurse's spell, resolved to grow a beard, not in an effort to appeal to Islamic extremists, as CNN pundits later speculated, but rather because he thought it looked better.

During one of Ellis's morning visits, Saddam revealed a softer, more romantic side. He asked Ellis if he had a family, to which Ellis answered that he had two sons and had recently been married for a second time. Saddam seemed genuinely curious to learn more about Ellis's family, and so Ellis resolved to retrieve some pictures of them from his room to show Saddam the next time he made his evening rounds.

When Ellis returned the next night, he handed the pictures to Saddam, who slowly started leafing through them, pointing to some of the people and asking who they were. He seemed to take a particular interest in Ellis's brother-in-law, Lionel, who was an entertainer in Las Vegas and was clad in a flamboyant suit and sun-

THE ACE OF SPADES

glasses. Saddam kept returning to the picture, finally pointing at Lionel, sitting back, and letting out a hearty laugh. When Saddam got to a picture of Ellis's wife, Rita, he looked it over, paused, seemed to consider something for a minute, and then volunteered, "I will write a nice story for her."

Sure enough, when Ellis returned the next day, Saddam proudly handed him one of his loose sheets of yellow legal paper, on which he'd written in Arabic:

> The night is defeated at the end of life
> The stars are getting lost and the dawn is of joy with you
> My heart has risen after winning his dream
> Comfort is settling and hardship has gone away
> My soul has flourished and his flower has matured
> And God has blessed us for the remainder of our lives.

Ellis was amazed that the former dictator had taken the time to compose something for his wife, and that he'd been so happy to present it to him. But *that* was Saddam, a man of extreme contradictions. The man who in an effort to extinguish threats posed by Shia militias had ordered the systematic draining of the Mesopotamian marshes—forcing the migration of hundreds of thousands of people—would now hover over his weeds as a doting parent would his child. The man who, prior to his capture, had struck terror in the hearts of millions of Iraqis, would save bread crumbs from his meals and carry them outside, where he'd feed them to visiting birds. Eventually they grew to expect these daily snacks from the old man and would sunbathe on the barbed wire. Saddam would greet them enthusiastically, proudly gesturing to Ellis and saying, "Look, they come!" One day the birds didn't arrive as expected, and Saddam seemed deflated. He lamented to Ellis, "They must have eaten earlier."

Ellis spent one especially long day helping to fill sandbags that were intended to protect against mortar attacks. After he finished, he remembered that the day before, Saddam had requested some sanitizing wet wipes. Saddam was a notorious germaphobe and was constantly trying to clean and disinfect. So that evening Ellis arrived at Saddam's cell with wet wipes in hand. Handing the box to the former Iraqi leader, Ellis was surprised not to receive his customary gratitude. Saddam, Ellis recalls, "looked at the box skeptically and pulled out one wipe, holding it between his index finger and thumb." After staring at it for a few long seconds, he said, "These are kind of . . . dainty."

Ellis couldn't believe that the man who sometimes feigned an inability to speak English had just used such an unusual word. Struggling to keep a straight face, Ellis dutifully promised to snoop around for some larger ones—"man-sized," he joked to Saddam. It just so happened that Ellis's wife, Rita, had recently included a box of large wet wipes in a care package she'd mailed, so the next day Ellis returned to Saddam's cell and, with not a little pride, presented them. This time he was greeted with the familiar smile of appreciation. Saddam chuckled to himself, looked at Ellis approvingly, and said, "Papa Noel."

Ellis would sometimes wonder if he was falling prey to the same desire to please Saddam that was ubiquitous among Saddam's deputies when he was in power. Having grown up observing the worst humans were capable of in his tough neighborhood in St. Louis, Ellis wasn't naive. He was well aware that Saddam was guilty of atrocious acts. And he recognized that the former president's apparent charm and graciousness could very well be an effort to manipulate him. *Watch your back, Ellis,* he told himself. *Don't let him get to you.*

Puzzlingly, the items for which Saddam was most grateful were often nothing special. If his behavior was simply a manipulative act, all he really had to show for it was an almost pathetic assortment of worthless scraps, such as his plastic chair with crude rubber armrests, large wet wipes, an old antenna radio that he was forever struggling to adjust to pick up a signal, an exercise bike that wouldn't be out of place in a 1980s YMCA, and perhaps his most extravagant indulgence, his beloved Cohiba cigars. One day

THE ACE OF SPADES

Ellis couldn't help but just ask Saddam, flat-out, how he seemed so content with so little, having gone from "silk sheets to an Army cot." Aside from the old exercise bike, it would be possible to shove what remained of Saddam's worldly belongings into a shopping cart. Yet the man who'd lost nearly everything remained unbothered. He responded to Ellis's question simply, saying, "I remember how I grew up. I was a poor farmer."

Dr. Ala Bashir, Saddam's personal physician for nearly twenty years, recalled about his former patient, "He actually lived a simple life. I saw him many times sleeping on a mattress on the ground. He would eat like any other Iraqi—I saw him frequently cook for his guards. He lived in ordinary houses and rarely stayed in those palaces he built. I have no doubt that Saddam genuinely didn't like the luxurious life."

There may have been other reasons for his surprising contentment. For the first time in decades, the dictator was essentially safe for the near term, as the mechanics of his eventual trial were still being worked out. On a daily basis, he was as secure as he'd ever been. Dating all the way back to when he was dodging the blows of an abusive stepfather, he'd known no extended periods of peace and security. For a man who'd narrowly escaped multiple assassination attempts, and spent much of his adult life engaged in cataclysmic foreign wars, ruthless internal power squabbles, and a desperate flight from capture, the secure simplicity of life in a cell may have seemed like a relief—at least for a short time.

Ellis was relaxing in his room late one night when he heard a knock on the door. He'd been watching a goofy comedy on his computer and sighed at being pulled back into reality. Unexpected late-night visits were never good. Reluctantly, he dragged himself from his cot and shuffled over to open the door. It was one of Saddam's American guards telling the medic that the dictator had asked for him. Shaking the cobwebs from his head, Ellis made the short moonlit walk to Saddam's cell and asked his patient what was wrong. Saddam told him his stomach hurt. Ordinarily, Ellis would have been annoyed if a detainee had interrupted his limited off time with what appeared to be such a mundane problem, but he decided to cut Saddam some slack since he rarely complained of any discomfort.

Ellis provided Saddam with a few over-the-counter options to lessen the pain, and the Iraqi selected some Tums. Upon taking them, Saddam seemed lost in thought for a few moments. Then, emerging from his reverie, he mentioned that he'd given the same chewable wafers to his daughter when she had a stomachache as a young girl. He reassured Ellis, "I break them in half for her."

Consecutive bursts of bad news issuing from back home in St. Louis would soon pull Ellis from Saddam's universe and interrupt his efforts to make sense of the Iraqi's psychology. Ellis received a flurry of increasingly troubling emails from Rita, reporting that his mother was gravely ill and wanted to see him. Taking a short break from his frantic efforts to arrange for an emergency leave trip home, Ellis called the hospital where his mother was being treated and heard the words that no son—much less one who is thousands of miles away in a war zone—wants to hear: "I'm so sorry, Mr. Ellis, I'm so sorry."

Feelings of guilt consumed him.

His sadness was compounded by his increasingly conflicted feelings toward this bizarre mission in Iraq. He had trouble accepting that he was ostensibly serving his country by providing medical care to a man accused of war crimes, who could end up dead anyway, while being unable to help his mother.

CHAPTER 13

Baghdad, Iraq—April 2004

The secure phone rang on FBI agent Rod Middleton's desk in the small shipping container in which he spent much of his time, diligently typing up summaries of Saddam's interrogations that had amounted to little more than a revisionist history of his rule. March had rolled into April, and Saddam's questioning still appeared to be yielding little of real value.

It was FBI Headquarters.

You think we should make a change? his supervisor asked, referring indirectly to Piro's leadership of the interrogation. Folks here aren't happy, the man continued, and you can imagine the pressure they're under to get something out of this guy.

Middleton could understand. An entire war had been launched in part on the premise that Saddam possessed weapons of mass destruction, and now, nearly a year after the invasion, they were no closer to finding anything than they'd been on day one. Further, there was an insurgency that seemed to be gathering strength. Still, Middleton thought Piro deserved more of a chance. Plus, changing the role of lead questioner would disrupt the team, and could even suggest to Saddam that they were desperate.

No, leave him in place, Middleton said. Give him some more time.

Tom Neer, the FBI's profiler, and some others on the team had suggested a phased approach. In it, Piro's rapport-building first phase would eventually lead to a "reckoning" phase that would feature subtle efforts to wound Saddam's pride and cause him to begin to doubt his legacy. That would be followed by a final "bartering" phase in which he'd be provided an opportunity to rehabilitate his image in exchange for cooperation. Neer's perception was that "the only reason Saddam got out of bed each day was to manage his legacy."

Piro remained wedded to the first phase, though. One team member recalled that he seemed "obsessed with his personal relationship with Saddam." This, of course, invites the question: Who was working whom? Was Piro cleverly developing what seemed to be a genuine relationship with Saddam to extract information, or was Saddam, in fact, co-opting the young agent?

"Eventually you have to change the tone," Middleton would later say about the Piro-led interrogation. "You can't just sit there and be all 'happy happy joy joy,' marching through history and drinking tea."

Middleton didn't remain to see whether Piro's approach would ever yield dividends, since it was eventually time for him to go home. He'd promised his wife, Barbara, that he'd only stay three months. His last day in the country found him nearing the completion of a four-and-a-half-hour interview with the notorious "Chemical" Ali. It was a warm day, about ninety degrees, but not oppressive. Middleton was wearing his standard cargo pants and untucked button-down safari-style shirt. Suddenly, incoming mortar fire rocked the camp, shaking the trailer in which they were meeting. As this was not entirely uncommon, Middleton and Ali paused, and then continued their discussion. Middleton tried to expeditiously wrap up what he considered to have been a successful session. Majid had provided valuable details on Saddam's gas attacks that could be used as evidence during an eventual trial. Eager to finally begin his long journey home, Middleton typed up his report, attached it to a secure email addressed to FBI Headquarters, and hit send.

After dodging incoming mortar fire as he raced across the base in his Toyota Hilux, Middleton caught the next C-130 out to Jordan.

He arrived at the Sheraton in Amman in the middle of the night and headed straight for the refrigerator, where he grabbed a bottle of vodka and took a deep breath, attempting to exhale the last three months of stress and frustration. He picked up the phone and dialed.

Across the world, Barbara was preparing dinner for their two children. Suddenly, the phone rang. Baby, I'm out, she heard her husband's voice say.

Middleton didn't know what *else* to say. The events of the past twenty-four hours had been too surreal to distill into anything that would make sense to a woman cooking dinner for her kids in Omaha, Nebraska. After the call ended, he flipped on the hotel's TV and tried to muster interest in its coverage of the Masters golf tournament, but he still felt deracinated, unable to grab hold of "real life."

The next day, as he trekked through various airports, completing the last legs of his journey home, he struggled to reconcile the sight of throngs of business travelers frequenting Cartier and Hermès with the heat, dirt, and violence he'd left behind. The brightly lit concourses he walked down were an overwhelming pastiche of perfection, shininess, and noise. Middleton's mind raced: *Something is wrong—things are too nice.*

At Omaha's Eppley Airfield he finally met Barbara, and they drove together to pick up the kids at school. When they pulled up to their home Middleton was amazed to see all his neighbors and their children gathered in his driveway, where they'd hung red, white, and blue decorations and posted cardboard "Welcome Home" signs. It was unexpected and overwhelming.

"It may have been the best feeling I've ever had in my life," he says.

Their gratitude had a purity that had been absent from the previous three months, during which he'd been exploring the darkest recesses of human nature. He was at once proud of what he felt had been a successful interrogation of Chemical Ali and frustrated by the nagging sense that Saddam had bested them. As much as anything, though, he was glad to be "out of that craphole with shells dropping on me."

The next day Middleton was standing on his back deck, overlooking the golf course. Staring out at it, he was overwhelmed by the bright green—such a departure from the barren Iraqi moonscape to which he'd grown accustomed. He broke down crying.

Just over a year later, Barbara would die unexpectedly. Her heart had quit at the age of thirty-seven from idiopathic spontaneous ventricular fibrillation. The doctors couldn't explain why. Middleton, it turned out, had spent some of the last months of his wife's life listening to Saddam Hussein pontificate, and now he was left to care for their two children, fourteen and twelve. The proud Air Force veteran, former SWAT team member, and terrorism investigator was crushed. Plans had already begun to be made for Middleton to return to Baghdad that July. This time, though, he wouldn't be going.

CHAPTER 14

Baghdad, Iraq—spring of 2004

Back at Camp Cropper, having buried his mother, Robert Ellis found Saddam seated on his small cot, his back against the wall, writing feverishly on his yellow legal pad. With each passing day, he appeared to be growing more fixated on getting his thoughts on paper. He'd always had an obsessive preoccupation with his legacy, and he must have recognized that this could be a final opportunity to ensure his reflections were captured for posterity.

There were a few evenings when Saddam seemed especially eager to unburden himself of issues that must have been weighing on him. Perhaps the afternoon interrogations had touched a nerve and he was still stewing. On this night, clearly agitated, he protested to Ellis what he claimed were the unfair accusations the Bush administration had leveled against him to justify the invasion.

"Why soldiers come?" he asked, appearing genuinely confused as he mimicked soldiers firing rifles. "They didn't find anything." He was referring, of course, to the search for WMD that had been the pretext for the invasion.

Ellis usually did the best he could to avoid getting too drawn into these discussions. He'd been instructed not to discuss controversial topics. Plus, he didn't really have good answers to Saddam's rhetorical questions. Still, he couldn't always extricate himself from conversations that wandered into fraught areas. Once, Saddam had asked how things were going with the American mission in Iraq.

Sometimes he heard explosions and gunfire from his outdoor rec area, so it was no mystery to him that the Americans had been encountering resistance in their efforts to establish security. That time, Saddam took Ellis down memory lane, recalling how under President Reagan his relations with America had been smooth. He made a gliding motion with his hand to underscore this point. Finally, he asked, What does America have to gain from this? He appeared puzzled.

Ellis was silent.

Then Saddam added, portentously, "They'll wish they had me back."

Late one morning, as he was enjoying a cigar with Saddam, Ellis got an urgent call over his two-way radio to report to his headquarters. Hustling over, he was given two notes, one of which told him to call his wife immediately, and the other to call the Red Cross. Ellis took a deep breath. He knew this drill, and it wasn't a good one. First he called Rita. She told him that his brother Larry was in the hospital in critical condition, with a blood pressure of 80 over 20 and bleeding from the esophagus. Ellis didn't need to hear much more to know that his brother was dying. Larry was only fifty-two, and the news dizzied Ellis. He fought to steady himself.

While the news came as a surprise, Ellis had long known that Larry had been traveling a dangerous and self-destructive road, mixed up with drugs, alcohol, and petty crime. After Ellis had taken a few minutes to collect himself, he hurriedly packed his bags and began what would be another marathon journey home.

That afternoon, sitting in Baghdad Airport's passenger terminal, coated in sweat and surrounded by an assortment of other soldiers heading home on leave, Ellis felt his mind wander. Moments like these, in which a person is suddenly yanked from the desensitizing daily grind, can sometimes engender brief epiphanies. He realized that it had been six months to the day since his mother had died.

Later, strapped into the seat of a C-130, Ellis felt red-hot anger boiling up. He was angry to once again be marooned overseas during turmoil at home, and angry at his brother for having made so many resolutions over the years to reform his ways, only to again succumb to temptation. Besides the deep ache of what he knew would likely be his brother's death, Ellis recognized that something else was nagging him; something he'd just experienced and couldn't make sense of.

Before he'd left for the airfield, Ellis had a made an impromptu visit to Saddam to let him know about his brother, and that he'd be going home and wouldn't be checking on him for a week or so. Ellis didn't want Saddam to wonder where he'd gone. The medic shared the truth partly out of a sense of duty, since he was responsible for Saddam's well-being, but also because, as much as he may have hated to admit it, he found himself not wanting Saddam to be upset. As it turned out, the feeling may have been mutual. After Ellis was done explaining that he was losing his brother and would be gone for a while, Saddam stood up, hugged him, and said, "I will be your brother."

CHAPTER 15

Baghdad, Iraq—late June 2004

Rod Middleton had already been home in Omaha for a few months—his life upended by the sudden loss of his wife—when George Piro finally got Saddam to admit that he'd abandoned his program to develop weapons of mass destruction and had never had a substantive relationship with Al Qaeda. When finally pressed by Piro, Saddam denied any contact with Osama bin Laden—the same denial he'd later volunteer to the Super Twelve. He explained to Piro, "I am a believer but not a zealot," before adding, "religion and government should not mix." To his CIA questioners he'd voiced similar concern about the danger of religious leaders infiltrating government, remarking that the "turbans" must never be allowed to wield power.

It had taken more than six months, and countless hours of listening to Saddam pontificate, but Piro considered this admission a success.

Just before Piro was to head to the airfield to board a plane back to the States, he went to see Saddam one last time. As they smoked a cigar, Saddam smiled. You know what, the former dictator said, maybe if I get off, we can start a consulting firm together.

Piro joined in on the joke. Sure, if you can shake these charges, I'll think about it, he said.

Saddam then embraced him, kissing him on the cheek three times. If the dictator felt that he'd been bested by the interrogator, it didn't show.

As Piro boarded his flight out of Iraq, he was full of pride. He felt his plan had worked—that his patient efforts to develop a relationship with Saddam had succeeded in eliciting valuable information. Others, including many on his own team, disagreed. After all, many in the intelligence community had been convinced for some time that Saddam no longer retained WMD, and few seriously entertained the notion that he ever allied with Al Qaeda in a meaningful way. Beyond those two admissions—if Saddam was even to be *believed*—what really had been accomplished?

The CIA's John Maguire later put it this way: "Saddam *did* win. We miscalculated who we were dealing with—he was all about framing history and his place in Iraq. For us to think we could befriend him, build rapport, and get him to tell all was naive in the extreme."

Conservative pundit Tom Joscelyn would be the most unsparing in his criticism, writing: "The truth is that the [interrogation] memos are almost completely worthless from an intelligence perspective. Saddam turned the FBI into his own personal stenographer."

Despite the fact that the interrogation had ended with the former president volunteering little of intelligence value, the FBI *would* go on to gather more than enough evidence from interviews with Saddam's codefendants, former government officials, and the testimony of victims—as well as from a large trove of archived Baath Party material—to build a solid case for Saddam to be tried for crimes against humanity.

The new question was, could Saddam be as effective in steering his trial as he was in steering his interrogators?

PART III

CONDEMNED

He lay as one who lies and dreams
In a pleasant meadow-land,
The watchers watched him as he slept,
And could not understand
How one could sleep so sweet a sleep
With a hangman close at hand.

—Oscar Wilde,
"The Ballad of Reading Gaol"

CHAPTER 16

Amman, Jordan—fall of 2005

Dr. Najeeb al-Nuaimi, a former justice minister in Qatar, was packing up and preparing to leave a human rights conference in Amman, Jordan, when a female Lebanese lawyer approached. Confronting him, she said: Raghad Hussein, Saddam's daughter, would like to meet with you. She'd like you to join her father's defense team. She lives here in Amman.

Saddam's trial for crimes against humanity had recently begun at the Iraqi High Tribunal (IHT) in Baghdad, and Raghad was looking for more legal firepower to help defend her father from the charge of ordering a crackdown in Dujail following the failed 1982 assassination attempt that resulted in the alleged killing of 148 Shiites.

Dr. al-Nuaimi had been no supporter of Saddam's regime.

No, no, he immediately responded to the woman's overture. This trial is a farce, and my presence would only give it legitimacy.

Please, the woman went on, undeterred. Raghad really wants to meet you.

After more entreaties and demurrals, Nuaimi finally relented, grudgingly. Despite his disapproval of Saddam's rule, he *did* believe that everyone deserved a fair trial. His commitment to this principle had previously led him to represent more than seventy suspected terrorists held at Guantánamo Bay.

• • •

Raghad had lived in Amman since fleeing Baghdad not long after the invasion of Iraq in 2003. It was the second time she'd sought protective asylum in Jordan, the first time being 1995, when she and her sister, along with their husbands and families, had fled following a feud with her unhinged brother Uday.

Raghad's Lebanese emissary arranged to have Nuaimi—a bear of a man with a forceful personality—picked up and delivered to Raghad's villa. Upon seeing Nuaimi enter, Raghad crossed the room to greet him. Her home had morphed into a shrine to her father, its walls blanketed with photos of Saddam and other mementos celebrating his time in power.

Thank you for agreeing to represent the president, she began, amiably enough.

She still carried herself as the daughter of a president, having inherited a charisma and presence that were familiar to those who'd known her father.

Nuaimi possessed his own gravitas, though, and wouldn't allow himself to be charmed by Raghad. I didn't agree to anything, Nuaimi politely corrected her.

Oh, I see, Raghad responded, thrown a bit off balance by this deviation from her script. It was clear to the former justice minister that she was a person accustomed to getting her way. Let me get you some tea, she said, trying to create an atmosphere of relaxed affability.

Thank you, Nuaimi replied, and gave a curious look around as the tea was delivered.

He commented on the nice furnishings, for which Raghad apologized, explaining that much of the furniture was actually made in America.

Nuaimi chuckled, and said that the Americans were also capable of producing nice furniture.

Raghad asked a few other women in the room to please excuse themselves, and they obediently followed her instructions. A moment later she asked, Why are you refusing to represent the president? You're a human rights advocate, and he's an Arab leader who is specifically requesting you.

First, Nuaimi replied, you keep addressing him as "president." He is not "president" anymore. He is your father, and I'll refer to him that way.

Raghad winced. It wasn't common for anyone to speak to her like this. Indeed, when she'd defected to Jordan with her husband back in the nineties she'd whispered conspiratorially to trusted Jordanians that she, in fact, was the decision-maker in her marriage. She forced herself to smile, feigning a relaxed insouciance in the face of Nuaimi's brusque declarations.

Second, the former justice minister said, I have a number of conditions before I would consider accepting.

But wait, Raghad said, confused as to why the encounter had gotten off to such a poor start; Ramsey told me this was a good idea. She was referring to Ramsey Clark, the former U.S. attorney general who'd recently agreed to defend Saddam. Since leaving government, Clark had undergone a radical transformation, using the exposure afforded by his defense of international pariahs—ranging from Charles Taylor to Slobodan Milošević—to lambast U.S. foreign policy.

I know all about Ramsey, Nuaimi said. I know he has lots of strong political views and motivations. I'm not like this. I do not know your father. I've been against his regime all my life. Politically we are not, and never have been, on the same side. He paused, as if to consider something, before continuing. On the human side he has a right to choose a lawyer, just as much as any person in this world. If your father wants me, he has to write a letter to me asking me to represent him, and he must sign it. I will accept that. I will not ask for one dollar in fees or expenses. If I do this, it will be voluntary. I'm not so cheap that I can be bought.

No, no, we can surely pay you, Raghad quickly offered.

I don't need your fees. I'm a rich man, Nuaimi said. I'm not looking for business. Having defined the initial parameters of the relationship, he felt compelled to confront Raghad with what he judged was an inescapable truth: You have to understand that your father will be hanged, he said.

Don't say that! Raghad responded. I received some messages saying that Bush may send someone to mediate, and that my father may be able to go to Qatar as a guest.

This kind of bullshit isn't going to happen, Nuaimi said, hoping that his bluntness would shake her of what he considered to be her fantasies. The trial will occur, and it will end with a ruling that your father must hang. You must understand, I was a minister in my country. I know how these things work. This will be a manufactured court, not a real one, and your father will never receive a proper defense. All of the judges will be motivated by ethnic politics and hatreds toward your father.

Raghad turned pale. There's nothing we can do?

Nuaimi didn't answer.

It was tough to tell if she was more upset by this sobering assessment of her father's situation, or by the implication that she'd never return to Iraq as part of an eventual restoration of Baath Party power. Nuaimi suspected the latter. I'm just telling you the truth, he finally said, bringing their meeting to a close.

CHAPTER 17

Iraqi High Tribunal, Baghdad, Iraq—summer of 2005

Salaam, Mr. al-Nuaimi, Saddam said to the newest member of his legal team. The former Iraqi ruler and the former Qatari justice minister were meeting in a bare subterranean antechamber beneath the courtroom at the Iraqi High Tribunal in Baghdad's Green Zone. Joining Nuaimi were other members of Saddam's defense team, including Ramsey Clark, Khalil al-Dulaimi, and Khamis al-Obeidi—the latter two being Iraqi lawyers. As greetings were exchanged the Iraqis kissed Saddam's hand in the traditional sign of respect and deference. Clark and Nuaimi did not.

The men then took their seats around a plain table. The room was filled with Saddam's cigar smoke—something that the health-conscious Nuaimi grew to find more and more unpleasant as their relationship deepened. A uniformed Iraqi man with a beard quietly took a seat near them by the door without identifying himself. Nuaimi looked the man over suspiciously, hoping that his icy glare would be enough to convince him he wasn't welcome. The Iraqi didn't budge.

Who are *you*? Nuaimi asked him coldly.

I'm a sheriff of the court, the man responded.

Nuaimi had no idea what that meant, and wouldn't be easily cowed. So what are you doing here? he pressed.

Nothing, just sitting, he said.

Is this a restaurant or something? Nuaimi asked, a sarcastic edge to his voice.

I have my instructions, the man responded.

Bring me your boss, demanded Nuaimi.

The man obliged, and returned shortly with a Marine officer.

What's wrong? asked the officer, suggesting by the tone of his voice that his intent was to defuse, rather than escalate, the situation.

There is something called confidentiality with a client, and this man won't leave, Nuaimi explained.

Let me ask my boss, the Marine responded.

Nuaimi bristled, fed up with the delay. Listen, if he doesn't leave, we're not meeting, Saddam will have no legal representation, and I'll tell the court and the world what a terrible operation you're running.

Okay, okay, let's go, said the Marine, ushering the mysterious bearded man to the door.

As the uninvited observer was being led out, Saddam let out a deep laugh and began clapping. You must have charisma to talk like this, he said approvingly. He shot a withering look at his Iraqi attorney and added, Someone always sat in my meetings with Khalil.

I am not Khalil, Nuaimi replied, as Khalil looked on, silently embarrassed but unwilling to spar with these two heavyweights.

Can we speak freely now? asked Saddam.

Sure, there are no dictators in the room, said Nuaimi, the double meaning in his choice of words intentional.

Oh, Dr. Najeeb, very clever, Saddam responded, laughing once again. He knew the Qatari was an accomplished lawyer, and no apologist for his former regime.

Before we start, is there anything you really need? Nuaimi asked Saddam. Not legally, just in general. Is there anything you haven't been provided and would like?

I can *ask*? said Saddam, appearing surprised to be afforded such an opportunity. Wasting little time in deliberating, he said, I need new shoes. I've been wearing these for two years and they're not mine. He then quickly gave Khalil his size, as well as sizes for some new suits and other articles of clothing he wanted. It would be the last time during the discussion that Saddam would perk up.

As Nuaimi pivoted into terrain less comfortable for the former dictator, it became clear that Saddam was more concerned about his appearance, and the optics of the trial as it was broadcast across the Middle East, than in actually developing a legal defense.

Nuaimi's pessimism certainly did nothing to encourage Saddam's more active participation in the development of a legal strategy.

There is nothing we can do to succeed in this trial, Nuaimi bluntly announced. These judges are just politicians, he continued, and this is nothing more than a play whose script has already been written.

No one spoke to Saddam with this kind of candor. After an uncomfortable silence, the former president quietly said, "I know." He added that because of this they would need to focus their energies on the media. They would need to communicate to the world that the proceedings were a farce. Let's forget about this as a court capable of making a fair judgment, Saddam went on, and use this as a platform to show the criminality of the entire occupation.

Before Saddam got carried away, Nuaimi felt compelled to again disabuse him of any delusions he might still be harboring. You *will* be hanged, the Qatari said.

That was enough to stir Ramsey Clark from his silence. Why are you talking like this? he demanded, frustrated by what he felt was Nuaimi's almost gratuitously candid pessimism.

Nuaimi explained to Clark that he had to be brutally honest to offset the influence of some Iraqis who'd been feeding Saddam's hopes that he'd be freed, that Iraqis were fighting and beating Americans outside the prison every day, and that his supporters would soon be able to break him out. This picture they're painting is garbage, Nuaimi continued, and they're cheating Saddam by misleading him.

What's *your* opinion, Mr. al-Nuaimi? Saddam asked.

The former dictator could sometimes seem downright reticent, something those meeting him for the first time could find disarming. Dr. Ala Bashir, his physician for nearly twenty years, once said about him, "When you talk to him, he listens to you. I've never known a better listener. He doesn't seem like the same man who does these cruel things."

My *opinion*? Nuaimi responded incredulously. What opinion? What I've said is fact.

Okay, if this is going to happen, it will happen, Saddam finally said with a curious mix of resignation and determination. Can you speak with the Americans and tell them that as the chief of the Iraqi military I need to be shot and not hanged? he asked. The notion that he might be hanged like a common criminal—an "Ali Baba," as Iraqis called them disparagingly, or worse yet, a traitor—seemed to bother him more than death itself.

Nuaimi then recounted to Saddam the story of Hermann Göring, who committed suicide on the eve of his scheduled hanging at Nuremberg.

I am a Muslim, I won't do this, replied Saddam, dismissing the idea but not lashing out at its messenger.

Years later, Nuaimi recalled that he'd expected to meet a "tough" Saddam, a poor listener who demanded obedience and acquiescence from his team. Instead, he said, "I liked him from that first meeting."

CHAPTER 18

Iraqi High Tribunal, Baghdad, Iraq—fall of 2005

"Shrugi," Saddam whispered venomously as he passed the chief prosecutor, Jaafar al-Moussawi. It was 12:21 p.m. on October 19, 2005, and Saddam was the last of the eight defendants to enter the Iraqi High Tribunal courtroom. He was there to stand trial for crimes against humanity, allegedly committed during the 1982 crackdown in Dujail. Saddam's slur was a crude insult used to deride Shia Muslims from regions bordering Iran as backward and uncivilized—it was akin to calling someone a hillbilly or redneck in the United States. Ancient sectarian hatreds were never far from the surface during the trial, and since the proceedings were televised, the hatreds would sometimes boil over for the world to see.

Unlike some of the other defendants, Saddam had had his handcuffs removed. On this day, he couldn't have looked more different from the bedraggled man pulled from the spider hole. Nattily attired in a gray suit with no tie, his beard freshly trimmed, he clutched a green Koran embossed with gold script. It was huge, the size of a large old-fashioned leather dictionary, and he carried it proudly and prominently, as he would throughout the trial. It was a symbol that played well with Sunni partisans despite widespread recognition that he'd hardly lead a pious life.

The room surged with energy as Saddam strode proudly into it, similar to when a musician finally takes the stage after a period of anxious anticipation. The swagger of Saddam's courtroom entrances reminded Paul Sphar—the portly American military policeman from Texas who, like the rest of the Super Twelve, didn't arrive in Iraq until the trial's late stages—of a WWE wrestler entering the ring. As Saddam entered, the other codefendants and his defense lawyers rose obediently in deference to the fallen leader, an embarrassing display of fealty that the authorities made sure wouldn't happen again. In subsequent court appearances, the deposed ruler was led in first.

Saddam stood before the Iraqi High Tribunal, the "internationalized domestic court" that featured statutes borrowed almost verbatim from the International Criminal Court and combined them with Iraqi criminal procedure. Five Iraqi judges would preside over Saddam and seven codefendants. Remarkably, Salem Chalabi, the nephew of Ahmed Chalabi, the prominent Iraqi Shiite expatriate whose shrewd lobbying had helped convince the Bush administration to go to war, had heavily influenced their selection. The close associations among the court, the Americans, and prominent Iraqi Shia politicians who'd been vocal opponents of Saddam's regime would almost immediately invite questions about the judges' objectivity.

Saddam had come full circle, as he was being tried just down the road from the Republican Palace, nerve center of the absolute power he'd wielded until a few short years ago. The tribunal had been established under the auspices of the American Coalition Provisional Authority (CPA). As the security situation in Baghdad continued to deteriorate, the concussive booms of nearby American artillery shook the courtroom walls with greater frequency. Some of the American civilians assisting the Iraqi government in the Green Zone spun this as a positive development, evidence that the military was really "taking it to the enemy." Others viewed the escalating violence with creeping dread. Most assumed that Saddam would be emboldened by the auditory reminders that the occupation wasn't going as swimmingly as the Americans would have him believe.

The chief judge as the trial began was Rizgar Amin, a Kurd with a receding gray hairline and mustache whose reading glasses often perched atop his hawk-like nose. He alone among the judges allowed himself to be broadcast on camera despite the obvious security risks that posed to him and his family. A black robe with white tassel was draped over his suit and tie as he sat on a large leather chair on an elevated bench in the front of the courtroom, flanked by his fellow judges. The defendants were led to their seats in a wooden dock, with two rows of three and a rear row of two. They were enclosed by a chest-high wooden railing connected to the ground by wooden legs, and seated in comfortable large black leather chairs. Behind them, on the other side of a Plexiglas wall, was a gallery stocked with media and "local observers," including a number of prominent Shia who'd either been persecuted by Saddam or worked to overthrow him.

Judge Amin began, saying: "If you please, your full name." As he spoke, he directed Saddam to the microphone situated in the front of the defendants' wooden dock.

The former Iraqi president responded, "In the name of God, the merciful and compassionate: Men said to them, 'A great army is gathering against you' and frightened them, but it only increased their faith. They said for us Allah sufficeth—"

"Mr. Saddam," Amin interrupted, "we want to record your ID information."

Saddam, unfazed, continued, "—and He is the best dispenser of affairs."

"Your full name, please," Amin asked again, growing impatient. "Mr. Saddam, all we're asking now is your ID information—that is, your name, surname, profession, and residence. You will then have your turn to speak. Could you please give us your ID information?"

"I do not want to trouble you, because your way of asking is acceptable and because you are acting as a judge," Saddam responded, oddly gracious in the middle of his calculated disruption.

"Mr. Saddam, we want your ID information."

"Now who and what are *you*?" Saddam replied with a question of his own.

"Please give us your ID information and things will become clear," Amin responded.

"I should know who is knocking on the door," Saddam retorted, using one of the folksy aphorisms of which he was fond.

"We are the Criminal Court of the First Instance at the Iraqi Supreme Crimes Tribunal," Amin responded, for some reason deigning to respond to the former president.

"And were you all judges before?" Saddam countered.

"These matters have nothing to do with you," Amin said, refusing to take Saddam's bait this time. "Please be seated, Mr. Saddam. We will get back to you after we have finished noting the ID information of the others," Amin finally concluded. He seemed to have resigned himself to failure in his very first attempt to move the trial forward.

"I hold no grudges against any of you," Saddam continued, "but for the sake of justice and out of respect for the great Iraqi people's desire when they chose me, I say this: I will not answer the questions of this so-called court despite my respect for its members, and I maintain my constitutional right as president of Iraq—"

Amin again tried to interrupt Saddam, who seemed poised to launch into a filibuster.

Undeterred, Saddam barreled on with his peculiar mix of faux deference and bullying. "I will not take up much of your time. I only wish to comment on your request that I identify myself. I do not recognize the party that appointed you and I do not recognize the assault [war on Iraq] because anything built on the wrong basis is in itself wrong."

"Meaning that you will not identify yourself," Amin responded, appearing more and more impotent from his perch on the bench.

"No, because I do not recognize you," Saddam said, growing more defiant, his rough Tikriti dialect now reverberating through the courtroom.

"Fine, please sit down," Amin finally ordered.

"Mr. Awad al-Bandar, please identify yourself," Amin continued, trying to move on and restore a semblance of normalcy to the proceedings.

"My identity is my headdress, but since they took it away from me on my way here, I no longer have an identity," Bandar said.

Bandar had been the former chief judge of the Iraqi Revolutionary Court, which had supposedly sentenced more than a hundred innocent Dujail residents to death in response to the assassination attempt on Saddam. He would prove to be a menacing presence throughout the proceedings. To those guarding him, his antipathy toward the Americans stood out dramatically, especially in contrast to the avuncular manner exhibited by Saddam. Some of the Super Twelve would take to calling him "the Judge" in a tone that was not without some fear.

"Give us your name, father's name, and surname," Amin continued, still trying to score his first procedural victory over the defendants, who were proving, unsurprisingly, to be a disagreeable and uncooperative lot.

"My headdress is my identity. Why was I not allowed to wear my headdress? I am an Arab and I am wearing a dishdasha—"

"All I want is your name," Amin pleaded.

"My headdress is my identity; you robbed me of my identity when you took away my headdress."

Amazingly, Amin again relented. "Who took it?" he asked, before ordering that the headdress be retrieved.

"Bravo!" cheered Saddam, no doubt both pleased and even amazed that this circus-like atmosphere he and his colleagues were fostering was rising to full spectacle.

"They took *all* our headdresses," he then piled on.

"Bring all their headdresses," Amin ordered, adding, "When you come to this court, you may wear whatever you wish as long as it conforms to public decorum."

There was a delay as the defendants' headdresses were retrieved and returned to them in the dock. As they were distributed to the waiting defendants, Judge Amin noticed that the sound system was malfunctioning, and he was forced to adjourn for five minutes so that it could be fixed.

Following a short break, the chief prosecutor, Moussawi, concluded the day by presenting the charges, accusing Saddam and his codefendants of committing crimes against humanity when 148 residents of Dujail were allegedly jailed, tortured, and, in many cases, executed by hanging following a presidential decree signed by Saddam on June 16, 1984.

Following a rather uneventful session sandwiched between lengthy recesses, the court reconvened on December 5 with Saddam's chief lawyer, Najeeb al-Nuaimi, contending that the court itself was illegitimate, as it had been established during an illegal occupation. He also presented the somewhat specious argument that the court should have no jurisdiction over crimes alleged to have occurred before the American-led occupation and the establishment of the tribunal. Nuaimi concluded by lamenting the "great interference by the current government in the affairs of the judiciary," an accusation that would prove prophetic, even if it didn't have a material impact on Saddam's ultimate guilt or innocence.

Next came the first witness from Dujail, who'd been only fourteen at the time of the failed assassination. He bravely agreed to appear on camera to provide an account of the persecution he suffered, and the crimes he witnessed. For that he would pay an awful price, as two of his cousins would be kidnapped following his appearance, a nephew would be killed, and a brother shot and paralyzed.

A perceived lack of security for trial participants would cast a lingering cloud over the proceedings. Within months of the trial's opening, two defense attorneys would be killed by gunmen as they drove through Baghdad, likely targeted for their role in defending Saddam.

As violence spread outside the courtroom, the testimony inside brought to life the violence of the previous era, no less horrific. The fourth session of the trial, on December 6, featured some of its most wrenching testimony as a woman, speaking from behind a screen, with her voice deepened and intentionally distorted to safeguard her anonymity, spoke haltingly as she provided graphic testimony of the suffering she endured at the hands of Saddam's security forces. She described how "I was forced to take my clothes off. They lifted my legs, tied my hands, beat me with cables, and gave me electric shocks. There were more than one, and it was as if I were their banquet." Cultural sensibilities likely prevented her from spelling out in any more detail the brutal sexual abuse she suffered.

Plunging ahead bravely, the woman recounted more of the horrors she witnessed and experienced, many of them at Abu Ghraib prison, which had been a house of horrors under Saddam long before the abuses of U.S. guards there made international headlines. She described how one of her relatives, who was mute and deaf, was brought in front of the women and stripped naked, whereupon the guards pulled on his penis and taunted, "What kind of creature is this?"

Saddam busied himself taking notes during her testimony, occasionally taking a break to look up and smile.

The day concluded with Saddam being provided the opportunity to cross-examine the witnesses, a peculiarity of Iraqi criminal procedure that the Americans had sought to avoid, as they knew it would afford Saddam countless opportunities to pontificate, not only to the gallery assembled in the courtroom but to the entire Arab world. It surprised few when he did just that.

He began solemnly, again referring to himself in the third person. "These testimonies, brother first judge, are meant to disparage a march of thirty-five years. During that time, we built a great Iraq with our tears. This march is being disparaged. I do not believe that any true Iraqi, and you are a true Iraqi, accepts this. As judges, you know how Saddam Hussein has taken care of the judiciary. Leave Saddam Hussein alone, for he is not the issue. But this is your history and you shed blood for this. You fought eight years to score victory against Iran. You fought all the Satans of the West and put them in their place. By God, if you had two percent of what the United States has, it would not have dared to attack Iraq. By God, two percent only . . ."

Somehow he managed to spit out 139 entirely extraneous words before Judge Amin finally cut him off, saying, "Please ask the witness the question that you want to pose."

Saddam ignored the judge, continuing his melodramatic oration. "The Americans and the Zionists want to execute Saddam Hussein. They will be smaller than a bedbug if they do not execute him. Why fear the execution? Saddam Hussein said he was ready to be executed if this served the people when he was a secondary school student. He was sentenced to be executed three times. This is not the first time. Saddam Hussein and his comrades do not fear execution."

Judge Amin tried once more to corral the dictator, who had now shifted fully into his stump speech—one he was able to deliver powerfully, and which he hoped would resonate with his Sunni Arab target audience.

"We will listen to the witness, and you have the right to question. If you have any question to the witness . . . ," Judge Amin interjected plaintively as the former dictator steamrolled on, commanding the world's stage once again. He hadn't yielded to one of his countrymen in thirty years, and he wasn't about to begin now.

CHAPTER 19

Baghdad, Iraq—2006

Vic, we're gonna move tonight.

No longer hesitant in the company of Saddam, the Super Twelve had grown confident issuing orders to the former president, though they continued to do so in a respectful fashion.

"Vic" was short for "Very Important Criminal," and a few of Saddam's American guards would sometimes call him this. After having returned to the Rock following a court recess, Specialist Rogerson had received word that they had to deliver Saddam back to the Iraqi High Tribunal late that night for a resumption of the trial. He wanted to provide advance warning so Saddam would have time to pack his bags for the late-night helicopter ride. Depending on the number of days court would be in session, Saddam and the Super Twelve might be bunking in the Crypt, the dark labyrinth of cells underneath the courthouse, for up to a week, so they needed to pack appropriately. Like many older men who become somewhat set in their ways, Saddam didn't like to be rushed or surprised, but he was generally pleasant and agreeable as long as he was given time to prepare for any changes to his routine.

Once Rogerson had given him the heads-up, Saddam began his usual pre-movement rituals. First he went outside and made sure to water his plants—weeds, really—growing in the small plot of soil in his rec area. Next he began to pack his olive green Army-issued duffel bags for the week or so he might be away.

He'd carefully make sure that the items he expected to need first were located near the top. Meanwhile, his suits, which the Army delivered for dry-cleaning on the Rock, were carefully placed in garment bags for him by the Super Twelve. The former president took his appearance seriously, as each public exposure since his ignominious capture was an opportunity to rehabilitate his image. Finally, he packed his notepads and pens, as well as his empty wet wipe box full of cigars, right near the top of his bag for quickest access when he arrived at court and would meet with his lawyers.

When he finished packing, Saddam stepped into his shower, where of course the guards were supposed to keep an eye on him to make sure he didn't slip and fall, or intentionally try to hurt himself. The shower was covered with a rubber mat that was pieced together like a jigsaw puzzle to further prevent the risk of injury.

As Saddam showered, Specialist Rogerson noticed that Perkins was staring at the prisoner for almost the entire duration of his soaping and rinsing.

Hey, Perkins, you don't need to stare a hole in the guy, said Rogerson.

Though Perkins was guilty of nothing more than scrupulously following his instructions not to take his eyes off Saddam, he'd pay for it in the remorseless environment that was deployed life for the twelve young men. Even Saddam sometimes joined in the banter, laughing when Rogerson told him the story of Perkins peeing his pants. The former president, who'd probably lived decades surrounded by people cowering in fear, seemed to relish the opportunity to "be one of the guys."

The rest of the Super Twelve could never quite figure out the eccentric Perkins. The older soldier's fashion style could be bizarre. Hutch remembered the time Perkins showed up at an Army "Company Fun Day" family picnic back at Fort Campbell clad in ankle-length Capri pants and Roman-style sandals, looking like a middle-aged German bureaucrat who'd taken a wrong turn on his way out for a Sunday stroll. The razzing Perkins caught wasn't really deserved. He was just sufficiently different to be the butt of bored soldiers' jokes.

Having packed and showered, Saddam lay down on his bunk and tried to fall asleep, since he knew that his night's rest would be interrupted by the movement to the IHT. Rogerson gently closed the cell door as Saddam pulled his sheets over himself, but it was more a formality than a security measure. During the day the cell door was generally left ajar so Saddam could move about to his rec area or access some of his storage space as he pleased. Between his cell on the Rock and freedom there were so many layers of security that escape would have been unthinkable. Hutchinson joked that life on the Rock was like the old *Andy Griffith Show*, where the town drunk, Otis, let himself in and out of his cells as he pleased.

Saddam would miss all of this when he was at the IHT; the Rock's space, his books and papers, the outdoor rec area, and, most of all, his privacy. (He was alone on the Rock, whereas the other codefendants were bunked in cells adjacent to his underneath the courthouse.)

It was the middle of the night when Rogerson warned Saddam that it would soon be time to go. Twenty minutes, he announced into the darkened cell.

Saddam had been asleep for hours and was still a little groggy. Okay, friend, thank you, he said quietly, gingerly pulling himself out of bed.

In the backs of their minds, the soldiers couldn't help but wonder if there might eventually be a day when they'd have to do this knowing that for a sleeping Saddam there'd be no more tomorrows, no reason to hurry. There was too much to do right now, though, so those thoughts were shunted aside.

Twenty minutes later, it was time to go. Are you ready, Vic?

"I am ready when you are ready," Saddam replied sportily.

As long as he received his twenty-minute warning, Saddam would almost always respond agreeably. Months later, the Super Twelve would find themselves parroting some of Saddam's favorite expressions, like this one, as they prepared to leave on missions. "I am ready when you are ready," they'd say to each other in faux-Arabic-accented English as they put on their gear.

Saddam had dressed and gathered his belongings for the journey. A few of the soldiers approached to help carry the heavier bags, as well as the garment bag containing his suits.

When Hutch reached over to help Saddam with one of them, momentarily struggling with its weight, he joked to Saddam, "What the hell, did you stuff Ali in this bag?"

Saddam laughed heartily, and would even repeat the joke to Chemical Ali after he arrived at the IHT and reunited with his codefendants.

They moved to the waiting Humvees outside. Whenever they left the Rock, even though they were safely within the larger, well-guarded perimeter of the enormous American Camp Victory, the Super Twelve left nothing to chance, with six of them pulling external perimeter security, weapons locked and loaded, and the other six escorting the prisoner to the Humvee.

Who is the driver? Saddam asked.

It's Hutchinson, same as usual, Lieutenant Andre Jackson replied.

Not yesterday it wasn't, said Saddam, apparently still smarting from the fact that the younger Dawson had driven too fast, the bumps rattling the Humvee and causing discomfort to the sixty-nine-year-old Saddam's brittle body.

Don't worry, today it's Hutch, the lieutenant reassured him.

Okay, that's good, said Saddam, looking relieved.

Despite his best efforts to drive carefully, whenever Hutch struck a bump in the road, he heard Saddam let out an exaggerated groan. Anyway, it took only a few minutes for the Humvee to roll across the darkened base to the two Black Hawk helicopters that stood waiting.

Though the ten-minute chopper ride to the Iraqi High Tribunal's courthouse had grown somewhat routine, it was still always a bit surreal. The city looked so peaceful, twinkling seductively in green through the soldiers' night-vision goggles. For just a moment it was possible to imagine that the roughly seven million below had made a pact to put aside the sectarian hatred and violence, to come together as one and do the things that people do when grudges are laid to rest: gather outside in cafes, laugh, debate the prospects of the local soccer clubs. But then, inevitably, the chopper would descend to the landing zone, and reality would wipe away all such thoughts.

CHAPTER 20

Iraqi High Tribunal, Baghdad, Iraq—December 21, 2005

On day six of the Dujail trial, prosecutor Jaafar al-Moussawi, who resembled a bulldog in both appearance and behavior, began to question Saddam about his claim that he'd been mistreated by his American captors. "Did they beat you? Did someone truly beat you?"

"Yes, many times, all over my body," Saddam responded.

"We will see who is responsible and hold them to account," the prosecutor responded.

Saddam would not be so easily mollified, however. "The Americans are your masters. How can you bring them to account?" he snarled.

Moussawi knew Saddam's game and went along with it—in fact, raising him. "If you've been tortured then I'll ask for all of you to be transferred into Iraqi custody," he said, fully aware that Saddam hadn't been mistreated, and that the defendants would be horrified to be transferred to the Iraqis.

Moussawi laughed during an ensuing break in the proceedings, proud to have beaten Saddam at his own game. He'd prevailed in the skirmish not because of his mastery of legal nuance, but because he understood the way his adversary's mind worked.

For his part, Saddam knew that he'd been bested—that his bluff had been called. He wasn't devastated, though. It had been worth a try. Indeed, as he was led from the courtroom that day, he was supposedly overheard joking with an American guard, "I know you've treated me very well, it was just something I said for the court."

The Super Twelve were always proud of the way they treated Saddam—never giving him more than he was due, but according him the dignity they felt the old prisoner deserved. Some might have said that going on "cigar runs" for the dictator exceeded the minimum incarceration standard—by a lot—but the money for that came from someone higher up. They never did find out who the source was.

It was in pursuit of cigars one late afternoon—as an oppressively hot day gradually gave way to a more tolerable twilight—that Privates Paul Sphar and Tucker Dawson drove from the Rock to the "hajji mart," only ten minutes away. They always looked forward to this errand, as it meant they could stock up on some of the supplies that made deployments less miserable. The hajji mart offered every kind of tobacco product and energy drink imaginable, as well as an endless supply of DVDs. Since the troops weren't allowed to drink alcohol, this was about as good as it got for soldiers looking to unwind.

The two young soldiers borrowed a Humvee for the short drive across the Green Zone to the open-air bazaar. Even as they embarked on these sunset expeditions they were aware of how ridiculous it was that two young "joes," to use Army parlance for junior-enlisted soldiers, were cruising around Camp Victory in search of tobacco for Iraq's deposed dictator. *No one would ever believe us*, they thought as they rolled past scores of unwitting American soldiers. The MPs were aware of the strict orders they'd been given to keep their mission a secret.

As they perused the plywood stalls, the two young men made an odd pair: the portly and tattooed Sphar, who was no stranger to punishment for appearance-related infractions, such as not having shaved prior to morning formation; and the young North Carolina native Dawson, who could have just stepped from an Army recruiting poster. Back at Fort Campbell, when Sphar had first seen the handsome Dawson emerging from his white Ford Bronco with a surfing bumper sticker on the back, he'd thought to himself, *This guy should be in a fraternity somewhere.*

The local merchants hawked their wares, cigarettes hanging from their mouths, as the two MPs navigated their way through the outdoor bazaar. They soon found a stall where they knew Cohiba cigars—Saddam's favorite—were sold, and handed the stall keeper several bills. They then turned their attention to the DVDs being offered at a neighboring stall. The discs were dirt cheap, sometimes two for a buck. The quality could differ wildly, though, with some literally recorded in a theater with a handheld camera and people occasionally visible as they wandered past during filming. Sphar picked out a horror movie eight-pack, featuring all of the *Friday the 13th* movies. It would add to his substantial collection; by the end of the deployment he'd have almost an entire footlocker of horror and B movies.

Having accomplished their mission, the soldiers climbed into their Humvee and rumbled back to the Rock, special acquisition in hand, looking forward to delivering the cigars to their prisoner and then settling in to watch one of their newly purchased flicks.

Saddam was, as always, pleased to receive his beloved cigars. He extolled their virtues to the two young MPs "almost as if he were trying to sell them to us," recalls Sphar.

CHAPTER 21

Baghdad, Iraq—2006

My boys were always getting in trouble when they were young, Saddam said to his interpreter, Joseph, and to Hutchinson one evening as they sat together outside at the Rock. As usual, the men relaxed on flimsy white patio chairs in the rec area, a cocoon of tranquility that Saddam could retreat to after having the eyes of the world on him in the courtroom. The prison walls insulated him from the violence ravaging Baghdad, though he could occasionally hear the faint crackle of gunfire in the distance. As the fall season set in, it could get cool in the evening, and on this night the men clustered around Saddam's "fire"—the name he'd given a small space heater that he'd sometimes bring out once the sun had faded below the concrete wall. Saddam seemed to enjoy naming inanimate objects, like the antiquated exercise bike he referred to as his "pony." He was in a good mood, reflective and talkative, puffing contentedly on his cigar and occasionally nibbling on dinner leftovers from a Tupperware container. One would never have guessed that he was on trial for his life.

Always getting in trouble, Saddam said again, almost to himself this time, as if replaying scenes of his boys' hijinks in his head. You couldn't take your eye off them for one minute, or they'd be grabbing sweets they weren't supposed to have, he continued. What about your boy, how is he doing? Saddam asked Hutch.

He's doing good, Hutch answered about his son, who was

THE PRISONER IN HIS PALACE

still a baby. I can't wait for him to get bigger so we can go fishing together. Hutch had always been an outdoorsman, and he was raring to teach his son a few tricks.

Saddam's eagerness to hear stories about the soldiers' children suggested to Hutch that maybe the anecdotes reminded him of raising his own kids. He was curious if Saddam ever had doubts about how he'd raised them. He couldn't be sure, but he felt that beneath the blustery facade he could detect a hint of regret at how Uday, in particular, had turned out.

While Saddam and Hutch enjoyed trading stories of their respective families, there frequently seemed to be an element of delusion on Saddam's part. When Hutch was having these discussions with Saddam he was unfamiliar with the extent of Uday's savagery, which subsequently became the stuff of nightmarish legend.

"All I knew at the time about Uday was from skimming a *Maxim* magazine article," Hutch recalls.

In fact, as all of Iraq and much of the world would come to know, Uday Hussein was a monster. Adjectives failed to do justice to his catalog of cruelty. When asked about Uday, everyone, even those who might be described as Saddam apologists, agreed that he was as close to evil incarnate as a human being can be. That Saddam could affectionately reminisce about his son's childhood, and feign parental indignation at the theft of some treats—as if that captured the extent of Uday's shortcomings—reveals either the depth of Saddam's delusion or the deliberateness of his manipulation.

While Saddam had busied himself with the affairs of state, gradually delegating more responsibility to his second son, Qusay, Uday descended deeper and deeper into a netherworld in which he gorged himself on perverse sexual pleasures and sadistic deviancy. His ravenous sexual appetite struck fear in attractive young women and their families across Baghdad. The terrifying reality was that no one was safe from his wolfish lust. He'd have friends and associates recruit scores of women five days a week—with the other two days reserved for what he called "fasting"—and deliver them to the Baghdad Boat Club on the Tigris. There, following gluttonous consumption of alcohol and drugs, he'd line the women up for inspection and select one or two for the evening. If they were lucky, they'd be released the following morning, perhaps rewarded with a few hundred dollars and some jewelry, along with strict instructions to keep their mouths shut.

Uday displayed a particular interest in young brides, whose husbands were often forced to stand by impotently as he had his way with them. One groom, devastated by the thought that his love had been ravaged by Uday on the night of their wedding reception at Baghdad's posh Hunting Club, shot and killed himself. Not long before the American invasion, an eighteen-year-old bride who'd dared to resist Uday's advances had been dragged by Uday's goons into a bathroom, where they tore her wedding dress from her body and locked her in to await Uday's arrival. Shortly after Uday got there, a maid heard screams emerging from a nearby bedroom. She later saw the girl's limp body dragged out on a military blanket, acid burns covering it, her life extinguished just as it had begun to blossom.

Uday's rampages, and the state apparatus that enabled them, reminded many of the reigns of the most depraved Roman emperors. Tongues were clamped in place with pliers so that they could be sliced off with a scalpel, ears were lopped off, and welder's torches were pressed against bodies convulsing with terror. One friend of the family says that "the day Uday discovered the Internet was a black day for Iraqis," as he took to researching ever more exotic torture techniques. He even obtained—or created—an iron maiden that was discovered at one of his properties following the U.S. invasion.

Uday was drunk with a power that only one man in Iraq could even try to restrain. Sadly for Iraq, Saddam didn't try very hard.

Uday's *least* destructive addiction was cars. In a country whose economy had been shattered as a result of ruinous wars and crippling international sanctions, he accumulated an extraordinary collection of hundreds of high-end sports cars. One staffer's entire job was to fill binders with pictures and information on expensive cars so that Uday could make his selections.

Saddam enjoyed discussing cars with his American guards, perhaps recognizing that this was one topic that could unite a sixty-nine-year-old former Arab dictator with his twentysomething American minders. Adam Rogerson specifically remembers one cool evening spent talking cars with Saddam. Specialist Art Perkins was also on duty, though he would periodically excuse himself to duck inside and freshen Saddam's glass of tea. While Rogerson did his best to maintain a degree of professional distance from the man he was tasked with guarding, something of a rapport had developed between the men.

"If you went in there and you were intimidated, he could smell it, and he'd have his way with you," Rogerson says. "But if you went in and were like, 'This is who I am, this is who you are, this is how it's going to work, and either we'll get along or we won't'—if you were stern but friendly, he respected you for that."

As the three men sat in the outdoor rec area on this night, Saddam's transistor radio spitting out its mix of American and Arabic tunes in the background, Saddam volunteered: *You know, I am looking for some love. When I get out of here, I'm going to get married again. I'm not done.* He was dressed in his dishdasha and favorite dark jacket to help ward off the evening chill of the Baghdad night.

Really? Rogerson asked, returning Saddam's lecherous smile, suggesting he was in on the joke. *How do you* do *it?* he said, feigning amazement at the old man's professed virility. Rogerson was amazed at how easily Saddam could transition from penning nostalgic poems about his family to fantasizing with his guards about bedding more women.

Soon the conversation shifted. *How is your family doing, my friend?* Saddam asked.

I miss them, sir, Rogerson responded. By this point in the evening he was tired, the result of one of the long runs across the sunbaked base that Sergeant Luke Quarles, who was training for

Army Special Forces selection, had dragged him on. Hopeful that some conversation would help the shift go by quickly, he explained to Saddam that he'd married his high school sweetheart when they were both very young by U.S. standards. He was only twenty, and his bride had just finished high school. He went on to tell Saddam how much he missed his three brothers back home, sprinkling his remarks with colloquialisms that may have been sailing over his listener's head. Saddam nodded, though, quietly visualizing the wholesome portrait of Americana that Rogerson was unself-consciously painting.

Something in the young soldier's narration must have stirred a memory, because during a lull in the conversation Saddam piped up with: My son had so many cars . . . you wouldn't believe it.

Oh yeah, Rogerson responded, what kind?

Just about all of them, Saddam said, laughing. One time, though, Uday made a terrible mistake. He made me very angry.

Sensing that Saddam was heading down a dark road, Rogerson braced himself for what might be coming. What happened? he asked.

I was very angry with him so I burned all his cars, Saddam said.

Rogerson was struck by Saddam's cavalier tone. The former president was at his most entertaining—and inscrutable—when his outlandish declarations weren't accompanied by the emotions one would expect.

I lit all his cars on fire. It became a huge fire, Saddam went on. As the memory crystallized in his imagination his laughter grew fiercer.

The event that had triggered Saddam's frenzied immolation was vintage Uday—a night of debauchery that predictably led to a violent outburst, only this time the victim would be Saddam's half brother Watban Ibrahim al-Tikriti. A fight between Watban and Luai Khairallah, the brother of Saddam's wife Sajida, over the most sought-after prostitute at a party had led them to seek the interces-sion of Uday, which proved—unsurprisingly—to be a terrible idea.

Uday had arrived at the party around 3:00 a.m. armed with a

new pump-action gun that, according to some observers, resembled one of the exotic weapons seen in a Stallone or Schwarzenegger movie. Wildly drunk by then, and irate to hear that Watban may have been making fun of a minor speech defect he had, Uday began spraying the crowd with bullets, killing three and wounding many more. Intoxicated by the gun's power, as well as the alcohol coursing through his veins, he turned his weapon on Saddam's half brother and shot him in both legs. Six young women, gypsy dancers and singers who'd been part of the evening's entertainment, were reportedly also killed by the indiscriminate fusillade. Watban's bodyguards stood by passively, aware that the shooter was the president's son.

Saddam seemed to enjoy recounting to Rogerson how, as punishment, he'd torched Uday's prized collection of Rolls-Royces, Bentleys, BMWs, Porsches, and Ferraris, which had been stored under guard in a garage in the Republican Palace.

Laughing wildly, the former dictator recalled how he gleefully watched the inferno, smoking one of his favorite Cohibas as the flames engulfed his son's treasured possessions. Saddam's almost maniacal laughter was contagious. Rogerson was unable to resist joining in, succumbing to belly laughs of his own. The mental image of the dictator dousing hundreds of his son's luxury cars with gasoline and setting them ablaze reminded Rogerson of "a Jerry Springer episode on steroids."

What had it been like, growing up with a father like that?

CHAPTER 22

Baghdad, Iraq—early 1980s

"Happy birthday to you, happy birthday to you, happy birthday dear Hala, happy birthday to you."

The singing was in Arabic, but the tune was unmistakable. Hala, Saddam Hussein's youngest daughter, appeared to be about ten, and was standing next to an enormous birthday cake—big enough to cover an entire park bench—adorned with candles. She stood among about a dozen children, her mother, Sajida, on one side and Saddam on the other. Sajida was wearing a flowing white dress while Saddam was wearing an olive military uniform. He surveyed the singing children approvingly, an enormous smile on his face. The party was broadcast on Iraqi national television, and the message was obvious: Saddam, Iraq's wise and benevolent ruler, is an iconic family man, as doting to his own children as he is to his people.

As the song came to an end, Hala enthusiastically blew out the candles to the applause of those assembled. She was wearing a formal dress, and the contrast between her grown-up dress and her youthful innocence made her shy smile even more endearing. Sajida leaned over to kiss Hala, who then bounded over to Saddam. He pulled her into a hug, her little body enveloped in his warm embrace. She clasped his waist in turn as he looked down at her and kissed her head gently.

Raghad, the oldest of Saddam's daughters and four years Hala's senior, would later say that she could recognize this expression "from a line of one million men." It was a gaze that could trigger panic in everyone from ordinary Iraqis to trusted aides, but to Saddam's girls, it was merely familiar, approving—a dad's delight.

Baghdad, Iraq—2006

One afternoon Saddam beckoned for Hutch to come over. Saddam was sitting outside in his favorite plastic patio chair, the one whose arms the Super Twelve had outfitted with rubber padding to make it more comfortable for the sixty-nine-year-old.

Look, Saddam said, peering at Hutch. A letter from Raghad. His eyes glimmered with pride. She writes backward, he explained. She writes from the left to the right, like Americans, he said, laughing. She asks me how I'm doing, and I tell her that my guys are treating me well.

Whereas at first Saddam's contact with the Super Twelve would usually take the form of a request of some kind—like he was "flagging down a waiter," according to Paul Sphar—he'd now begun to motion them over when it seemed that he just wanted someone to talk to. Usually, the soldiers welcomed the distraction.

Saddam's reading glasses were perched on his nose, and he'd been absorbed in the paperwork that occupied much of his time these days. Before Saddam had beckoned him, Hutch had been working his way through a Harry Potter book, which he enjoyed reading since it gave him something fun to discuss on the phone with his young daughters back home in Clarksville.

Hutch appreciated Saddam's comment about his guys "treating him well." While he was surprised to find himself enjoying his time with the old man, part of him was still frustrated, though, that he wasn't able to get out on patrol more often, roam outside the wire and mix it up with insurgents—the sort of activity he thought he'd be doing on this deployment. The number of hours he and his fellow MPs spent cooped up in the relatively safe confines of Camp Victory observing a famous prisoner made them envious of soldiers whose assignments gave them more mobility.

Since Saddam had brought up Raghad, Hutch volunteered to the former president: You know, I have daughters myself, ages six and four. I just talked to them on the phone the other day.

Really, how are they doing? asked Saddam. They must miss their father.

They've been dressing up as princesses, Hutch said. They're crazy, I love it.

He was a tough but loving dad—his kids sometimes calling him the "Drill Sergeant" in response to the discipline he tried to instill in them. He'd sometimes even have them "toe the line" in the kitchen before they headed off to school in the morning, a last-minute inspection borrowed from the basic training ritual of the same name to make sure they were ready to go and not forgetting anything.

Saddam quietly listened as Hutch talked about his daughters. Likely sensing the young soldier's nostalgia, the older man said, "Every daughter is a princess."

Saddam, too, could be a doting father. Ramsey Clark, the former U.S. attorney general who served on Saddam's legal team, spent considerable time in Amman, Jordan, with Saddam's daughter Raghad as she helped manage his legal defense. "I've never seen a more loving commitment to a father from a daughter," Clark says, pointing out that she was "the kingpin behind the defense operation."

Clark remembers sitting at Raghad's comfortable villa one evening when she got up too quickly and became dizzy, briefly passing out. He suspects that the combination of stress over her father's situation and physical exhaustion resulting from having difficulty sleeping contributed to her collapse. She was delivered to an emergency room in Amman and soon released. The episode would have been forgettable were it not for one detail. Raghad had grown surprisingly upset at having broken a necklace during her fall. Clark was surprised by this reaction, since Raghad was widely assumed to possess a small fortune—one that had been plundered from the Iraqi treasury. Why get so stirred up over a single broken necklace?

As they sat together in Raghad's well-appointed living room, she explained to him why the necklace was so meaningful to her. She told him how, as a young girl, she'd been perched atop her father's shoulders one Friday afternoon as he traversed busy streets "campaigning for office." Suddenly, Saddam lost his footing, perhaps bumped by the surging crowds, and Raghad fell to the ground. As she started to get up, she noticed blood on her scraped knee and broke down in tears.

Saddam bent down to dust her off and console her. After he'd settled her down, and they'd begun to walk again, he took her to a nearby jewelry stand. He pointed to the necklaces. Which one is the most beautiful, he asked, as a treat for being such a brave little girl?

That one! Raghad exclaimed.

Very well! For a beautiful girl!

Saddam purchased the cheap necklace and gently placed it around his daughter's neck.

Clark made a point of relaying Raghad's recollection to Saddam the next time they huddled in the austere meeting room underneath the courthouse preparing for trial. Clark says Saddam remembered it like it was yesterday, even though it had been more than three decades since Raghad had tumbled from his shoulders.

CHAPTER 23

Baghdad, Iraq—2006

Raghad had grown up to marry a murderous incompetent named Hussein Kamel, who, by virtue of little more than marrying into the family and dutifully playing the role of loyal stooge, had risen to prominence as the head of Saddam's weapons development program. Kamel's brother, Saddam Kamel, had married Rana, another of Saddam's daughters. Following a rumored fallout with Saddam's son Uday, the four had fled to the safety of neighboring Jordan. Their defection had been devastating to Saddam, for whom loyalty was sacrosanct, and, eleven years later, the betrayal was apparently weighing on him as he sat outside in the Rock's rec area, legs crossed, reading the paper.

Perhaps sparked by something he'd come across in an article, Saddam began to ruminate aloud on the 1995 defection. His interpreter, Joseph, with whom he enjoyed discussing the latest headlines, sat next to him. Hutch was on guard duty, sitting across the courtyard from the two. Saddam had positioned his chair so that the glare of the hot afternoon sun came down over his shoulder, warming the pages of the paper, rather than shining in his face. He was clad in his dishdasha, which was considerably cooler than Hutch's long-sleeved Army combat uniform.

I would never hurt my daughters, Saddam said, as if responding to an unspoken criticism.

Still, when they left, it endangered everything. My daughters weren't happy in Jordan, and I had to find a way to get them back.

Hutch couldn't have known that this was a lie—that the two girls had, in fact, been afforded the opportunity to return to Iraq without their husbands, and had refused. Hutch was unfamiliar with the story of their defection, and therefore had a tough time following Saddam's broken English as he labored to recount it. But he was able to grasp what seemed to be the highlights.

My daughters were scared, Saddam continued to his audience of Joseph and Hutch. They were scared of what I might do to their husbands and to them. I'd never have hurt them, but I knew that if I couldn't convince the boys to return I might never see my daughters again. I also knew I couldn't trust those boys.

Saddam was panicked by what Hussein Kamel could have been telling foreign intelligence agents.

I would never hurt my daughters, Saddam repeated. But I couldn't let the boys live. It would have shown weakness.

Baghdad, Iraq, and Amman, Jordan—August 1995

The soldier approached General Ra'ad al-Hamdani gravely. Sir, you're needed on the palace phone.

Hamdani moved across the open room in the Iraqi First Division Headquarters and picked up the red hotline. He knew that only three people were permitted to call it: Saddam, his son Qusay, and his secretary, Abed Hamoud.

Hamdani gingerly picked it up. He heard a flurry of shouts and curses, interrupted by shuffling and ominous echoes. Hello? Hamdani asked. As he tried to make out the indistinct voices, he clearly detected Saddam's thick Tikriti accent. The president sounded unhinged and panicked. Hamdani had never heard him like this.

He heard movement. Then, a new voice. "Abu Ahmed."

It was the familiar voice of Qusay, Saddam's son, addressing him by the patronymic.

Hamdani had gotten to know Qusay when Saddam assigned the young man to his unit during the Iran-Iraq War. There was a brief silence, followed by more commotion.

Dad!

It was Qusay's frantic voice again. He was calling out to his father. It would be the only time Hamdani ever heard one of Saddam's boys call him that. Hamdani tried to imagine the scene unfolding inside the Presidential Palace. While morbidly curious, he was also grateful for his distance from it.

Tell Hamdani that there is a conspiracy against us from within the family, he heard Saddam bellow. Hussein Kamel betrayed me.

Hamdani's stomach sank further. A more serious betrayal was scarcely imaginable.

Not long after the hotline in General Hamdani's headquarters had rung, another phone rang about five hundred miles to the west in the CIA's Amman, Jordan, station. Dave Manners, the new CIA station chief, had just arrived in the country with his six children. He picked up the phone.

Hello, Dave, Ali Shukri said in flawless, Oxford-accented English. Are you getting settled in? Ali Shukri was a senior advisor to Jordan's King Hussein and former head of the Jordanian Royal Court.

Sure. I'm living out of a suitcase, we haven't found a house yet, but my family and I are getting there.

The boss would like for you to come over and visit now. He wants to welcome you to Jordan. Shukri was referring to King Hussein.

Manners quickly rifled through his suitcase, pulled on the least wrinkled clothes he could find, and left for the palace. When he arrived, he found Shukri out front smoking. Looking like he could have stepped from the pages of a Brooks Brothers catalog, the advisor escorted the trim CIA officer into an elegantly appointed diwan where they found King Hussein, also smoking. The room's furniture and decorations were understated yet refined, free of garish extravagance.

The king politely welcomed Manners to the Hashemite kingdom and went on to reveal that the previous day an Iraqi entourage, including two of Saddam Hussein's daughters and sons-in-law, had sped across the desert border in a heavily armed convoy of luxury sedans. The sons-in-law happened to be brothers, and one, Hussein Kamel, had headed Saddam's weapons development program. The Iraqis were reported to have flagged down an Egyptian taxi driver in Amman and asked for directions to a hotel. They received directions to the Amra Hotel, a comfortable, though hardly luxurious, spot in leafy East Amman. When King Hussein learned of their arrival, he had them relocated to the unoccupied Hashmiya Palace.

When they met with King Hussein, the Iraqis explained that they no longer felt safe in Iraq, and they asked if they could find refuge in Jordan. King Hussein had gotten along well with Saddam in the 1980s, but the goodwill had dried up when the latter invaded Kuwait. The king was a shrewd strategist, though, and with the Kamel brothers' defection he saw an opportunity. To offer protection to the fleeing Iraqis would at once honor the tribal code upheld by descendants of the Bedouin and provide a chance to repair relationships with the West that had been damaged by his refusal to join the coalition against Saddam after his invasion of Kuwait.

The king chose to welcome the Iraqis without qualification.

And so it began. Intelligence agencies from across the globe began dispatching their WMD experts to Amman for a chance to debrief Hussein Kamel and learn more about Iraq's suspected clandestine weapons program.

The Jordanians would host an introductory dinner to provide American intelligence agents an opportunity to meet the Kamel brothers. The dinner was held at the Hashmiya Palace. The Americans, clad in the Joseph A. Bank–style suits favored by American bureaucrats, arrived to discover the Kamels' entourage clad in Hawaiian shirts, guns tucked noticeably into their waistbands, with the exception of Hussein himself, who was wearing a dark suit. It felt like a scene from *Miami Vice*—as if the Iraqis had seen too many movies and embraced the image of hedonistic outlaws.

The dinner started off poorly, and never improved. In a culture in which patiently developing relationships is critical, the Americans engaged in little small talk. For his part, Hussein Kamel—an abstemious psychotic whose eyes, when they weren't staring blankly, darted crazily—volunteered a number of ridiculous proposals.

If you deliver five thousand Mercedes to the Iraq-Jordan border, and use loudspeakers to explain to the Iraqis on the other side that the first five thousand soldiers to cross the border will be awarded one, the Army will experience mass defections and crumble, he suggested.

It was a patently absurd idea.

Undeterred, his wild eyes now furiously scanning the room, Kamel floated what was perhaps an even more ridiculous idea. I ask that you support Hussein Kamel as a replacement for Saddam, he said, referring to himself in the third person, in a manner eerily similar to his former patron. Provide an American military division for me to command, he continued, and I can take Baghdad.

The Jordanians said nothing. Meanwhile, the Americans tried to be receptive and polite while aware that these ideas were nonstarters. Recognizing that the discussion was destined to go nowhere, Dave Cohen, the Americans' lead negotiator, eventually turned to Manners and whispered, I can't say anything more to him . . . what do we do now?

We leave, Manners replied flatly.

The Americans stood up. Thank you very much, gentlemen, for your hospitality. It is late and we must go, they explained. Walking out the door, the men eyed each other quizzically. None of their training could have prepared them for such a preposterous discussion. As they slid into their waiting car, Cohen, still nonplussed, asked Manners, That guy was a big deal in Iraq? How?

Despite the inauspicious start, the Americans and Jordanians persisted in their efforts to see if they could pry any useful information from the brothers. It became more and more clear, though, that "something was off" about them, says Ali Shukri. Even Saddam Kamel's young boys, who could be observed playing at the palace guesthouse while waiting to meet with their father, shared their father's vacant look, more reptilian and cold than human.

At first, little the Kamel brothers said was of any intelligence value, though they did provide another window into the ghoulish landscape of Saddam Hussein's Iraq. Saddam Kamel boasted that his brother, Hussein, had punished an aide for not punctually completing an assigned task by forcing him—at gunpoint—to drink a gallon of gasoline, before loading his weapon with an incendiary munition and shooting the man so that he'd explode.

He was glowing with pride as he recounted the story.

Hussein Kamel then offered: Everyone thinks that my brother, Saddam Kamel, is the nice and soft one. Well, let me tell you about the time that a soldier argued with one of his commands. He started beating him until he lay on the ground bleeding, at which point he stomped on his head until the man's brains came out.

The Kamel brothers' Jordanian interlocutors, working to develop a rapport to elicit information from the two, simply nodded at these tales of violence, concealing their revulsion. Though separated from Amman by only about five hundred miles of desert, Baghdad under Saddam Hussein had clearly become a largely unrecognizable place where over-the-top cruelty was routine.

Ali Shukri would meet with Hussein Kamel a mind-numbing 181 times, adapting to his preferred nocturnal schedule, with the marathon meetings beginning around 10:00 p.m. and sometimes dragging on until the sun began to creep up over Amman. He was struck by how Kamel would never refer to Saddam by name but always as "the president," even as he was scheming to overthrow him, so deep was fear of the regime ingrained in his psyche.

By the end of these meetings, Shukri was convinced that Iraq no longer possessed weapons of mass destruction.

As weeks dragged into months and the Iraqi guests struggled to find ways to pass the time sequestered in their guesthouse, disenchantment increased for both hosts and visitors. Hussein Kamel seemed unable to adjust to the fact that, once his utility as a defector had run out, he'd become a nobody.

Meanwhile, Saddam hadn't given up trying to get the Kamels and his daughters to return. He enlisted Uday and even his wife

Sajida to help lobby them, promising immunity if they chose to come back. Saddam even called Hussein Kamel directly, assuring him in an almost hypnotic voice, "Do you think I could harm the father of my grandchildren?"

Recognizing that his dreams of leveraging international support to unseat Saddam and install himself as Iraq's new ruler had no chance of being fulfilled, Hussein Kamel made what just about everyone but himself would agree was a suicidal decision: he chose to return to Iraq.

This is madness. If you return, you're a dead man, Kamel's Jordanian hosts told him.

I've been granted immunity, Kamel responded, with a blank stare.

Even Hussein Kamel's none-too-swift brother, Saddam Kamel, recognized that this was a disastrous idea. "You donkey, you want us to go back to our deaths?!" he shouted at his brother. But Hussein Kamel had always wielded authority over Saddam Kamel, and he was determined to leave.

Hussein Kamel had sent Saddam Hussein a groveling letter a few days before the defectors left Amman. The letter was filled with tortured explanations for Kamel's defection, along with shameless flattery. One of the more egregious portions reads:

> I want Your Excellency to know that your photo and the photo of your kind family is hanging in every angle of the house. Our children do not know until today the reason for leaving Baghdad . . . they will always recall Papa Saddam and Mama Sajida. I hope that Mr. President, the Commander, will forgive us and permit us to return to our country, Iraq, so that we can live under your umbrella and large tent.

On the day of their scheduled departure, Saddam Kamel took ill, perhaps in part from the stress of what he suspected was an avoidable march to his death. At gunpoint, Hussein Kamel forced his brother, who was wrapped in a blanket to ward off his feverish chills, to get into a car for the return drive.

As the convoy of returning Iraqis, accompanied by a Jordanian government escort, sped through the eastern Jordanian desert, creeping ever closer to the border they'd crossed with such
grandiose plans just months before, there is evidence that Hussein
Kamel began to get cold feet. Every half hour or so he'd command
the fleet of Mercedes to stop on the side of the desert highway,
explaining that he needed to relieve himself. In fact, all he did when
exiting the car was "pace up and down as if he were making up his
mind." After each of these bouts of doubt, he'd eventually climb
back into the waiting car and continue his fateful journey back into
Saddam's deadly orbit.

If the Jordanian escorts had any doubt as to the fate that the
Kamel brothers would soon meet, it was dispelled when they
arrived at the border and saw what was waiting on the other side. In
a scene that was something of a hybrid between a western, with a
desert wasteland as a backdrop, and the gangster film *Scarface*, with
Saddam's son Uday playing the role of debauched villain, two helicopters stood idling on the Iraqi side of the border. Uday emerged
from one, smoking a large Cohiba cigar. He embraced his sisters,
before ushering them into one of the waiting helicopters. He then
politely escorted the Kamel brothers into the other. The Jordanian
intelligence officers, behind the safety of the border demarcation,
joked to each other, in the dry manner unique to those who've
spent careers observing the uglier sides of human nature, that they
wouldn't want to be going wherever Uday was ferrying the men.

While waiting for the helicopters to lift off, the Jordanians placed
macabre wagers on how many more days the Kamels would have
among the living. A week was the longest anyone gave them.

As the helicopters pulled skyward, banking to the east toward
Baghdad, one of the Jordanians entered the border checkpoint and
phoned the king's palace in Amman.

"*Khallas*," he said. "They're finished."

Upon the Kamel brothers' return, Saddam forced them to
divorce his daughters. He then ordered the Kamels' uncle, Chemical Ali, to lead a tribal hit squad to exact revenge for the "dis-

honor" the brothers had brought upon their tribe when they defected. Within days, an assault force of roughly forty al-Majid family members, led by Chemical Ali, made their way to a house in a southern suburb of Baghdad where the Kamels had holed up. Uday and Qusay, forbidden by Saddam from participating in the act of revenge, were eager spectators, parking nearby in the hope that they might get a look at the brutal spectacle.

The ensuing shoot-out would last for nearly thirteen hours, in a bizarre scene that could only take place in the phantasmagoria of Saddam's Iraq. In keeping with tribal tradition, Ali had even sent a Honda packed with weapons to the Kamel stronghold in advance to ensure they could put up a fight.

Dr. Ala Bashir, Saddam's personal doctor, reports being on call at Ibn Sina Hospital that day as wounded family members who were carted in provided real-time updates on how the gun battle was going. At one point, impatient to see an end to the Kamels' stubborn resistance, Chemical Ali decided to launch a rocket-propelled grenade at the besieged home. It killed Saddam Kamel, as well as his sister and her three young children, who were between the ages of three and six and had been hiding in a bathroom of the house.

Hussein Kamel fought on.

As the sun began to set, he finally staggered, wounded, from the house, shouting operatically, "I am Hussein Kamel."

He was cut to pieces by automatic weapons fire. As the smoke of hot lead rose from his fallen body, Ali strode up to him and stood on his face, a grave insult, before emptying one final magazine into the dying body.

"This is what happens to traitors," Ali shouted.

Accounts differ as to what happened next. Some say that Ali severed the bloodied head from the mangled body and delivered it to Saddam. Others report that the al-Majids put meat hooks in the eyes of the slaughtered brothers and dragged them away.

That night Saddam arrived at Ibn Sina Hospital to check on the wounded. He appeared somber but relaxed as he calmly surveyed the collateral damage of his decision to make the Kamels pay. As he did so, Dr. Bashir was reminded of something remarkable that had occurred at Ibn Sina years before.

Dr. Bashir had patched up Saddam Hussein after he'd been injured in a car accident during an American air strike in the first Gulf War. Also wounded in his car that night had been Saddam Kamel, the son-in-law who'd just met his end in the bloody shoot-out with Ali's hit squad. Dr. Bashir would never forget how, on the day of the bombing many years before, Saddam Hussein, wounded himself, had visited the room in which Bashir was preparing to operate on his son-in-law. Saddam politely asked, "May I come in?"

Following Bashir's approval, the president entered the room and quietly took Saddam Kamel's hand. He'd hold it for the duration of the forty-five-minute procedure, asking Bashir to do his best to make sure there'd be no scar left on the young man's face.

The affection that Saddam had once felt for the boys wouldn't be enough to spare them from the deadly punishment they'd earned with their defection. After they'd breathed their last breaths, Saddam—from his vantage point next to the Ibn Sina emergency rooms—wondered aloud, "I can't think how they could have left Iraq, and I certainly don't understand how they could have thought of returning."

CHAPTER 24

Baghdad, Iraq—2006

Saddam no longer wielded the power of life or death. His day-to-day existence was now entirely in the hands of others. Still, he did the best he could to derive happiness from his daily routine, even as he stood trial with his life in the balance.

If there was time, the first thing he'd do after being shuttled from the Rock to the IHT courthouse was to go to the small underground rec area near his cell—really nothing more than an empty room with a few steel folding chairs where he could visit with his codefendants—and light a cigar. Since he didn't smoke during transport out of deference to the soldiers who didn't like it—a paradoxical display of manners from a man who'd unblinkingly sanctioned the execution of his sons-in-law—he'd be craving the pleasant tobacco taste and hit of nicotine by the time he arrived. Before lighting up, though, he'd often ask the soldiers guarding him if they'd like one. He'd sometimes be joined by his codefendants. Together, they shared Saddam's cigars and the assorted sweets the former president had gathered from the care packages prepared by his daughter Raghad and delivered to him by his lawyers, who shuttled back and forth to Amman with some regularity. Just as Saddam had parceled out extravagant gifts to his loyalists while in power, he continued to dispense perks now that he was powerless, even if those perks were paltry.

Once he got word that the trial was about to resume upstairs,

Saddam would slowly make sure that he looked presentable, and then step into the elevator to be delivered to the courtroom. He knew that as soon as he exited the elevator, he was stepping back out onto the world stage.

Day eight of the Dujail trial brought a major surprise. Mild-mannered Judge Amin had been replaced by Judge Rauf Abd al-Rahman, a Kurd from the town of Halabja, which had been the site of one of Saddam's most egregious crimes when he'd launched chemical gas attacks against Iraqi Kurds during the Iran-Iraq War.

"The chief judge has been replaced," Rauf began, explaining that this was "an administrative and procedural action, and that the rights of the defendants would be preserved."

The balding sixty-four-year-old Judge Rauf couldn't have been much more different from his predecessor, as evidenced by his efforts to take command of the courtroom immediately. He wasted no time trying to set a new tone, saying, "We will allow you to speak, but not political speech. If anyone insults the law or the court or members of the court they will be removed."

He would soon be tested, like a substitute teacher confronting a classroom of schoolchildren accustomed to misbehaving. Barzan Ibrahim al-Tikriti, Saddam's half brother who'd headed the Iraqi intelligence service, would be the first to see how far he could push the new judge.

"I am convinced that the court is illegal and the daughter of adultery," Barzan began.

"I am asking you to address the court respectfully and I will not allow you to insult it," Rauf responded.

"Before you there was a brave man, and you took his place," Barzan continued, suddenly having developed an affinity for poor judge Amin, whom he and the defendants had so tormented.

"I didn't take his place. This is an administrative procedural action," Rauf replied, repeating his talking point.

In reality, the removal of Amin rightly aroused the suspicion of trial observers, as it looked to skeptics as if he'd been ousted for being too lenient with the defendants. Adding to the suspicion that the Iraqi government was meddling in the trial was the fact that Amin was initially to be replaced by Judge Sa'eed al-Hammashi, who, unlike Rauf, had been one of the original five judges in the trial. Al-Hammashi was dumped at the last moment, however, due to unsubstantiated charges that he'd been a Baathist. His removal was the handiwork of Ahmed Chalabi, who chaired the De-Baathification Commission and whose fingerprints were all over so many of the sectarian missteps that occurred during the early years of the American occupation.

Barzan, seemingly relishing his role as the trial's chief agitator, continued his disruptive protestations.

"I want to explain my medical situation," he blustered. "I need tests but the machine is broken and I can't have them. My sickness needs observation and it needs medical and psychological treatment and I can't have it in the prison. Iraqi law admits releasing sick prisoners. Why don't you release me?"

Judge Rauf responded evenly, but firmly. "Listen, make this demand through your lawyers and when we get it we'll refer it to the medical committee. Sit down."

"I will not sit down," Barzan thundered, his voice now more menacing.

Rauf had had enough.

He motioned for the guards to remove Barzan, who was then marched out after some pushing and shoving.

Saddam couldn't resist getting in on the act. He rose to his feet and shouted, "Down with America! Down with the traitor! Long live Iraq!" Soon some of the other codefendants and their lawyers joined him in cursing the judge.

"Bring in the court-appointed lawyers!" Rauf ordered as Saddam threatened to once again hijack the proceedings. Recognizing that Saddam's chosen legal counsel might not fulfill their duties, the court had appointed Iraqi defense attorneys to observe the trial and remain on call in an adjoining room to fill in as necessary. Thus it was that one of Rauf's first official acts was to eject Saddam's entire disagreeable lot of lawyers and replace them with the court-appointed ones. Saddam's chosen attorneys weren't banished from the trial permanently but rather, like unruly schoolchildren, just removed for the day and allowed to return for future sessions (though as the trial progressed expulsions and walkouts of defense counsel would result in the same disruptive scenario repeating itself).

As the court-appointed defense team appeared on command, Saddam glared malevolently at them. "We reject and refuse you," he said, sneering. "If you stay, you are devils." He then demanded to be allowed to leave the courtroom, a request Rauf was more than happy to accommodate.

"Remove him," Rauf ordered.

Saddam continued his protest, saying, "Don't say 'Remove him.' I was your leader for thirty-five years."

"Remove him," Rauf repeated unflinchingly, refusing to back down.

Rauf's hope that establishing a more firm presence from the bench would restore some normalcy to the trial proved to be wishful thinking, as the circus-like atmosphere continued. As the proceedings entered their eleventh day, Saddam marched into the courtroom shouting, "Long live Iraq! Long live the Arab nation! Down with the traitors! Down with Bush! You are not a judge, you are a criminal."

Rauf appeared unfazed, responding, "Enough speeches. Call for the next defendant."

Barzan was the last to enter, shouting, "Long live Iraq! Long live the Iraqi people!" Remarkably, he was dressed in what appeared to be white long underwear, as if he'd just rolled out of bed in a winter cabin rather than shown up for the most high-profile trial in his country's history.

Saddam eagerly joined in on the sideshow. "Shame on you, Rauf!" he shouted.

Not to be outdone, Barzan growled, "You are not *rauf*" (which in Arabic means kind).

"You are not *rahman*," he continued, seizing on the judge's last name, which means compassionate.

"Enough! Sit him down!" Rauf ordered from his perch in front of the courtroom.

Saddam then shouted, "This is the behavior of the traitors. God is great! God is great!" Using one of the catchphrases that had featured so prominently in many of his presidential speeches, he added, "And curses upon the evildoers." Not finished, he delighted some in the audience by hurling the base Arabic insult "Curse the father of your mustache."

Of course, the persona of raging showman that commanded the world's attention in the courtroom disappeared the moment the elevator doors shut and Saddam was returned to his cell on the floor below. Chris Tasker was sitting outside Saddam's rec area beneath the courtroom one day, observing Saddam alone in what was little more than a "steel cage with four chairs," when Saddam suddenly looked up at him.

The former president was seated on a metal chair with his legs crossed, puffing on a cigar. Tasker, not entirely sure how to react to the prisoner's stare, felt the need to say something to break the uncomfortable silence, and decided to go with the innocuous, That sure smells good, sir.

You want some? Saddam asked gamely, gesturing for Tasker to join him in the cell.

Sure, Tasker replied, trying to appear nonchalant.

Tasker slid the cell door open and entered the room. He took the cigar from Saddam's outstretched hand and inhaled the sweet tobacco smoke, careful not to cough in front of Saddam, before exhaling and sending it arcing into the cool air of the underground cell.

Soon, though, the mounting silence that accompanied the shared cigar again grew awkward. Tasker searched for something to say. How did you get started with cigars? he came up with—a natural question for the Cohiba-loving Saddam.

Fidel, Saddam responded, smiling.

Saddam liked to share the story with the guards of how Fidel Castro had taught him how to smoke cigars. Sometimes he'd even show pictures of the two of them together, likely taken during one of his rare foreign trips—a 1979 visit to Havana.

Tasker thought that this was pretty cool. What would his buddies back in Ohio think when they heard that he'd smoked a cigar with Saddam Hussein? That is, if he could *ever* tell them, he thought, remembering his instructions not to discuss this mission with anyone. Trying to keep the conversation going, he saw a magazine sitting nearby with a picture of a car on it and gestured at it. "Which kind is your favorite?" he asked Saddam.

"Mercedes," the former president responded without hesitation.

Tasker thought that steering the conversation to cars had been a good idea—it was something he knew a lot about.

Suddenly, a man burst into the rec area. "You can't be in here," he announced breathlessly.

"Okay," Tasker said. He immediately knew what had happened, and kicked himself for not having expected as much. Someone watching the bank of closed-circuit TV screens in "mission control" must have seen him sitting with Saddam, smoking a cigar, no less. The alarmed monitor had hustled down to put a stop to the fraternizing. Both Saddam and the soldiers were under more of a microscope at the IHT, making it difficult to enjoy the casual interaction that marked life at the Rock.

Saddam, meanwhile, was oblivious to the drama taking place between his American minders as he continued to puff away contentedly on his cigar.

CHAPTER 25

Baghdad, Iraq—2006

Dressed in his dishdasha and clutching his prayer beads, Saddam paced in his outdoor rec area and silently mouthed a string of words. Hutch was on duty and looked on quietly as Saddam traversed the "little lap that he walked all the time": from the side of Hutch's plastic chair, across the rec area to the assortment of overgrown weeds he cared for, and back. Hutch later recalled that when Saddam walked back and forth like this, mumbling to himself, "you'd think he'd lost his mind if you didn't know him." Sometimes his cadence and mannerisms suggested to the Super Twelve that he was rehearsing things he planned to say in court. Saddam himself may have suspected that his behavior appeared odd, as he'd sometimes look up, catch the guard on duty observing him, and offer an almost sheepish smile.

Hutch was absentmindedly flipping through one of the *People* magazines he'd grown hooked on during the deployment when he noticed that Saddam had stopped pacing and was looking at him. Sir? Hutch asked, anticipating a request he'd be expected to help out with. But it was not a request. Saddam just wanted to talk. And that was fine with Hutch.

Me and Barzan, we used to fish right near here, you know, Saddam began. Oh, very big fish there, not so many there, he explained, trying to describe the various fishing holes in the nearby man-made lake.

Despite the Super Twelve's efforts to keep their location a secret, Saddam knew exactly where he was. Sometimes he'd even catch a glimpse through the white sheet that the soldiers had installed over the windows of his Humvee, and at such times he'd volunteer observations on landmarks they were passing.

The fish Saddam described could indeed grow quite large. American soldiers took to calling the hulking carp "Saddam bass" after hearing rumors that he'd stocked the lakes with them. As with most stories surrounding Saddam, this one wasn't without a darker legend. The Super Twelve heard tales that Saddam's henchmen had dumped into the lakes the dying bodies of enemies they'd shot, causing the large fish to develop a taste for human blood.

Even with Saddam out of power and on trial, the gruesome violence hadn't abated. The only difference was that now, instead of regime opponents, it was victims of Iraq's worsening civil war who sometimes found their way into the water. Hutch would sometimes fish these "floaters" out of the lake, parts of the decomposing corpses disintegrating in his hand as he struggled to retrieve them.

As sectarian death squads ramped up their efforts to ethnically cleanse mixed Baghdad neighborhoods, ghastly discoveries became routine. That same year, for example, twelve corpses got caught in metal grates intended to block debris from floating into the Tigris. The victims had been bound, blindfolded, and shot in the head before being dumped in the river, yet their discovery prompted little more than a shrug from Baghdad's citizens. After three years of escalating violence, such macabre finds had become the new normal.

Saddam—who'd predicted this societal breakdown would occur, confidently telling his CIA interrogators shortly after his capture that "you will need someone like me to hold this place together"—seemed remarkably upbeat as he recalled his fishing exploits. Rather than growing dejected, he seemed energized as he shared memories of a life he no longer enjoyed.

Barzan, he was tricky, Saddam said, as he continued his account of fishing with his half brother.

Oh yeah, Hutch replied, who usually caught more fish, sir?

Barzan would lie and tell me that his fish were bigger. But mine were really bigger, Saddam said, using his hand to illustrate the difference in size between fishes they'd argued about years ago, trying to find the right words to communicate how much they differed in weight.

Those sound like some big fish, sir, Hutch volunteered agreeably, as Saddam stood before him, a big smile lighting his face.

Yes, they were—big and mean. I like them that way—I like them mean so they fight back, Saddam said. I used to prepare and cook them myself, he added with pride.

He then continued his pacing, a serene expression on his face as he thumbed his prayer beads and in his imagination was transported back to those peaceful afternoons on the water.

Baghdad, Iraq—1980s

Saddam watched his fishing line dangle in the man-made lake, admiring the water's tranquil surface and the contrast it made with Baghdad's throbbing energy just a few kilometers away outside the palace walls. Blending into that urban buzz were the screams of anguish issuing from prison cells across the city. On this day, Saddam was joined by two of his close confidants, Taha Yassin Ramadan and Tariq Aziz, as well as Jordan's King Hussein and a few of the king's senior officials.

Saddam enjoyed spending time with King Hussein. They were an unlikely pair, Saddam having risen from nothing to become a peer of the urbane king, who hailed from the largest tribe in the Arab world. The two rulers and their top aides gathered on a small platform jutting out into the lake's cool blue waters. None actually held their rods; instead they simply laid their hooked lines beneath large stones at the platform's edge, where they could dangle in the placid water. Perhaps not surprisingly in a country where everything was engineered to keep the dictator happy, Saddam's line jerked sharply every few minutes, even while the others lay dormant in the water. Saddam acted surprised—and gleeful as a child—every time he reeled in one of the Tigris carp.

As King Hussein and a few of his top ministers relaxed on the short one-hour flight back to Amman, the king feigned exasperation that Saddam's line had attracted a seemingly endless number of fish while the others rarely rated a nibble. Mostly joking, but with a hint of frustration, the king went on to speculate that maybe there was a diver under the water attaching the fish to Saddam's hook—or perhaps a cage full of fish had been positioned directly beneath the spot where Saddam had cast his line.

On a subsequent visit things changed. Finally, the king felt a bite on his line. Almost simultaneously Saddam felt one. The king speculated, according to his tongue-in-cheek conspiracy theory, that perhaps the underwater diver had placed the fish on his hook before quickly recognizing his mistake and affixing one to Saddam's as well. Much to the king's pleasure, and probably to the horror of Saddam's entourage, when the two heads of state pulled their catches from the water the king's fish appeared to be the bigger one. Saddam wasn't pleased, but he didn't miss a beat. He summoned an aide and turned over the two fish to him with instructions to weigh them and determine which was larger.

The aide soon returned, earnestly reporting that Saddam's was a quarter kilogram heavier.

Baghdad, Iraq—2006

My friend, Saddam said to Hutch, I'm ready to move inside now.

His words briefly startled Hutch, who'd lost himself in a daydream as he watched Saddam pace almost hypnotically back and forth across the rec area.

Okay, sir, let's do it, replied Hutch as he gathered up his radio and the magazines he'd been leafing through. Leaving behind the outdoor patio, which was ringed by concrete walls topped with concertina wire, he led the former president back inside, walking in front of him as he always did so that the old man had someone to grab on to and steady himself should he lose his footing.

Once they'd completed the short walk inside, Saddam stepped aside and waited for Hutch to open the cell door for him. A germaphobe, the deposed ruler avoided touching door handles whenever possible.

At the guard desk just outside Saddam's cell, Hutch set down the items he'd taken outside with him and settled his large frame into one of the guard chairs. As soon as he had sat down, however, Hutch noticed that Saddam had remained standing, looking at him with that unmistakable expression that suggested something was amiss.

Saddam then took his foot and kicked the cell door open. Hutch hadn't closed it behind Saddam, and this was Saddam's not-so-subtle way of expressing his displeasure that it had been left open. While Saddam sometimes liked the freedom of movement an open cell door enabled, since it allowed him to access his storage closet more easily or wander out to the rec area with one of his guards, at other times he preferred it to remain shut.

"My friend, my friend," Saddam said to Hutch, gesturing at the door, which was now fully ajar.

Dammit, thought Hutch, who knew what this meant. Reluctantly, he dragged himself out of his chair, walked over, and dutifully shut the cell door.

Saddam appeared relieved. Thank you, my friend, Saddam said, before taking a seat at his desk.

Despite himself, Hutch couldn't help but smile.

CHAPTER 26

Baghdad, Iraq—2006

If you play that damn song one more time, I'm going to kick your ass, Private Paul Sphar shouted across the room to Private Tucker Dawson. Dawson had been playing "Fireman" by Lil Wayne just about every morning in the cramped room they shared, and it had begun to drive Sphar crazy. Minor aggravations and annoyances were magnified by the forced proximity of deployment—and further compounded by unrelenting heat, grinding stress, and testosterone. Friction was inevitable and eruptions bound to take place.

When they did, the Super Twelve often resolved them in a somewhat brutal though surprisingly effective manner. Specialist Rogerson later recalled that "if we got sick of each other, we'd take each other to the Pit and that was it." "Taking each other to the Pit" meant squaring off in hand-to-hand combat—or what was called in Army training "combatives"—while the rest of the squad circled around and watched, ensuring that things didn't get too out of hand. Striking with the fists was frowned upon; rather, the men would try to grapple each other into submission. Sometimes mutual exhaustion simply led to a draw, at which point the two soldiers would help each other to their feet as they gasped to catch their breath. These bouts had a familial quality to them. It was "kind of like I can mess with my brother, but you can't," Rogerson recalls. "I would beat the shit out of Perkins more times than I can count, but if someone from the outside bothered us we'd have each other's back."

In this instance, though, Sphar didn't have the patience to wait until later to deal with Dawson. The two had always had a rocky relationship, having entered the Army from very different worlds. Sphar was a tattooed "gamer" while Dawson, an avid hunter and fisherman, was more the embodiment of southern preppiness.

As Lil Wayne continued to blast from Dawson's computer, Sphar couldn't take it anymore. He charged across the small room and, lowering a shoulder, crashed into the young Carolinian, his considerable girth helping to send both tumbling to the ground. Neither of the young soldiers actually wanted to hurt the other, but the steam had reached a boil and needed release. They crashed about the cluttered space, slamming into plywood walls separating them from soldiers bunking next door. Eventually the stocky Sphar gained the upper hand, pinning Dawson to the floor. That's when Sergeant Tom Flanagan burst into the room, having heard the commotion from the hallway as he passed by.

Cut that shit out! Flanagan shouted.

The two combatants slowly peeled themselves off each other, secretly relieved to have a face-saving opportunity to call a truce. There was never any doubt that Flanagan's command would be obeyed. The sergeant was universally admired for being hardworking and a straight shooter. Sheepishly, Sphar and Dawson headed to the showers to clean up and get ready for another day—another twenty-four hours that stood between them and eventually going home.

Life for soldiers consists of an endless succession of countdowns. They begin during basic training—with the ubiquitous "[xx] days and a wake-up" scrawled on port-a-potties across base, denoting the number of days the trainee has left until graduation—and never really end. Once soldiers get to a unit in wartime there are countdowns to deployment; once on deployment, there are countdowns to midtour leave back to the States; once on leave, there are countdowns to returning downrange; and once returned, there are countdowns to the end of the deployment. Occasional flare-ups, such as Sphar and Dawson's wrestling match, were just one of the ways soldiers vented frustration with their *"Groundhog Day"* existence.

One afternoon Sphar and Dawson were out in Saddam's rec area at the Rock. They'd come from the old man's cell, prompted by his half-joking, half-serious comment "My cage cannot hold me." While they played chess Saddam sat smoking a cigar, absorbed in his reading and writing. In the background, his old radio played its curious mix of American and Iraqi tunes. He'd been working his way through ten volumes by the fourteenth-century Tunisian philosopher and historian Ibn Khaldun that he'd asked his daughter Raghad to procure for him. He'd also requested of her some volumes of Arabic poetry and scholarly studies of the Koran. Raghad would collect the books and give them to Saddam's lawyer Nuaimi when he traveled to Amman. Raghad's dutiful support suggests she was no longer troubled—if she'd *ever* been—by her father's role in having her husband gunned down following the couple's return from Amman in 1995. Like her father, she was a survivor, and by all accounts opportunistic, and she must have known that she had little to gain by falling on a sword for her dead husband.

Sphar and Dawson were careful to keep an eye on Saddam even as their chess match grew more heated. As they periodically looked up they noticed that their prisoner had begun to steal glances at them as well. He seemed curious about something but didn't beckon to them, as he usually would if he wanted to talk.

Saddam then set his papers down and walked over. He hovered over Sphar and Dawson as they concentrated on their next moves, puffing on his cigar as he watched the two young soldiers play. He was studying the game carefully.

"Can I play?" Saddam finally asked.

Sphar had been winning, and so he assumed that Saddam was challenging him. Hold on one second, sir, let me check, Sphar said. He called Sergeant Flanagan, who was in the control room watching the closed-circuit TV camera feeds.

Is it okay if I play chess with Vic? he asked.

Sure, Flanagan said.

As Dawson stood up to make room for Saddam at the chessboard, Sphar rearranged the pieces to their starting positions. Do you want black or white? he asked.

It's okay, you choose, the former president responded. I haven't played in many years, he added, perhaps trying to manage expectations in the event of a loss.

He needn't have worried, as he went on to beat Sphar in a blitzkrieg attack. Saddam didn't say a word after his demolition of the young soldier. They played again, and Saddam won again. Sphar says, "It was like he was playing a child, and I'd been playing chess for years."

While the soldiers had been instructed not to engage Saddam on potentially inflammatory topics, they sometimes couldn't help but succumb to their curiosity. One afternoon Dawson, who believes that Saddam "probably did most of the crap he was accused of before I was even born; he'd killed a lot of people," came right out and asked Saddam a couple of the questions that had been on some of the soldiers' minds.

"What do you think about the war? Are you glad the terrorists are out there hitting us with IEDs and bombs and shooting us?" Dawson asked Saddam.

No, Saddam responded. All I ever wanted for Iraq was peace. But, he added, let me ask you this. If we came into your country, and we were running things, what would you do if you didn't want us there?

Well, yeah, I see what you're saying, Dawson replied.

Exactly, so I can't really blame them, said Saddam, referring to the insurgents, and I really can't stop them.

Dawson may have felt emboldened to broach these sensitive subjects since it was clear to many of the soldiers that Saddam had taken a particular liking to him, perhaps because he was the youngest member of the Super Twelve. Saddam would often ask Dawson about his girlfriend, telling him he should be at home going to college with her rather than fighting in Iraq. One afternoon Saddam even promised Dawson that he'd pay for him to go to college if he could ever access his bank account.

Late one night at the Rock, Dawson surprised his buddies by parading down the hallway of their living quarters—nothing more than a row of small dwellings partitioned by plywood walls—dressed in one of Saddam's suits. Saddam gave it to me, he announced buoyantly. The fact that Saddam's suit, which was tailored for a paunchy man, didn't come *close* to fitting Dawson made the scene even more ridiculous. The soldiers cracked up as Dawson took exaggerated steps through the austere living area as if on the catwalk at a fashion show.

Months later, explaining his relationship with Saddam, Dawson would say, "I don't think he ever would have tried to hurt me. If I were to hand him a gun—a loaded gun—I bet you he wouldn't shoot me. I'm pretty darned sure. He never tried to do anything to harm us. If he called you friend, you were his friend."

Presidential Palace, Baghdad, Iraq—September 11, 1994

Ra'ad al-Hamdani, the Iraqi patriot and decorated veteran, was in command of the elite Al-Medina Al-Munawara Republican Guard Division headquartered at Camp Taji, about twenty miles north of Baghdad, when the phone in his office started ringing one September afternoon. It was Qusay, the more disciplined of Saddam's two sons, calling.

"General," the young man said, "we are gathering all the military leaders. Please report to the palace immediately." And then came the words that "felt like lightning striking my body," says Hamdani. "The president wants to reinvade and occupy Kuwait."

Hamdani had been against the first invasion, and after witnessing firsthand the carnage inflicted by the vastly superior American-led coalition, including nearly being killed himself—the "sword had reached my neck," he later recalled—he resolved to do anything he could to prevent a repeat of that disastrous mistake.

When Hamdani arrived at the palace, he was greeted by Qusay, who privately confided in him that he, too, was concerned about the prospect of launching another foolhardy invasion. We are not capable, are we? Qusay asked Hamdani, his tone suggesting he already knew the answer to his question. What shall I tell the president?

Tell him we cannot do it, Hamdani said.

The young man's expression indicated that he recognized the gravity of the situation.

The commanders gathered in the palace. Others spoke first, sycophants to the last, assuring Saddam that "we are not only capable of occupying Kuwait, but can make it all the way to Oman." Qusay then turned to Hamdani and asked, "How come they're all saying this would be easy and you're saying it's impossible?" Qusay asked the question respectfully, with the confidence of a lawyer who knows what his expert witness is about to say.

If we get the order, I will salute and carry it out, as I always have, Hamdani answered, and the results will show who is telling the truth. The implication was clear—they would not be good.

Hamdani had returned to his headquarters, unsure of how his message had been received by the president. His uncertainty wouldn't last long. Late that night, around 10:30 p.m., the red hotline rang in Hamdani's office at the Division Headquarters in Taji. Only three people ever called on this line: Saddam, Qusay, or the president's private secretary, Abed Hamoud. This time it was Abed.

"Ra'ad, Our Uncle wants you," Abed said, referring to Saddam by the affectionate—but slightly menacing—nickname his deputies sometimes used. Hamdani quickly jumped in an official military sedan to make the roughly forty-five-minute drive south to the Presidential Palace in Baghdad.

Late-night summonses like this weren't entirely uncommon, as Saddam worked long and unpredictable hours. As Hamdani's driver steered his way to the palace, aggressively navigating the city streets, the general tried to divine what kind of Saddam he was about to encounter. He weighed the danger of upsetting Saddam with his candor against the risk of another ruinous war, and asked for God's protection as his car rolled inexorably forward.

Upon arrival, Abed Hamoud did nothing to assuage Hamdani's fears. "The president is very angry with you," the secretary said. A deep, paralyzing fear enveloped the general, the kind one feels late at night when one has slipped into a nightmare.

Can the guard accompany me? Hamdani asked, gesturing to a member of the security detail working the night shift in the palace. The general was hopeful that the presence in the room of another person might somehow diffuse Saddam's anger.

No, he wants you alone, Abed replied.

Taking a deep breath, Hamdani opened the door.

General Ra'ad Hamdani, he announced formally as he snapped to attention and saluted the president. Both of the men were in olive-colored military uniforms. Anger was etched across Saddam's face—a face that, even when calm, could cause Hamdani's pulse to beat 120 times a minute. The president took a final inhalation from the cigar he was smoking before setting it down deliberately. There was a moment of uncomfortable silence and then he began:

Ra'ad, I cannot respect any commander who says he can't do something.

Sir, there was never a command I did not obey. In this instance I was commanded to provide an opinion, Hamdani explained, which I did.

A few excruciatingly slow seconds of silence ticked by. Hamdani continued to stand frozen at attention while Saddam observed him impassively. Hamdani was familiar with Saddam's claims that he could tell what people were thinking before they opened their mouths. Sit down, Saddam finally said.

The two men sat, Saddam on one side of the room's lone desk, Hamdani on the other. The office was surprisingly cramped and utilitarian, the only items on the desk an assortment of papers stacked underneath two paperweights and some scattered pens and pencils.

Explain yourself, Saddam commanded. What is the justification for your negative assessment?

Sir, I compared our capabilities with those of our enemy—America, Hamdani began. According to these models we're incapable of defeating them.

Oddly, despite the fact that Hamdani's words were presumably not what Saddam wanted to hear, his body appeared to grow less rigid. He seemed to be calming down.

Can I take some items off your desk and use them to demonstrate something to you? Hamdani bravely asked Saddam, who nodded assent.

See this paperweight? This is a Russian T-72, our most sophisticated tank, Hamdani explained, picking the paperweight up to signify the tank. Imagine that this has a value of 1.5 on a scale of 1 to 5, Hamdani said. I got this tank at the beginning of the eight-year Iran-Iraq War, and it has never been upgraded due to the sanctions that were imposed on us.

He then picked up the other paperweight and said, This is an American M1 tank. It is a 5 on a scale of 1 to 5.

Saddam appeared to be concentrating, and remained eerily silent.

Hamdani continued: On top of this M1 tank the Americans can fly an Apache helicopter with Hellfire missiles. This multiplies their effectiveness by 5. So now they have 25 and we still have 1.5. Hamdani then reached for a pen and held it over the paperweight signifying the tank. This pen is an F-16 and the Americans can fly them above the tank and the Apache. This multiplies their effectiveness again to 75. We still have 1.5.

Hamdani was poised for Saddam to lash out at any minute. These were Saddam's military capabilities that he was denigrating, after all. Remarkably, the explosion didn't come.

Above the F-16 there will be a B-1 bomber, Hamdani went on, slightly emboldened by the fact that he hadn't yet been cut off. And above that they have satellites, he added, having extended his analysis from hypothetical tanks squaring off in ground combat all the way to outer space.

Taken all together, Hamdani said, my analysis suggests that the

Americans possess capabilities of 125 in comparison to our 1.5. That is why we cannot win this war, and why we should not reinvade Kuwait. With that, he exhaled. He'd done it. He'd articulated his heretical thoughts to Saddam.

Saddam finally broke his silence. I know that you have fought against Israel, Iran, and America, and that you are courageous, he began. Hamdani briefly felt the suffocating fear start to dissipate—but suddenly Saddam pivoted. That is why you don't need all these numbers, Saddam said.

Saddam was indirectly referring to his deeply held, primitive belief that somehow sheer courage and bravery could propel Iraqis to victory over enemies who enjoyed vastly superior technological capabilities. This was Saddam the Bedouin, placing faith in mystical warrior virtues over rational computer-driven metrics. Saddam stood and extended his hand for Hamdani to shake, signaling that the meeting was over. Go back to your command, Saddam said, adding ominously, I *was* thinking something else for you. The unspoken, though deadly, implication was clear.

Saddam was still grasping Hamdani's hand. What do you want from Saddam? he asked.

Hamdani knew that Saddam had something like a car or money in mind. This, again, was Saddam the Bedouin, wanting to appear magnanimous to his tribe, and make them dependent on his largesse. While audiences with Saddam always had the potential to result in death, many visitors emerged with gifts, some quite lavish. Hamdani was a proud man, though, and didn't want to become any more beholden to Saddam than he already was by virtue of being a senior leader in his military. I am just a soldier doing my job, he responded, and I'd never ask for anything.

As if he hadn't heard Hamdani's answer, Saddam repeated, What do you want from Saddam?

Thinking quickly, trying to appear respectful while not actually asking for anything, Hamdani said, God protect you so you can protect Iraq. That is what I want.

But Saddam pressed Hamdani for a third time, continuing

to refer to himself in the third person. What do you want from Saddam?

Hamdani strained to come up with a satisfactory answer. Finally, he replied carefully, "Since I am in the military, I do not need anything, but if I leave, please let me knock on your door with any needs I may have at that time."

This answer finally satisfied Saddam. He released Hamdani's hand and allowed him to leave. As Hamdani emerged from the office, Saddam's secretary, Abed, cut him off and asked him to wait in the reception area for a moment.

A few moments later, the secretary came out and said, "Our Uncle thinks that it is better if this conversation stays here, as your analysis could negatively impact morale."

You have my word, Hamdani responded.

Then he shook Abed's hand before walking out into the night, slumping into the backseat of his waiting sedan, and beginning the lonely drive home through the deserted late-night streets.

CHAPTER 27

Baghdad, Iraq—2006

One afternoon Saddam looked up at Hutch from a magazine he was reading out in his rec area. The sun bore down on them, as it always did, coaxing beads of sweat from their foreheads.

The Iranians, Saddam began . . .

That's all Hutch needed to hear to know where Saddam was going with this. He'd made no effort to disguise what was clearly an obsession with threats—both real and imagined—posed by his neighbor to the east, Iran. Saddam jabbed angrily at what he said was a picture of an Iranian leader in the article he was reading.

He told me he would have tea in Baghdad one day, Saddam said, sneering, implying to Hutch that the Iranian had boasted of conquering Iraq. Well, I made sure he never did, Saddam added triumphantly.

The notion that he'd thwarted what he believed to be the Iranians' nefarious goals brought him pleasure, and he paused, savoring the satisfaction the memory brought him. Regret over the hundreds of thousands of soldiers and civilians who perished on both sides of the Iran-Iraq War didn't cast a cloud over his fond recollection.

They want Iraq, Saddam went on, summoning increasing energy as he spoke. They've tried to trick our citizens into supporting them for years, he hissed, his rising anger striking to Hutch, who was more familiar with the relaxed Saddam, content to putter around the rec area, water his plants, and feed the birds.

Hutch had a hard time following this diatribe, since the more complicated the topic, the more Saddam struggled with his English. From what he could gather, though, the article contained some favorable references to Iranian leadership—ones suggesting that their ambitions were more peaceful than belligerent.

The former Iraqi president cursed the article, dismissing it as nonsense.

This was a different side of the man. It caused Hutch to consider whether currents of rage always rushed beneath Saddam's characteristically placid exterior, like a still river whose depths are roiled by turbulence.

He simply nodded in agreement, content to listen passively until Saddam eventually ran out of gas. Clad in his simple dishdasha and sandals, and with unstylish glasses perched on his nose, Saddam appeared much different from—but sometimes acted like—the crotchety old men reading the morning paper at the local Waffle House back in Hutch's native Georgia, loudly complaining about certain articles to anyone who'd listen. *Hell, at least this makes the shift pass by more quickly,* Hutch thought, as opposed to the two of them alone with their thoughts and a film of sweat from the midday sun.

Baghdad, Iraq—day 17 of the Dujail trial

Indeed, the Iranians never did drink tea in Baghdad. Saddam had made sure of that, no matter how much it cost. As the Dujail trial resumed, everyone in the courtroom strained to hear Saddam's voice on an old video recording:

"Anyone who stands in the face of the revolution, even if they are one thousand, two thousand, three thousand, ten thousand, I will cut off their heads without raising a hair or my heart beating for them. I have a heart—and I am not exaggerating—if an ant stops breathing, I feel pain in my heart for it. However, such type of people, by God, no matter how many they are, I feel no compassion in my heart for them."

After that statement, the video showed people cowering on the ground as Iraqi security officers during the Saddam era beat them with sticks. Saddam could be heard again, saying, "If a person dies in interrogation, he has no value." The tape played for one minute, but captured the essence of an era.

The defense lawyers objected that the content of the tape had nothing to do with the Dujail case. While they may have been factually correct, Saddam's sinister words, coupled with the disturbing visuals, mattered in a trial that, as Saddam himself recognized, was being adjudicated not only by five judges in the courtroom but by millions at kebab shops and teahouses across Iraq and the Arab world.

Saddam did his best to hijack the day's proceedings, making his familiar claims that the trial was illegitimate, and continuing his rant from a previous session in which he blasted "the invaders, criminal dwarfs, and the infidel slaves of foreigners." This time he complained that the trial had been set up "under the spears of the invaders," pointing to the "U.S. tanks around this palace" as evidence of the impossibility of a fair process.

Next came poetry. Relishing any opportunity to send the trial careening off the tracks, Saddam proudly announced that he'd composed three lines of poetry for the unamused Judge Rauf, "because I noticed you enjoy listening to poetry." At this, Rauf determined that he'd heard enough of Saddam's clownish rambling and cut the mikes.

Eventually Judge Rauf managed to redirect the court's attention back to the charges being leveled against the former president, focusing on the accusation that 28 juveniles were among the 148 whose death sentences were reportedly endorsed by Saddam. Iraq's former leader vehemently denied the charge, saying, "I would not order the execution of a young Iraqi, even if you take out my eye." Informed that the prosecutor had the identification cards of the victims, Saddam simply responded, "I think they are forged." He added that it wasn't the responsibility of the head of state to know their ages.

CONDEMNED

Many trial observers couldn't help but wonder why so much energy was being poured into prosecuting Saddam for crimes committed in response to Dujail, which, after all, only focused on the fates of 148 people rounded up following a failed assassination attempt, in light of Saddam's far more egregious crimes against humanity, the most notable being the notorious Anfal campaign in 1987 and 1988, in which at least fifty thousand Iraqi Kurds—and likely closer to a hundred thousand—were reported killed.

Anfal, meaning "spoils" in Arabic, and referencing a battle in 624 A.D. between Muslims and non-Muslims, ostensibly targeted Kurdish militias who'd allied with Iran during the Iran-Iraq War, but was more broadly designed to extinguish Kurdish resistance to Saddam's rule once and for all. Reportedly, there were chemical weapons attacks and mass executions from which no one, not even women and children, was immune.

Chemical Ali oversaw the massive operation. According to documentary evidence gathered by the FBI and presented in their "Prosecutive Report of Investigation Concerning Saddam Hussein," Ali ordered Kurds to leave their homes, issuing military orders warning, "The villages shall be regarded as operational zones that are strictly out of bounds to all persons and animals and in which troops can open fire at will, without any restrictions." Ali ordered "random bombardments, using artillery, helicopters, and aircraft, at all times of the day or night, in order to kill the largest number of persons present in these prohibited zones." Ali told subordinates he had "no objection to beheading the traitors," with the caveat that "it would have been preferable to send them to security for interrogation before executing them."

Witness accounts were chilling. Testimony included an account of three men who were "blindfolded and made to stand on chairs, arms raised above their heads. The chairs were then kicked away, leaving the prisoners' feet dangling a couple of feet from the ground. Next, guards attached one end of a string to an empty gas container and the other to each prisoner's scrotum. When the signal was given, the guard would drop the gas cylinder, ripping out the man's testicles. Within half an hour, all three were dead."

Another Kurdish witness described "thirty large, windowless trucks arriving at the camp. We were herded onto the trucks and rode all day with no food and little water. Three children between the ages of six and seven died during the ride. A woman went into labor and was foaming at the mouth from dehydration. . . . When the trucks stopped for the last time I saw pits which had been dug into the ground. Standing behind each pit were two soldiers armed with AK-47s. We were forced out of the truck and fell into the pit where we laid, tired and starving. The soldiers started shooting. I looked around and saw the woman who had gone into labor riddled in bullets."

Only by playing dead and lying motionless amid the pile of sweaty bodies as they bled out did the witness survive.

Years later, the man Saddam had tapped to oversee the genocidal operation, Chemical Ali, would tell his FBI interrogators: "There are two faces of Saddam, one who went out of his way to share with those in need and was sometimes reduced to tears when stopping to assist a poor person, and the other a lonesome man with no friends, either inside or outside his family, who didn't even trust his own sons." This second "face of evil" was "so cruel you couldn't imagine."

CHAPTER 28

Baghdad, Iraq—summer of 2006

BOOM! The explosion reverberated through the Rock's outdoor rec area, shaking the concrete where Saddam sat alongside his interpreter, Joseph. Private James Martin, one of the Super Twelve, sat across from them. For a brief moment the lines of sight of the men converged, then Saddam locked eyes with Martin and simply shook his head, as he always did when gunfire or explosions interrupted an otherwise quiet day. The soldiers sometimes wondered if that look was meant to suggest that all of this could have been avoided if he were still in power. There was also the possibility that he saw the occasional explosions and distant gunfire as evidence his loyalists would eventually try to set him free. His secretary, Abed Hamoud, would defiantly warn CIA interrogators of that eventuality: "This is a wild place, and you will struggle mightily to hold it together. It's not over yet. You are in control now—you have me in prison. But I can hear the bombs and gunfire outside. We'll see what happens."

Years later, the Canadian attorney William Wiley, who was tapped by the State Department's Regime Crimes Liaison Office to advise Saddam's defense team, would say, "Saddam had no sense of worry that he was going to be executed—he thought this was a temporary inconvenience, and that he'd again rule Iraq."

Private Martin, a burly Pennsylvanian who looked like he could be a bouncer back home, would later recall that after the nearby explosions Saddam would express concern and ask, Were your friends nearby? Are they okay? Martin could never tell whether Saddam's concern was real or feigned. But at least in his and the other soldiers' presence, the former president rarely, if ever, spoke ill of the U.S. military. He generally acknowledged that they were just doing their job. For the Bushes, Secretary of Defense Rumsfeld, and the Iraqi officials whom he reviled as American "puppets" and "stooges," though, he had nothing but scorn.

Sometimes Saddam couldn't resist volunteering advice to the guards on how the Americans could more effectively manage the occupation and pacify the country.

"The people are used to being ruled," Saddam would say, before offering one of the folksy analogies he liked to use. "You wouldn't leave the doors to a bank open," he said, the implication being that only with sufficient force could chaos and lawlessness be avoided. After the soldiers' talks with Saddam, it was sometimes hard not to wonder, as Adam Rogerson did, if they "were just over there trying to stop something that's been going on forever."

Saddam seemed to particularly enjoy the company of Joseph, the Lebanese-American interpreter who by now had spent a year with him, the two having first met when Joseph began his assignment in the summer of 2005. Joseph was a big man in his fifties, and carried himself with a confidence—bordering on cockiness—that belied his status as an interpreter and likely helped him develop a rapport with Saddam. Prior to meeting the dictator for the first time, the interpreter had no doubt that Saddam was a "brutal tyrant who deserved to be wiped out" for his crimes. Over time, though, he grew to enjoy his daily interaction with the former president. He found himself impressed by some of the same things that had struck Doc Ellis and the Super Twelve—for example, the former president's habit of rising to greet his guest and ceremoniously waving him into his cell. It was as if Saddam was subconsciously trying to convince his visitor, and perhaps even himself, that he was still a head of state, formally welcoming visiting dignitaries into his private quarters.

The closeness that developed between Saddam and Joseph contrasted with the few, if any, meaningful relationships Saddam had over the course of his nearly three-decade rule. As the CIA's John Maguire later pointed out, "Saddam had no friends. A lot of people had affection for him, but it was not reciprocal. He was alone as a leader." The one thing, after all, that Saddam could not decree during his reign was genuine human interaction. A victim of his own paranoid personality, he evidently craved the kind of honest conversations that his brutal nature ensured would never happen.

Terrible fates befell senior advisors who dared speak the truth. One minister made the mistake of suggesting to Saddam that he temporarily step down in order to end the war with Iran and secure more favorable postwar terms. The mere suggestion that he relinquish any power—even for a brief time—constituted an impudence that Saddam couldn't countenance. His overpowering narcissism, which according to psychologists was most likely rooted in deep underlying insecurity, conditioned him to lash out against any perceived challenge. The unfortunate minister was immediately detained by Saddam's security forces. His wife, alerted to his abduction, pleaded for Saddam to show mercy and send her husband home. Saddam did indeed send him home a few days later—in a black canvas bag, chopped into small pieces.

Joseph never saw this side of Saddam. He knew only an older man who "showed sincerity and love to others," who was "humble . . . normal . . . like any other." Joseph was especially impressed when, during one visit, Saddam motioned to him and explained that he had a special gift. It was a book, entitled *Zabiba and the King*. Saddam explained that he'd written it. He was proud of his work, and in handing it over he insisted that Joseph promise to read it.

Joseph was flattered by Saddam's attention and assured him he would.

Zabiba and the King was one of a number of books Saddam claimed authorship of. His retreat into the realm of his imagination had begun years earlier, when he was still in power, and as his tenure lengthened he would spend increasingly more time escaping into art, history, and poetry. In fact, toward the end of his rule, he'd grown so detached from the daily administration of his country that Taha Yassin Ramadan, his former vice president, said that even in periods of crisis it could sometimes "take three days to get in touch with him."

Farouq Palace, Tikrit, Iraq—fall of 1996

General Ra'ad al-Hamdani, then head of the elite Republican Guard in Tikrit, heard his phone ring.

General Hamdani, you're being summoned to the Farouq Palace, one of Saddam's aides informed him. The president wants you and the other commanders to join him immediately.

What now? Okay, I'll be right over, Hamdani said, but it will take a few hours to get the brigade commanders from Mosul, Kirkuk, and Baghdad.

A few hours later, Hamdani and his deputies drove down the long boulevard toward the enormous domed gate to the Farouq Palace compound in Tikrit. It was a beautiful fall day in Iraq, the skies a clear blue. The approach to the palace was fantastically over-the-top. There was a giant arch that towered over a long entrance drive, like a misplaced Champs Élysées rising from flat scrubland. Once the officers were waved in by security, they beheld a different world. Blanketing the palace grounds were date palms and lush manicured lawns, which led down to the Tigris as it flowed languidly south toward the capital.

The assembled military leaders wondered why they were there, imagining that perhaps there'd been an emergency and they'd soon be led to a military operations room. Instead, they were ushered into a large, plushy ballroom. Upon entering, they instinctively jumped to attention at the sight of the president, who was wearing casual civilian clothes and greeted them with a large grin. Scanning the room, Hamdani noticed that Saddam appeared to be presiding over a gathering of artists and poets, some of whom he recognized. The attendees, a Who's Who of Iraq's creative community, were assembled on elegant couches facing Saddam, who was seated on a throne-like chair at the room's front. Next to him was a podium at which the artists would take turns delivering presentations and lectures.

"God salutes the Republican Guards," Saddam said affably, at once responding to their salute and introducing the military men with a broad smile to the assembled artists. Even though Saddam appeared to be in one of his more carefree and voluble moods, one of Hamdani's deputies was so struck with fear at the sudden audience with the president that he froze as he saluted, his mouth unable to get out the words to introduce himself.

Saddam simply smiled at the officer's nervousness, and invited the new arrivals to sit down.

They still had no idea why they were there. Their confusion was not allayed as poets began to take turns at the podium, reading their work to Saddam, who appeared as relaxed and happy as Hamdani could ever recall. He would sometimes interrupt the orations to clap, otherwise sitting back and puffing happily on his cigar. The officers, meanwhile, remained rigid in their seats.

The poets took breaks to nibble on pastries and sip tea and coffee, but the military men felt too out of place to mingle, and so they remained awkwardly fixed in their seats. After nearly two hours of poetry, Saddam took his leave from the assembled artists, who proceeded to retire to an outdoor garden. Hamdani followed the poets outside. Feeling like someone who'd crashed a party, and self-consciously aware of how much he stood out in his military uniform, he approached one of Saddam's aides and gingerly asked if the officers were still needed by the president. No, the man said, and so they finally left.

They never did discover why they'd been summoned to the palace in the first place.

No one from the afternoon's gathering could have known where Saddam had gone after he disappeared, but these impromptu artistic salons seemed partially aimed at stoking his creative energies.

Brought by the country's great artists into closer connection with his muse, he would hunker over sheets of paper and try his hand at composing his own works of literature—works such as *Zabiba and the King*, whose themes seem telling.

The allegorical tale features a king imprisoned in a palace that is rife with disloyal advisors, perpetually scheming in the shadows. The king craves genuine human interaction, and discovers it in the person of Zabiba, a plainspoken peasant woman who wins his heart with her candor and affection. She says to him, "Isn't loneliness the worst enemy of one in power? And to put an end to this loneliness, one must flee it." When the King remarks that he loves to "have a good laugh with the common folk," Zabiba responds by asking him why he stays "locked up in the palace . . . sitting in house arrest even though nobody ordered you to do it." She continues, "Your palace is a den for breeding demons. It looks like a place where Shaitan [Satan] himself chose to breed . . . and where Shaitan dwells, you can be sure betrayal is being plotted."

CHAPTER 29

Baghdad, Iraq—summer of 2006

Saddam was losing weight, and the Americans were getting nervous. Recognizing that his physical well-being was a form of leverage, Saddam had launched a hunger strike—in part to protest what he claimed was insufficient security for his defense lawyers. Indeed, Khamis al-Obeidi had recently been gunned down in Baghdad, the third member of the defense team to be killed. With Saddam's initial handpicked lawyers packing their bags and decamping to Amman, the court-appointed Iraqi legal team was forced to assume the defense duties.

The results of Saddam's hunger strike were beginning to show. He wasn't under the illusion that his protest would impact the results of the trial, but he knew that at a minimum it would cast another cloud over the proceedings. All of this worried the Americans, who were intent on ensuring that the trial and detention were carried out as professionally as possible. The Americans were "terrified that Saddam would die," recalls William Wiley, the Canadian lawyer participating in Saddam's defense.

Whether as a result of pressure from Saddam, or out of solidarity, the former president's codefendants made at least a token effort to turn down food—though one of Saddam's deputies, former vice president Taha Yassin Ramadan, would have a particularly tough time of it. Ramadan had previously achieved notoriety in 2002 by suggesting that the growing tension between Iraq and the United States be resolved by staging a duel between Saddam and President George W. Bush, to be presided over by then U.N. secretary general Kofi Annan. A man of apparently large imagination, he also proved to have a large appetite. When the courthouse guards dutifully delivered him a tray of food, he must have thought that he could quickly wolf it down without anyone seeing. He was either unaware of, or had forgotten, the closed-circuit TV cameras blanketing the bowels of the IHT, monitored around the clock by scores of security personnel. Sure enough, they noticed the mustachioed former vice president looking around furtively before proceeding to scarf down his meal. Remarkably, Saddam also found out—even in prison, he could seem all-knowing—and, predictably, Ramadan received a "good bollocking" from his former boss, recalls the lawyer Wiley.

Increasingly concerned by Saddam's refusal to eat, a representative from the Regime Crimes Liaison Office (RCLO), the office that had been established by the Americans to help manage the trial, asked Wiley if he could find a way to get Saddam's defense team to convince their client to break his fast. Wiley possessed natural charm coupled with a raconteur's wit, so he was a good choice to play the role of ambassador. No one on the defense team seemed willing to deliver this message to Saddam—except for one man, Wiley would discover. There was a retired brigadier general from the Iraqi military's legal services branch, an older man who possessed a certain gravitas and who appeared remarkably unafraid of Saddam. The old officer's reward for his apparent courage was to be deputized by the group to ask Saddam to please start eating.

Losing no time, the older general immediately raised the former president on the video-teleconference (VTC) terminal connecting the defendants' subterranean cells to an aboveground room used by their lawyers. Choosing his words carefully, the general began: Mr. President, we're very worried about your health, as you haven't eaten in quite a few days.

Surprisingly, he was not cut off, and so, slightly emboldened, the general went on to say, All of us are concerned about you, and we would encourage you to resume eating, whatever you think of this process. He then concluded, And you *have* to do what I say . . . because I'm older than you.

The other lawyers assembled in the VTC room held their breath and braced themselves.

After a tense silence, Saddam burst out laughing. Okay, he agreed, I will eat.

The old man had understood Saddam's character and had intuited what kind of approach would be most likely to yield dividends. According to Wiley, the general had smartly bet that the former president was "probably looking for a face-saving way out of the hunger strike and had appealed to Saddam's vanity by first saying how worried they were about his health, and then taking a bold chance to lighten the mood by finishing off with a joke." Wiley believes the stratagem also worked partly because the deliverer of the message was a respected military man, and not a political hack.

Meanwhile, closing arguments in the Dujail trial had begun, and Saddam hadn't appeared in court for a few weeks. Wisely, to maintain order the judge had decided to bring in the defendants one at a time. It was Saddam's turn as day thirty-five of the Dujail trial began, and he immediately complained that he'd been on a hunger strike for nearly twenty days, and in the hospital for the last three, where he said he'd been force-fed from a tube.

On this day Saddam was without the international defense team that he and his daughter Raghad had retained, most choosing to hunker down in nearby Amman, Jordan, in continued protest over their security. They also felt that their attendance served to legitimize what they'd concluded was an inherently unjust trial. Saddam had long considered the trial a sham, and in strategy sessions with his defense team he'd often seemed more interested in Ramsey Clark's stories about working in LBJ's White House than in the particulars of his case. Saddam's closing argument in response to the charges stemming from the Dujail crackdown was, therefore, in the hands of the substitute Iraqi lawyers put in place by the RCLO.

Saddam immediately set out to intimidate his court-appointed

Iraqi defense lawyers, since he saw them as complicit in enabling what he considered a fraudulent trial to move forward. With the courtroom crowd and those watching on television as his audience, Saddam menacingly jabbed a finger at his court-appointed attorneys and shot them an icy glare of the kind that in earlier years might have constituted a death sentence. He warned, "If you present the argument, I will consider you my personal enemy and an enemy of the state." Building a head of steam, he continued, "You're going to read what the Canadian man [William Wiley] wrote. I challenge you, did you write it? I don't want history to be stained by this defense." In fact, Saddam didn't want court-appointed lawyers to present *any* defense, since he feared it would make the trial appear more legitimate.

"You do not write history, people write history," Judge Rauf interjected, trying to cut off Saddam's threats and grandstanding.

When it finally came time to deliver the closing argument, the court-appointed defense lawyer given the task grew so nervous that he claimed to fall ill, and a colleague was designated to take over. The essence of the latter's argument—which the Canadian Wiley had, in fact, assisted with—was that the prosecution hadn't presented any convincing evidence that Saddam exercised control over the state organs that carried out the crackdown following the failed assassination attempt in Dujail. The lawyer argued that there was no established chain of command or forensic evidence linking Saddam to the subsequent imprisonments and alleged executions.

Though it was a clever defense, the suggestion that he hadn't been in charge of what his subordinates had allegedly done was more than the narcissistic Saddam could bear. He interrupted the defense presentation, thundering, "Not a single plane can fly without my order."

His sudden proclamation was at once fabulously revealing, and entirely self-defeating. Nothing could have made his priorities more clear; defending his imagined status as all-powerful ruler was of more importance than exploiting a nuanced legal argument to bolster his defense.

Saddam then pivoted to the subject that had *really* been bothering him. "When you issue the death penalty, it should be by firing squad. Remember that I am military and I should not be hanged like a normal criminal." The judge reminded Saddam that the trial was not yet over, and that the court hadn't yet issued a verdict. Nonetheless, discussing the possible execution had sparked Saddam's belligerence. "I'm sure that you hear the sounds of weapons just as we hear them, though we are in jail. This is the sound of the people," he said.

"You are provoking the killing of people by car bombs," Rauf responded.

"I provoke against America and against the invaders—I urge the people to kill the aggressive invaders," Saddam fired back.

Judge Rauf then made what would perhaps be his most controversial comments of the trial. "Around sixty Iraqis die daily, while just two American soldiers are killed. Who are the victims here?" the judge asked.

"I do not incite killing," responded Saddam.

"Well, if you command your groups of mujahideen, or whatever their names, ask them to attack the Americans in their camps, not the civilians in the streets, they are innocent," said the judge.

Rauf's comments, while remarkably tone deaf in light of the American blood that had been shed to bring Saddam to justice, nonetheless made sense when viewed from the perspective of an Iraqi nationalist trying to show Saddam that Iraqi civilians bore the brunt of the suffering caused by the insurgency.

Saddam's fiery call to kill Americans, meanwhile, was dramatically at odds with the avuncular demeanor of the prisoner who was affectionately nicknamed "Abu," or "Father," by his Lebanese-American interpreter, and who once referred to his American guards as his "sons."

Who was the *real* Saddam? All that could be said definitively was that his demeanor would change the instant he joined his guards in the elevator following a court appearance. Whether he'd had a good day in court or a bad one, "he left it in the courtroom," says

Private Dawson, recalling how "even if Saddam had just gotten mad at the judge, he would step out of the courtroom and joke with me."

One moment Saddam would be in the courtroom "yelling and swinging his arms and calling the judge a sissy boy," says Hutch, and the next he'd be relaxing contentedly in his subterranean cell, "like he was proud of himself for giving them hell." The former president effortlessly downshifted from "game time" to "play time."

Often, Hutch would fetch for Saddam some of the Raisin Bran Crunch that he liked and watch as the old man enjoyed it with some tea. Then the courtroom firebrand of a half hour earlier would peel off his suit and fire up a cigar, puffing on it for a few minutes before collapsing onto his cot for a nap, "exhausted from the show."

CHAPTER 30

Baghdad, Iraq—fall of 2006

If there was only a day or two between trial appearances, the American soldiers would keep Saddam at the IHT to avoid exposing him to the unnecessary risk of shuttling him back and forth from the Rock by helicopter. At the Crypt, the Super Twelve were generally more focused on the prosaic concerns of everyday life than on the history-making drama unfolding in the courtroom above. They accepted that their contribution to the trial was ensuring that Saddam was properly cared for.

Among their daily responsibilities was making sure Saddam was well fed, and for this, like everything, they developed a routine. Hutch would pick up Saddam's food from the chow hall and deliver it to his cell in a cardboard box. He made sure that each item on the ridged paper plate was segregated from the neighboring types of food, using a napkin to carefully wipe off the rims between the sections. Saddam loved seafood or red meat as an entree. If the food wasn't presented to his liking, he sometimes wouldn't touch it. He wouldn't complain, but he could be stubborn. He'd simply open the box, examine it, close it, and quietly push it to the side.

When Hutch was at the Crypt and neither guarding Saddam nor sleeping, he liked to log on to the Internet in the media room, which the soldiers could use when the computers were available. He'd spend most of his online time emailing his wife and kids, and occasionally check to see how his Longhorns were faring as college football season heated up.

There was also a small room near the Crypt where the soldiers had been able to hook up a DVD player and a PlayStation as another way to pass the limited amount of time they weren't on shift. One afternoon Private Dawson was in the fourth quarter of a heated *NFL 2K5* game when another Super Twelve member, Lieutenant Jackson, not long removed from his commissioning as an Army officer, walked in. The young lieutenant announced, "You're done," and, as Hutch later recalled, demanded that Dawson turn off his game and allow Jackson and an officer friend to watch "some female show like *Sex and the City*." Hutch was as annoyed by the officers' imperiousness as he was puzzled by their choice of programming.

A veteran of a number of combat deployments, as compared to Lieutenant Jackson's zero, Hutch jumped to young Dawson's defense, declaring, "No, sir, that's not how things go." He was sick of what he saw as the lieutenant throwing his weight around unnecessarily, especially as he was "straight out of college and shouldn't have been ordering soldiers around in their off time." Eventually, a captain and a first sergeant rushed in to defuse the situation. Hutch didn't have a dog in the fight but was responding to what he felt was a violation of the unspoken code governing the relationship between young officers and enlisted soldiers. Maybe, too, the grind of this deployment had him chafing at Army life, a mode of existence in which rank so often determined what a guy could or couldn't do.

When they got back to the Rock, Hutch noticed that Saddam's cell was growing increasingly cluttered with papers and books. While the outdoor rec area provided the former president a place to escape his claustrophobic cell and enjoy a change of scenery and some more space, it sometimes got uncomfortably cold out there in the evening as the days grew shorter and winter approached. There was a small room between Saddam's cell and the outdoor rec area that was nearly empty. It occurred to Hutch that they could clean up this room and convert it into a small office and indoor smoking area for Saddam. That way he'd have some more space to read, write, enjoy his cigars, and manage his correspondence. Without being asked, Hutch, Tasker, and a few others set to work transforming the old storage room into an "office" for the former president.

They spent an afternoon clearing out the ten-by-sixteen-foot room and preparing it for Saddam. Hutch spent a few hours scrubbing scuff marks off the walls. The soldiers managed to dig up a small wooden desk and leather office chair that had been abandoned elsewhere in the old palace, and they installed the furniture in the center of the room. They hung a small Iraqi flag behind the desk to make it seem more official and befitting a head of state.

Hutch looked forward to being the one who escorted Saddam to the new office they'd constructed for him. After the soldiers had completed the finishing touches, Hutch led Saddam out of his cell and toward the rec area, but at the right moment he took a detour and surprised the old man, revealing to him the newly outfitted office space. Hutch smiled with pride as the former president absorbed what he'd been gifted with.

Saddam had thought he was headed to the rec area so, when they entered, he was carrying his wet wipe box full of cigars and a water bottle. Hutch explained what he and the soldiers had done. Saddam slowly examined the room, almost as if inspecting it, making small adjustments to the location of the desk and checking the stability of the chair. While he did so, Hutch quickly scrubbed some residual dust off the desk and chair with a baby wipe.

Saddam stepped back, surveyed the new space one final time, and beamed.

He went back to retrieve stacks of his yellow legal pads from his cell, purposefully delivering them to his new office. While wearing a dark jacket over his dishdasha, he sat behind the desk and rifled through his paperwork. Meanwhile, Hutch and another guard sat across from him—the same place those who were summoned for an official audience with him in years past would have sat. The scene felt a little unreal—almost as if Saddam were pretending, a child playing make-believe.

The former president would go on to spend a portion of each

day there, busying himself with his reading and writing. He even carried his beat-up old transistor radio into his new work area, listening to that curious mix of Iraqi and American music as he went about his business. He worked with a sense of urgency, scribbling entries in a journal he kept so that "the people . . . may know the facts as they are and not as those who want to counterfeit them," as well as composing his poems.

The soldiers enjoyed pleasing Saddam, in part because he was pleasant in turn and surprisingly low-maintenance. Hutch would later recall that "everyone brought things to him, but he didn't require it. You always hear stories of the rich and famous people having a fit because somebody didn't take all the green M&Ms out of their bowl of candy or something like that. He was never like that. He appreciated everything he had; he took very good care of his clothes and things, because that was the way he was raised."

While that assessment was generally true, it did overlook some of Saddam's pickier habits, such as refusing to eat "torn omelets" or, out of a fear of germs, his insistence that the guards get up and close his cell door for him. As junior enlisted soldiers—many from working-class backgrounds—most of the Super Twelve appreciated a former head of state showing them a respect that they sometimes didn't get from their own superior officers. For this, they'd indulge the former president some of his eccentricities.

The Super Twelve had never gotten to know Saddam the dictator, only Saddam the imprisoned old man. They believed they were doing the right thing in bringing some dignity to his existence. The Saddam they went out of their way to accommodate was a man that Iraqis like Shameem Rassam, who'd sat across from him in different circumstances back when his power was absolute, couldn't imagine.

Baghdad, Iraq—late 1970s

"It's the palace calling," said the maid.

Shameem Rassam was a popular female news anchor in Baghdad.

Since there were only two television channels, she was a recognizable figure around the city. Her status wasn't unique for a woman at the time, since Saddam prided himself on progressive policies with regard to women in the workforce, and even in his military, where they could rise to positions of some prominence. In fact, he was even reported to have commented that he preferred the insights of women, which he felt were characterized by more candor.

None of that reassured Shameem, though, when she picked up the phone and immediately recognized the unmistakable, deep voice of "Our Uncle." It was late in the afternoon, and the sunlight streaming into Shameem's comfortable, well-appointed living room was beginning to soften. Shameem had just gotten home from work when she fielded the call, still wearing the fashionable outfit she'd worn on air.

"Good afternoon," she said, working hard to make sure her voice didn't betray fear.

"Can you come and see me now?" Saddam asked.

Confused but careful to sound as calm as possible, she managed to utter a hesitant "What?"

After all, despite her job as a prominent TV anchor, it was still exceedingly odd for Saddam—or the Anointed One, as he was sometimes called—to call her at home.

In his deep monotone, revealing nothing of his intentions by the intonation of his voice, Saddam said, "This is Saddam. You are coming now."

Before she left, Shameem made sure to tell her husband about the bizarre summons. He was upset at the news but recognized there was nothing they could do. As she eased her Toyota sedan into Baghdad's busy rush-hour traffic for the short fifteen-minute drive, her mind began to race. What could it be? She couldn't help but remember the people she'd worked with over the years who'd been "sent away with no explanation and for no reason." In this she was similar to so many others who'd received summonses from Saddam over the years, minds furiously churning to divine why the dictator wanted to see them. Trying to anticipate the nature of his interest, and strategize on how to respond, was like preparing for a job interview where the result of a poor performance could be death.

As Shameem drove, she reassured herself that Saddam, who sometimes took a keen interest in what was being broadcast, probably just wanted to discuss the programming at her station. She couldn't imagine that it had anything to do with her brother and father, who'd been detained by Saddam's security forces a few years prior—but one never knew. Following their release, the two had rarely spoken of their captivity in the nightmarish Abu Ghraib prison, their silence leaving little doubt that whatever *had* happened had left an indelible scar.

At the Parliament building men ushered Shameem into a visitors' center, where she was searched and forced to surrender her belongings. Saddam was extremely paranoid, so anyone invited to an audience with him could expect elaborate and invasive security protocols.

She was then led into a reception area outside Saddam's private office. It was a nice waiting room, with comfortable couches surrounding a coffee table in the middle. A handful of others were waiting there. No one said a word.

After a short wait, a guard beckoned, and Shameem got up to approach Saddam's office. The guard told her he'd watch her purse while she met the president, and he provided one instruction: Do not shake the president's hand.

Shameem didn't need to ask why. She was aware of Saddam's fear of germs.

It was around 6:00 p.m. Late meetings like this weren't uncommon for Saddam. He possessed impressive stamina and a strong work ethic and, at this point in his rule, still often worked fourteen to sixteen hours a day.

Taking a deep breath, and willing her heart to stop racing, Shameem entered the president's office, trailed by the security guard. Saddam slowly rose and seemed to wince from what appeared to be a recent back injury. Almost reflexively, Shameem offered a traditional Arabic expression, roughly translated as "Thank God for your health."

Saddam replied, "The curse of being tall." At roughly six foot one, and with a ramrod posture in public, he looked down on most Iraqis. This counted for something in a tribal culture in which size was sometimes still equated with masculinity and power.

He then walked around from behind his desk and extended his hand. Shameem felt a surge of panic. She'd just been instructed *not* to shake his hand, and now here he was inviting her to. Seeing her hesitate, he asked, "Aren't you going to shake my hand?"

She managed a confused smile and gestured to the guard who was still hovering behind her. "He told me not to." Seeing Saddam's hand still extended, she shook it with as much confidence as she could muster. It was a cold handshake, and surprisingly limp for such a big man.

The door behind Saddam's desk opened, and a uniformed aide delivered a tray with two cups of tea. Saddam gestured for Shameem to take a seat, and returned to his chair behind the desk. The aide who'd delivered the tea also had a file for Saddam to sign, which he quickly did.

Shameem was too nervous and self-conscious to take anything more than furtive glances at her surroundings, but she couldn't miss the stately floor-to-ceiling cabinet behind Saddam, lined with ornaments and books, and an Iraqi flag hanging beside it. Some Arabic magazines rested on the president's desk, not far from the tea that sat in front of her. She was afraid to take the first sip, so it remained untouched.

Perhaps noticing her discomfort, Saddam looked up and said, Please, help yourself.

Still nervous, she responded: After you.

Saddam took a sip, and smiled. It was an odd smile, lacking in warmth. His mouth muscles had moved, but the rest of his countenance remained blank. He began the conversation with her matter-of-factly: Your father has a property in Mosul. We *want* it. He explained that the need to expand a government facility in Mosul made it imperative her family's adjacent land be seized.

How *is* your dad, by the way? Saddam asked almost offhandedly.

The question sounded innocent enough, but Shameem knew that answering it could lead her into a potential minefield, as there was a chance he was aware of her father's detention a few years ago. She searched for a response, but before she could say anything, Saddam preempted her. Tell him we're going to take the land, he said. As was often the case, his expression didn't betray what he was thinking. While studying her carefully, he didn't quite look her in the eye.

Shameem nodded, knowing that with Saddam there was no debate. All she could think about was getting out of there as quickly as possible. Then, without another word, he began rifling through some files and paperwork on his desk, as if she were no longer there. She had no idea what to do. After what felt like an eternity but was probably less than a minute, a security guard came in and ushered her out of the president's office. She breathed a sigh of relief as she made her exit.

As soon as she arrived home, she told her husband about the meeting, relaying the news about her family's property in Mosul. His expression showed anger, but such was life in Saddam's Iraq—where saying anything critical of the president was punishable by death—that he smartly bit his tongue, and simply said, "Thank God everyone is alive."

Shameem wasn't yet ready to tell her father the bad news about his property. He was still weak from a recent heart attack, and in some ways had never been the same since his release from Abu Ghraib. It was as if he were somehow still "stuck in the trauma of detention, still stuck in a different world," she would say later. She didn't want to add to his stress. Still, she knew she had to eventually tell him. When she did, he quietly cursed the unfair confiscation, but assured her that more than anything he was just relieved to see her back unharmed.

Shameem was home, and that was what was important.

CHAPTER 31

Baghdad, Iraq—November 5, 2006

The streets of Baghdad were even more tense than usual as Saddam's verdict drew near. It was November 5, 2006, nearly three years since Saddam had been captured. Baghdad was hazy and humid as temperatures reached the mid-eighties. Passing storm clouds seemed an augury for what was about to happen below. The prime minister, Nouri al-Maliki, had imposed an around-the-clock curfew in the city, as well as other areas where the government feared unrest. Both Iraqi and American troops were on high alert. American fighter jets streaked overhead at low altitude, just about disappearing across the horizon by the time their sonic booms shocked those on the streets below. Their presence was a show-of-force gesture meant to dissuade anyone who might be inclined toward violent protest. The Iraqi High Tribunal, always well defended, was protected on this day by an even more stifling security cordon. In armored vehicles guarding approaches to the building, soldiers alertly manned turrets, anxiously fingering the safeties on their weapons.

Saddam Hussein entered the courtroom that day with his trademark strut, like a prizefighter entering the ring. His still imposing aura, not easily described but immediately evident to onlookers, was on full display. Ushered to his leather chair in the defendants' dock, he sat down, clad in a dark suit and white shirt, his jet-black hair and eyebrows standing in sharp contrast to his salt-and-pepper beard. Only the bags under his eyes betrayed the fact that, at age sixty-nine and facing a severe sentence, he was nearing the end of what had been an exhausting life's journey.

Anxious to get started, Judge Rauf peered through large glasses perched on his hawklike nose and commanded Saddam to "stand up."

"No, I want to sit down," Saddam replied.

The judge again demanded that Saddam rise, this time gesturing for security to force the former president to his feet.

It was about 12:30 p.m. when Judge Rauf delivered the verdict. "The court hereby sentences the defendant, Saddam Hussein al-Majid, to death by hanging."

As soon as the words began escaping Rauf's mouth, Saddam jabbed his right hand in the air and launched into a fierce denunciation: "Long live the people. Long live the nation. Down with the traitors. Down with the invaders. God is great. God is great. God is great. Long live the people. Long live the nation. Down with the traitors. Down with the invaders." The hate in his eyes recalled a description of him once offered by a former prime minister of Jordan. Said the Jordanian, while "Saddam was often charming and humorous, cordial and friendly," there were other times when one felt one was "looking into the eyes of the devil."

Judge Rauf continued to recite the specific charges and verdicts as Saddam plowed ahead with his vehement protestations, the two men trying to out-shout each other. Saddam held aloft the ever-present large green Koran and gesticulated wildly with it. He almost appeared to be enjoying the raucous spectacle, at one point even showing a trace of an amused smirk. He'd again hijacked the proceedings and ensured that he, and not the judge, would be the one the TV cameras focused on. The English-language interpreter for the broadcast chose to translate nearly every word of Saddam's angry monologue, allowing much of Rauf's verdict to go untranslated.

It almost looked as if Saddam had begun losing interest as the judge continued reading the lengthy sentence, but, unwilling to cede the limelight, the former president continued dutifully with his tirade: "Down with those of base blood. We do not fear death. We are the cradle of humanity while the invaders are the criminals. They are the enemy of humanity. The traitors are the enemy of humanity. God is great. Long live the great Iraqi people. You cannot make decisions. You are tyrants. You are the servants of the occupation. Long live the noble nation and death betides the enemy."

Finally done with reading the verdict, Rauf instructed the security guards to "take him out." As the guards approached Saddam to lead him from the courtroom, he could be heard hissing to one, "Don't push me, boy."

Saddam had been found guilty of willful killing, deportation or forcible transfer, torture, and other inhumane acts, according to the Iraqi Penal Code and Iraqi High Tribunal statutes. The charge of willful killing was the one for which he'd been sentenced to death by hanging. His defense team would have thirty days to file an appeal, though there was little reason for optimism, given that the government was dominated by Shia who hadn't hidden their desire to exact retribution on Saddam for his crimes.

As soon as Saddam's day in court had ended, he was returned to the Super Twelve. The handoff occurred at the door of the elevator that would deliver him back to his cell in the bowels of the Iraqi High Tribunal, where he'd await a trip in a Black Hawk back to the Rock.

As they rode down in the elevator following the verdict, Private Dawson noticed no change in Saddam's demeanor. It is God's will, Saddam said matter-of-factly. I'm a soldier, and what God wants, God does.

It was almost as if he was going out of his way to project an attitude of cocky disdain, brushing aside the verdict as a nonevent. I've been sentenced to death before and it never happened, Saddam said.

Adam Rogerson later recalled that even with his death looking like a near certainty, Saddam remained convinced that "he was going to get out, get married again, and this was going to be put behind him. He was one hundred percent sure."

Hardened as many of the Super Twelve were by tough upbringings and—in all cases—by military training, and admiring of such virtues as strength and courage, they couldn't help but be impressed by Saddam's stoicism. Private Jeff Price, who had not grown as close to Saddam as some of the others, would, in looking back, nonetheless still accord him grudging respect: "He deserves credit for taking it like a man—you've got to be pretty doggone strong to do that."

The local and international response to the verdict was revealing. President Bush would say, "Saddam Hussein's trial is a milestone in the Iraqi people's efforts to replace the rule of a tyrant with the rule of law. History will record today's judgment as an important achievement on the path to a free and just and unified society." The headline of the independent Iraqi paper *Azzaman* read, "Iraqis Divided over Saddam Death Sentence." Regional coverage tended to predictably break along Sunni-Shia lines, with the Qatari paper *Al-Sharq* denouncing the verdict as a "death sentence for Sunni Arabs, shattering all hope of a dialogue between the various sections of the Iraqi people." Most prescient may have been the Palestinian *Al-Quds* daily, which predicted that the death sentence would "aggravate confessional divisions instead of ushering in a new era of entente between Iraqis."

As soon as the verdict was announced, Shiite neighborhoods such as Baghdad's Sadr City rang out with celebratory gunfire, dancing, and the giddy honking of car horns. Meanwhile, Sunni demonstrators in Saddam's adopted hometown of Tikrit took to the streets, proudly holding aloft pictures of the former leader and fellow tribesman, angrily vowing to exact revenge for what they saw as his unjust sentence.

The man who was at the center of this maelstrom remained serene as he was returned to his cell at the Rock. He soon resumed his comfortable routine of puffing on his cigars, watering his plants, writing his poems, and chatting amiably with his interpreter,

Joseph, and the Super Twelve. He didn't appear to be burdened by guilt. In his mind, everything he'd done had been consistent with the code he articulated in his novel *Zabiba and the King*: "Any means are justified if they achieve the goals dictated by the interests of power and security."

For now, Saddam could again retreat to the cocoon of his prison cell, insulated from the madness he'd helped spawn. Whether his calm bravado was a true stance or something manufactured—a great piece of performance art—he gave every impression that if death *did* come for him he'd be ready.

CHAPTER 32

Baghdad, Iraq—fall of 2006

Hutch was leafing through a *People* magazine while guarding Saddam in his cell at the Rock. Much had changed since those awkward first encounters when they'd feared the man inside the cell—the dictator whose sinister visage had become synonymous with evil. Now guard duty sometimes felt like waiting for a haircut at the barbershop and skimming magazines to pass the time. If anyone had an excuse to be anxious it was Saddam. Though his lawyers would scramble to appeal his sentence, he knew his country well enough to recognize that his deliverance wouldn't come from the Shia-dominated government appreciating the force of his lawyers' arguments.

As Hutch sat watching Saddam, his mind drifted to the days he'd spent with another old man approaching his death—his grandfather, a Navy veteran. Hutch had been struck by the fact that his grandpa and Saddam shared the same birthday, April 28. Thinking back, Hutch remembered the living room in which he'd kept his grandfather company those final months—before he succumbed to the cancer he'd likely picked up from cleaning asbestos-lined insulation in submarines. Hutch had always made time to visit his grandfather as the old man's health deteriorated, even when he was in a tough place himself, partying too hard and on an uncertain career path.

An image came to Hutch of his grandpa sitting in front of

the television set, watching one of the John Wayne westerns he enjoyed, connected to his oxygen tank. One of the Afghan throws Hutch's grandma would knit would be draped carefully over the back of the chair. Once grandfather and grandson were left alone and all of the house's other occupants were out on errands, the old man would ask in a conspiratorial tone, "So, you got 'em?"

Sure, Hutch would say, pulling a contraband cigarette from his pocket and handing it to his grandpa. But I feel bad giving these to you.

Oh hell, the old man replied, I should have been dead a long time ago.

As the disease slowly ravaged his body, Hutch's grandpa was confined to his modest home, but, like Saddam in his cell, his mind still roamed the vast expanses of his past.

You know what, Hutch's grandfather liked to say with the oxygen tank hissing in the background, the only thing you have at my age are your memories. So make sure your memories are good ones.

One of his more cryptic observations sometimes crept into Hutch's mind as he sat observing Saddam. Westerns always have good guys, who wear a white hat, and bad guys, who wear black hats, his grandpa said. It's the sneaky guys in the gray hats, whose allegiances are always shifting, that you have to watch out for. If you're going to make a choice, the old man continued, go all the way.

The unspoken implication was that those who inhabited the wishy-washy world of gray were the least honorable of all.

Hutch felt a hand grasp his shoulder, and a surge of adrenaline shot through him. *Holy shit*, he realized, *I was sound asleep.* He'd been exhausted as he began his shift at the small desk located just outside the door to Saddam's cell. The Super Twelve had been up much of the night preparing to move Saddam back from the IHT to the Rock, before finally making the trip in the early-morning hours. The last thing Hutch remembered had been leafing through the *People* magazine.

Now Saddam was standing over him, large hand clasped on his

shoulder. Excuse me, my friend, he said, peering down at Hutch, who was still trying to shake off the mental cobwebs.

What can I do for you, sir? sputtered Hutch. He was trying as best he could to feign alertness, as if sudden hypervigilance would somehow disguise the fact that he'd been caught sound asleep on duty by the very man he'd been charged with guarding.

Time to go outside for a smoke, my friend, Saddam said. His tone was patient and relaxed, as if he was allowing Hutch a moment to clear his head and wake up.

Okay, sir, no problem, replied Hutch.

I am ready when you are ready, continued Saddam.

Hutch let out a faint curse as he got up, wincing. The cumulative effect of his four deployments had been more creakiness in his back than he should have had at his age.

"You get up like an old man," Saddam teased.

Hutch smiled and gathered his clipboard, radio, a bottle of water, and the magazine he'd been flipping through.

Once he'd collected everything he needed, Saddam stood back and allowed Hutch to lead the way through the short hallway and out into the rec area. The former president always insisted on the guards walking first, the opposite of the standard protocol. It was familiar to him, mirroring how he was escorted years before when he was in power. Hutch didn't object to the deviation from the norm. Indeed, it could be useful, since on a few occasions he'd feel Saddam's outstretched hand suddenly grasp the back of his arm for support as they navigated steps or bumps in the path.

Though the former president fought never to exhibit any signs of weakness when in the courtroom or in the public eye—he "moved like a twenty-five-year-old in public," Hutch would marvel—in the privacy of the Rock, Saddam would sometimes show signs of the sore hip, bad back, and swelling feet that bothered him.

Once they made it outside, Saddam positioned the plastic patio chair carefully so that he wouldn't be directly facing the blinding Baghdad sun, and then he slowly lowered himself into it. He groaned as he sank down. Then he lit one of his cigars.

I used to enjoy American movies, Saddam volunteered, looking up from his cigar. And you know which ones were my favorite?

No, responded Hutch, which ones did you like, sir?

Cowboy movies, Saddam replied.

Really? I like them, too, said Hutch, smiling.

John Wayne, cowboys and Indians, Saddam added, suggesting that these were his favorites.

The way Saddam would just start telling a random story, out of the blue, reminded Hutch of his grandfather. Like his grandfather, Hutch realized "that was what Saddam was left with—his memories—and I was letting him talk."

CHAPTER 33

Baghdad, Iraq—December 2006

The cold December air blew in over the man-made lake, gusting up against the walls of Saddam's former palace, now his prison. Overnight temperatures dropping into the high thirties ushered in a new season, providing a bracing reminder that Saddam's likely execution was fast approaching, barring a successful appeal of his death sentence, which no one expected.

As Adam Rogerson sat outside with Saddam in the Rock's rec area, the former president looked over at him and asked, You want to sit by the fire with me? He gestured to a plastic chair near the space heater he liked to call his "fire."

Rogerson had grown up inured to harsh Cleveland winters. Nonetheless, the air had a bite to it, and so he took Saddam up on the offer.

The former president fired up one of his large Cohibas, the smoke from each exhalation wafting gently into the night sky. Rogerson would have liked a cigarette, but he and his fellow guards weren't allowed to smoke while on duty, a policy that impacted a number of the Super Twelve, many of whom smoked. In addition to Rogerson, so did Hutch, Tasker, Perkins, Dawson, and Flanagan. Some, like Tasker, even supplemented their cigarette-supplied nicotine with chewing tobacco.

Rogerson had brought a small package his wife had sent—care of his deployed Army Post Office (APO) address—outside with him into the rec area that night. In it were some candles she'd purchased at Walmart back home in Ohio. Mail delivery had an odd way of connecting his wife's peaceful existence back home to his life in Iraq. Seeing a postal stamp from his hometown could be a source of both comfort and melancholy.

Rogerson noticed that Saddam was studying him carefully as he opened the package, and appeared intrigued by its contents. My wife has been sending me these candles recently, Rogerson volunteered.

I see that, Saddam said. What do you do with them?

Actually, I don't really need them, Rogerson said, laughing, but I suppose I can use them to make our living area smell better. You know how it is when a lot of guys spend so much time together—it can smell pretty nasty.

Both men chuckled.

Rogerson would end up using the candles to help illuminate, and freshen the smell, of the smoke pit where the Super Twelve would huddle to enjoy their cigarettes. The smoke pit was a tumbledown plywood enclosed area alongside the palace where they guarded Saddam on the Rock. It stood beside an abandoned pool; what had once been a shimmery surface of cool blue water was now an empty concrete hole in the ground.

The scented candles were a funny sight in the hands of the burly, tattooed military policeman. He handed one to Saddam so he could take a closer look.

Do you think maybe I could have one? Saddam asked.

Sure, Rogerson replied.

Thank you, my friend, said Saddam with a smile. He produced a pen and began to inscribe Arabic words in the candle, his hand moving across it with as much precision as he could muster. I've written a poem for my daughter, he said, before asking Rogerson to please give it to the Red Cross for delivery to her.

Years later, moments like these would lead Rogerson to reflect that "Saddam had the best life you could possibly have in prison, and he liked us. I'm a true believer that if one of our helicopters went down and the insurgents came to get him, he wouldn't have hurt us. We had a good relationship. I don't think he would have hurt me. I *know* he wouldn't have hurt Dawson. I know for sure he wouldn't have hurt him."

A few weeks later it was Christmas Day, 2006, and Saddam remained at the Rock, awaiting a decision on his appeal. It was still freezing by Baghdad standards—temperatures would drop to thirty-five degrees overnight. There were few decorations to mark the holiday season, aside from a small Christmas tree that someone had bought at the Post Exchange (PX) and set up in the room where the Super Twelve's three computer terminals were located. Little else distinguished Christmas from a normal day, save for a few more care packages arriving in the mail. Rogerson had been thrilled to open an especially large package that contained enough Cap'n Crunch Christmas cereal, along with other snacks and toiletries, for the entire squad.

Private James Martin huddled with Saddam outside near his "fire." Saddam was wearing his dishdasha with his favorite dark peacoat over it. The soldiers had noticed very little change in Saddam's demeanor in the days following his sentence. He was sitting under the solitary outdoor light, intently focused on another of the candles Rogerson had given him, which was cradled in his lap. He had a pen in his hand and was writing on the candle—about the size of a large glass—marking it carefully in Arabic script. After laboring at his task for a while, Saddam looked up at Martin, who was trying to stay warm on the other side of the rec area.

This is for my wife, the former president said.

Really? Martin asked, somewhat surprised, as Saddam had never spent much time discussing his wife. When the subject of family came up, he generally steered the conversation to his children.

Yes, we have a tradition, Saddam replied. Every year on the Christmas holiday we light a candle. I'm writing a poem for her on this one.

Martin thought he detected in the old man a certain melancholy. Despite Saddam's randy musings weeks before about finding a younger woman, on this particular night he seemed to miss his wife. Perhaps, too, he sensed that the end was near. For years now, gunfire and explosions could occasionally be heard in the distance, but, however much he talked up the possibility, no one had come to rescue him. Though in the courtroom playing to the cameras he'd projected great strength, in moments like this he appeared more vulnerable, his proudly erect bearing collapsing into a slump.

Saddam's odd observance of a Christian holiday tradition wasn't the first time he'd displayed a surprising affinity for something Christianity-related. He'd recently surprised Private Jeff Price when he asked to watch *The Passion of the Christ*. He'd never before taken advantage of the opportunity to use the DVD player he'd been provided, preferring instead to busy himself writing poems. To watch this particular film, with its potentially incendiary religious content, he had to sign a waiver. He'd signed obligingly and after the film was finished expressed anger at the way the Jewish characters in the movie had treated Jesus. Saddam maintained that "Iraqis would have treated him better." He went on to volunteer that it had been the best movie he'd ever seen, a response that Price thought was "pretty nice."

The next day, December 26, 2006, Saddam's appeal was denied by the Iraqi judges in an eighteen-page decision that had been issued with remarkable speed. He would now most assuredly face death by hanging, required by law to take place within thirty days. The decision's haste had caught American leadership by surprise. The U.S. ambassador and many other senior American officials stationed in Baghdad were taking holiday leave back in the States. Likely they'd underestimated the extent to which festering hatreds had accelerated the review process.

The appeal's rejection didn't surprise the Super Twelve. Most had little doubt that Saddam was guilty of the violence for which he'd been charged, and they hadn't expected him to get off. While spending time at the IHT, they'd heard some of the horrific testimony surrounding his chemical gas attacks on the Kurds. Still, they struggled to connect the brutality of Saddam's past with the pleasant man they dealt with on a day-to-day basis.

"When I'd see the trial going on, and what he'd done to his people," Rogerson later recalled, "I'd be like 'Holy shit,' there's a shit-load of dead people, he just killed an entire city. I'd think, 'You've got to be kidding me,' but then I'd see him, and I never looked at him like 'You're a psychopath,' because [that person] wasn't with me. . . . He was more like a grandpa."

In fact, Saddam would write an additional poem on one of Rogerson's candles that Christmas. It was for the Super Twelve. Translating, he told them that it said he wished they could be back home in America with their families to celebrate Christmas, instead of guarding him in Iraq.

CHAPTER 34

Baghdad, Iraq—December 30, 2006

Saddam was sleeping comfortably in his cell inside the Rock. The Super Twelve had been on standby for a few days, aware that orders to carry out the execution could come at any time. As the soldiers went about their daily tasks, they had an abstract understanding that their time with Saddam would shortly be over, but, having never participated in an execution before, the gravity of the situation hadn't really sunk in. It somehow didn't seem real that this charismatic older man, with whom they'd spent so much time, would soon be dead. Other than a bad back and some creaky bones, he seemed fine.

Chris Tasker remembers that a few of them had even been annoyed that the impending execution meant they'd have to miss a performance by Kid Rock, who'd flown in for a Christmas visit to the troops. The visit wasn't a complete bust, though. Tasker managed to spot the famous rocker as the soldier went for a smoke outside the chow hall after dinner one night.

It wasn't until the day before the execution, Friday, December 29, that they learned the mission was a go. Saddam had just enjoyed what would turn out to be his last meal, eagerly devouring the lobster tails that the soldiers had delivered to him from the Coalition Café dining facility on Camp Victory. Saddam had gained weight while in custody, and at one point jokingly lamented that he'd gotten "fat like an American."

A few hours later, Saddam said good night to Specialists Adam Rogerson and Art Perkins, who'd been quietly observing him from the small desk outside his cell. The guards turned out Saddam's light after he'd lain down on his cot, taking care to speak in hushed tones so as not to disturb him. Hours before, Sergeant Battaglia had secretly broken Saddam's small transistor radio to ensure he wasn't inadvertently alerted to the timing of his execution, since news programs had already begun to report that he'd soon be put to death.

Specialists Rogerson and Perkins sat vigil outside Saddam's cell, quietly flipping through magazines as the old man slept his typical deep sleep, untroubled by what fate might have in store. The guards' mood was somber, "Old Man" Perkins volunteering none of the random trivia that would alternately annoy and entertain his partners on long overnight shifts.

At around 3:00 a.m., Lieutenant Jackson and the burly Lebanese-American interpreter, Joseph, arrived at Saddam's cell. Nothing Jackson had learned in the course of his ROTC training, or his subsequent training to be a military police officer, had really prepared him for this moment. They turned on the light and went in.

Tonight's the night, they said, telling the former president that he needed to get up and begin making final preparations for his execution, which they explained would take place in a few hours. They knew that he didn't like to be rushed, and so they were providing him plenty of time to get ready.

Saddam took the news calmly, almost appearing to have anticipated it. He'd been sentenced to death before, he said, and it didn't bother him.

Joseph, who'd grown close to Saddam over the fifteen months they'd spent together, would later say that delivering this news was the most difficult moment of his life, since he now saw their relationship as "more of a friendship than that of criminal and translator."

It was early Friday night back in the States, and most Americans were going about their business, perhaps beginning the long New

Year's holiday weekend with a dinner out, or maybe just relaxing on the couch and watching college football bowl games. Hutch wished he could be watching his beloved Longhorns take on Iowa in the Alamo Bowl. Those watching the holiday football games back home had no idea what was taking place half a world away. Most Americans' minds had already drifted from the violence that was plaguing Iraq, content to return to the pleasant rhythms of life in an America where little had really changed since the attacks of 9/11, despite the breathless pronouncements that things would never be the same.

Stephen Hadley, President Bush's national security advisor, informed the president of the impending execution before he retired for the evening.

The fact that the Iraqi authorities chose to execute Saddam early the following morning, at the beginning of the joyous Eid al-Fitr holiday marking the end of Ramadan for Sunni Muslims (Shiites wouldn't observe the holiday until one day later), was an ominous sign to those with an understanding of Islam. It looked like a gratuitous display of disrespect from the Shiite government that would inflame sectarian animosities even more.

When they got the orders, Rogerson was unsure of what to expect. Tasker was worried that things could get wild, that there might be the Baghdad equivalent of a "last stand at the Alamo." Suddenly, Saddam's fanciful ruminations about being sprung from prison seemed a little less outlandish. Trying to quiet his anxiety, Tasker focused on doing what he'd been trained to do. He cleaned his weapon, checked his ammo magazines, and made sure he was as prepared as possible should things get hairy. Despite the unique nature of their assignment, the Super Twelve had experienced little real combat thus far in their deployment. In fact, they'd been so out of the fray that one would later describe them as little more than "babysitters" up to that point.

As the rest of the Super Twelve began preparing for what would be their final mission escorting Saddam, two of them chuckled at an inside joke. Saddam heard them and, irritated, asked if they were happy at what was taking place. This frustration would prove to be one of the few lapses from his otherwise stoic demeanor.

Saddam asked to bathe, and he began to purify himself according to Muslim tradition at the sink in his cell. There's a vulnerability that comes with stripping naked in front of a bunch of strangers. The former dictator who'd caused so much pain and suffering during his lifetime looked like any other old man as he washed himself for the final time. As individual Super Twelve members occasionally looked Saddam's way, the knowledge that they'd soon play a role in the execution of this living, breathing human being— one who'd always been good to them—began to gnaw at their psyches. Saddam had spent a lifetime numbed—either by his brutal upbringing or by the violence that had punctuated his rule—to just this sort of empathy.

The former president continued to deliberately prepare for his final appearance on the world stage. He had trouble finding the right pair of socks, and so a few soldiers helped him rummage through some bags before finding them. Though a bit more harried than usual as he scrambled to prepare for his movement to the execution site, Saddam seemed, even now, to be genuinely concerned with the well-being of the Super Twelve, even asking whether they'd gotten enough sleep prior to the early-morning mission.

Saddam spent some time taking a mental inventory of his small collection of belongings, "just sitting there and looking at his stuff," Hutch recalls. The soldier from Georgia was struck by how, "out of everything Saddam had ever owned and controlled," he was now reduced to this almost pathetic collection of old books, papers, and a few suits. The former president took a few moments to leaf through some of the materials he'd written, appearing to be checking them one last time to make sure they accurately communicated his thoughts.

After spending a few more minutes going through his things, Saddam looked up and called out, "My friend," as he usually would when trying to get a guard's attention, beckoning for Hutch to come over.

Hutch first thought, *All right, what does he want now?* Then he noticed that Saddam was holding a blue box. He handed the box to Hutch through the bars. Next he extended his arm through the bars, took off the expensive Raymond Weil watch he was wearing, and also handed it to Hutch.

It took a moment for it to register: Saddam was actually offering him his watch. Hutch didn't quite know how to respond. He fumbled for words, then said, "No, I can't take this."

Saddam responded, "I want you to have this—you are a good friend."

Hutch knew that this was the fancy watch that Saddam preferred to wear when he made his courtroom appearances. He was partial to a simple Timex when alone in his cell. Hutch was concerned that he might not even be allowed to accept a gift like this, since he knew that the Army had rules and regulations governing every aspect of their existence.

He hesitated, telling Saddam, "I'm going to have to ask," at which point the former president insisted, "You have it." He smiled and said, "It will be for you and me to know. I'm not going to tell anyone."

Saddam then clasped Hutch by the wrist with one hand and slid the watch on with his other. Hutch didn't want to make a scene, and so he allowed the old man to put the watch on him. He rationalized that taking it would help ensure that this final night ran smoothly.

Saddam then carefully picked out one of his best suits to wear, as he always did before leaving the cell and appearing in public. He put on lots of cologne. One of the soldiers would later say, "You could smell him from a mile away."

By now most of the Super Twelve had gathered near his cell to begin movement to the execution site. They were dressed in "full battle rattle," complete with Kevlar vests and helmets mounted with night-vision goggles. They each carried a full combat load of hundreds of rounds of ammunition.

Noticing the cluster of guards assembling nearby, Saddam took a break from making his final preparations and walked over to them. Standing tall, with his chest out, he told the twelve American military policemen that they'd become "more family to him" than any Iraqis had been. He said he was going to die like a soldier, and thanked them for having treated him so well. He then shook their hands in gratitude.

There was no longer, after all, any reason for the condemned man to fear germs.

A few of the soldiers noticed tears sliding down his face.

CHAPTER 35

Baghdad, Iraq—December 30, 2006

It was one of the coldest mornings the Super Twelve would spend in Iraq, with temperatures dropping to thirty-two in the chilly pre-dawn hours. After a short helicopter ride over a sleeping Baghdad, followed by a quick drive squeezed into the armored Rhino, the heavily armed soldiers—whose mission had always been to ensure the safety and well-being of the dictator—delivered Saddam Hussein to his final destination.

The execution was to take place at the old Istikhbarat military intelligence headquarters in Baghdad's Kadhimiya district, which ironically was rumored to have housed torture chambers where supposed "enemies of the state" had suffered during Saddam's rule. The compound, by then known as Camp Justice, was nestled alongside the Tigris River, a few hundred kilometers downstream from the rough village into which Saddam had been born sixty-nine years earlier. Security was tight, with an American brigade providing external perimeter security and a sea of Iraqi security forces controlling the immediate area surrounding the gallows. The Americans were under strict orders not to enter the site, as it was considered imperative that there be no doubt this was an Iraqi operation.

As Saddam exited the hulking armored vehicle, his resolve appeared to stiffen with each descending step. It was almost as if he was consciously willing himself to a stoic acceptance of his fate, fortified by a defiant pride that he was dying for his country.

Specialist Rogerson would later say, "You can watch a million movies and be like 'That guy's about to be *executed*,' but to actually physically see someone who is not about to die by natural causes, but, rather, have someone wrap a rope around their neck and kill them—just knowing that is so deflating. And to have him thank us, it was like 'Oh my fucking God.'"

The Super Twelve waited just outside the building that housed the gallows. The building in which Saddam was scheduled to be hanged was constructed out of cinder block and a flimsy tin-like material and partially open to the outside, almost like a barn. While from their vantage point outside the soldiers couldn't see the gallows directly, they could see spectral shadows of the elevated stage with the rope hanging from it.

As they waited, Hutch found himself bothered by the fact that he knew Saddam hated the idea of being hanged—almost more so than being sentenced to death in the first place.

The Iraqi to whom Saddam was turned over, and who was responsible for managing the execution, was Mowaffaq al-Rubbaie. Rubbaie was serving as Iraq's national security advisor. He had once been a member of Iraq's Shiite Dawa Party—the same party responsible for the assassination attempt on Saddam in Dujail that had triggered the draconian response for which Saddam had been tried and was now to be executed. Rubbaie himself had reportedly been tortured repeatedly by Saddam's security forces prior to fleeing to London in 1979, where he would remain in exile until 2003.

Rubbaie received the handcuffed Saddam from the Americans and led him into a room where a judge read the list of indictments out loud to him. Saddam was carrying his Koran and appeared to Rubbaie to be "normal and relaxed." He showed no regret as the charges were read.

Rubbaie then led Saddam to the gallows.

At that point, a curious incident took place. As they mounted the first steps, Saddam stopped, looked at the gallows, then looked Rubbaie up and down, and said, "Doctor, this is for men." Saddam seems to have been trying to exude an almost theatrical fearlessness.

The former president was then escorted by masked executioners up a flight of stairs and toward a large noose and waiting trapdoor. None of the executioners were in uniform. One wore a leather jacket and the other a tan coat. Saddam, by contrast, appeared almost statesmanlike, clad in a dark overcoat with a white shirt visible underneath, a few inches taller than his killers. His unflinching bearing was striking, as he maintained his erect posture and businesslike expression throughout. He seemed to be channeling whatever reserves remained of the flinty and emotionless resolve of his younger days, when he would coolly send Iraqis to their deaths, casually puffing on his cigar as their lives were extinguished. He succeeded in denying the crowd the satisfaction of seeing him tremble. Rather, he followed the executioners' instructions obediently, with no visible fear.

He refused to wear a hood.

Saddam had often, somewhat cryptically, instructed his subordinates to "preserve the last scene," recalls his former general Ra'ad al-Hamdani. It was a Bedouin idea: that life has many scenes, but the one that will be etched in history is the last one. Hamdani recalls how, on a visit to the front lines during the Iran-Iraq War, Saddam had rallied a motley collection of exhausted troops, still licking their wounds from a recent defeat, telling them that no matter the result, they'd be remembered forever if they died fighting bravely.

Saddam knew this would be his last scene, an opportunity to rehabilitate his image and erase the shameful memory of being dragged out of that spider hole in abject surrender three years before. His unflinching attitude in the moments before his hanging was "typical Saddam," according to Hutchinson.

That he was the only person visible on the gallows without a mask lent him a certain dignity in what otherwise was a sloppy, unprofessional affair. The entire scene was a grim reminder that despite the civilized trappings of modern courts like the Iraqi High Tribunal, hanging remains a most primitive physical operation. Using unsophisticated implements like ropes and scaffolding, execution by hanging inflicts catastrophic trauma on the human organism, often fracturing vertebrae, tearing muscles and blood vessels, and leading to the discharge of feces and urine. There was something especially haunting about the way in which one of the hooded executioners carefully, almost gently, put a scarf around Saddam's neck, as if to avoid causing undue discomfort mere moments before the neck would be snapped.

Pro-Shiite shouts of "Muqtada, Muqtada, Muqtada" pierced the morbid stillness. Camera flashes went off, adding to the tawdry and spectral aura. Saddam chuckled, and mockingly responded to the sectarian taunts, "Do you consider this bravery?"

A voice shouted, "Go to hell."

Saddam replied, "The hell that is Iraq?"

The taunts were almost as revealing in *how* they were uttered as in what was being said. The former CIA officer John Maguire says, "If you listen to the video with Iraqis, everyone says that the people in the room are scared—there is fear in the room. Those aren't voices of triumph—'we are going to kill this motherfucker'—but rather, 'we need to kill him now, before something bad happens.'"

"They were scared shitless," he says, "because Saddam wasn't scared."

CHAPTER 36

Baghdad, Iraq—December 30, 2006

The Super Twelve were quiet as they sat outside the gallows. The hasty preparation that had preceded their departure from the Rock, and the anxiety of delivering their prisoner without a hitch, had dwindled to uncomfortable silence as they waited for the trapdoor to open under Saddam and end his life. Some of the soldiers had already begun feeling a strange unease. They didn't fully recognize it at the time, but it was dawning on them that playing a role in the death of a person one has grown to know is radically different from shooting an anonymous insurgent two hundred meters away.

Finally, after about an hour, their morbid thoughts were interrupted by a thunderous crash. It echoed through their bodies. Hutch recalls that it sounded like a bomb going off, and it took his breath away.

Saddam had been midway through reciting the Shahada, the Islamic profession of faith, when the floor dropped from under him, an audible crack echoing inside the execution room as his neck was broken. His body remained suspended for a few minutes before a doctor listened for a heartbeat with a stethoscope and, hearing none, pronounced him dead shortly after 6:00 a.m. A cacophony of gunfire followed, momentarily spooking the Americans into thinking there was a last-minute rescue attempt. Rather, it was just a show of jubilance from Saddam's enemies now that the moment they'd long hungered for had become a reality.

Saddam had stood out as the most dignified person in the sordid affair, an especially self-willed victory for a man whose lifelong barbaric crimes had hardly earned him nobility in death. Even Mowaffaq al-Rubbaie, who'd suffered grievously at the hands of Saddam's regime, was struck by Saddam's equanimity as he approached the end.

"A criminal? True. A killer? True. A butcher? True. But he was strong until the end."

The Super Twelve stood by silently as Saddam's body, wrapped in a white shroud, was carried from the gallows to be placed in the back of a waiting Humvee. Before the corpse could be loaded, though, a crowd of frenzied Iraqis formed a conga line around it, dancing wildly, chanting with unrestrained joy, and spitting on and kicking the wrapped flesh of the leader they'd loathed. Specialist Rogerson couldn't believe they had to stand by idly as the Iraqis were "shooting into the sky, screaming, carrying him, kicking the shit out of his dead body . . . it made me so upset. Why were they doing this? I'm watching this, and I'm like 'You've got to be kidding me.'"

Hutch, too, was appalled at what he was seeing, and that they'd been ordered not to interfere. "I was raised tough—I don't cry at funerals, and none of the men in my family do," he said later, "but I was emotional when I saw what happened at that execution. It was a betrayal. We'd tried so hard to make it honorable, and in a short period of time they destroyed everything."

Having spent their entire deployment working to ensure that Saddam was safe, healthy, and treated with respect, it was painful for the Americans to be forced to stand by impotently as the Iraqis made a perverse mockery of what was their first critical "post-Saddam" mission.

Joseph, the interpreter who'd grown very close to Saddam, was the most upset. Enraged, he lunged toward the fracas, hoping to give the old man he'd come to know—and against all expectation, *like*—some last shred of dignity. Hutch was worried about what might happen to Joseph if he got overpowered by the mob, and so he grabbed the big man from behind by his body armor, keeping him a safe distance from the wild scrum.

The Bush administration had long promoted the idea that Saddam's execution would usher in a new era of Iraqi reconciliation. This new era did not last five minutes.

The sectarian violence outside the gallows was also exploding elsewhere across the country. Saddam Hussein would have plenty of company in violent death that day, much of it the result of incensed Sunni militants targeting Shiites. Within hours of the execution, five Iraqis were killed by a suicide bomber in Tal Afar; four were tortured and shot to death in Mahmudiya; thirty-six were killed and fifty-eight wounded when a car bomb ripped apart a market filled with holiday shoppers in the Shiite holy city of Najaf; thirty-six were killed and seventy-seven wounded when three car bombs tore through a Shiite neighborhood in Baghdad; and twelve tortured bodies were discovered strewn elsewhere across the capital.

The sun was beginning to come up as the Super Twelve drove back to the Rock from the execution site. Some of the soldiers had been up for nearly twenty-four long hours, and were barely able to keep their eyes open as they navigated their way back through Baghdad to the place they now considered home. When they finally got to the Rock, they found Saddam's cell eerily untouched, just as they'd left it. His clothes, papers, water bottles, and cigars were still there—all that remained of the man who'd once constructed forty-eight palaces at a reported cost of $2.2 billion.

The Super Twelve organized Saddam's remaining possessions so that they could be collected and returned to his family by his lawyers.

Meanwhile, a helicopter transported Saddam's dead body from the execution site to Prime Minister Nouri al-Maliki's residence in the Green Zone, almost as if it were a trophy kill from a hunting expedition. The body had to be put on the floor of the helicopter, which then flew with the doors open, as it was crowded, and the body was too long to fit otherwise. Mowaffaq al-Rubbaie accompanied the corpse as they passed over the city Saddam had not long before ruled with absolute power. Upon arrival, Rubbaie displayed the body to Maliki, who replied, "God bless you."

Rubbaie couldn't have been *too* troubled by the ghoulish spectacle over which he'd presided, since he later asked for, and kept, the noose in which Saddam's neck had snapped.

Saddam's body was then flown up to Tikrit, his ancestral homeland, and returned to Sheikh Ali al-Nida, the head of his Albu Nasir tribe (who would himself be assassinated two years later). Iraq's former president was buried in the dead of night, near his two sons, Uday and Qusay, who'd been killed in a shoot-out with U.S. troops a few years earlier. Saddam the poet might have appreciated the dramatic symmetry. The once all-powerful dictator had come full circle. Born near Tikrit with nothing, and armed with little more than ferocious ambition, ruthlessness, and guile, he'd amassed unrivaled power. Decades later, stripped of it all, he would return a fugitive, hunted by the world's most powerful military, seeking refuge in a dirty barn before finally being discovered in a small underground hole. And now, he'd come home one final time, leaving behind a decades-long trail of blood and sorrow, the collateral damage of his unquenchable thirst for power.

In Washington politicians and diplomats hoped that Saddam's execution would mark a new, more peaceful phase in Iraqi history. While President Bush acknowledged that the execution wouldn't end the violence in Iraq, he said that it would mark "an important milestone on Iraq's course to becoming a democracy that can govern, sustain, and defend itself, and be an ally in the war on terror." White House spokesman David Almacy reported that on the morning of the execution, "President Bush arose shortly before five a.m. Central Time and had a ten-minute phone call an hour later with National Security Advisor Stephen Hadley to discuss world reaction to the execution."

Almacy then said that the president had received his daily intelligence briefing and "planned to spend the rest of the day cutting cedar on his ranch, taking a bike ride, spending time with First Lady Laura Bush, and pondering his next steps in Iraq."

The soldiers who'd successfully carried out the president's wishes wouldn't be spending time with their families anytime soon. They were still in a war zone, where they'd remain for months, working seven days a week in dangerous conditions, some unable to shake the memory of that cold December morning. Though they never doubted the justice of Saddam's sentence, many were disgusted by the ugliness of the old man's death.

"It didn't really hit us until we had time to distance ourselves," Specialist Adam Rogerson said later. "But once the dust settles and you're lying in your bed at night, your mind wanders, and you think, *Did I really just do that?* We'd gotten so close to him . . ." At that point, his voice trailed off, and he said, barely audibly, "I feel like I let him down."

The execution would be the first time that young Tucker Dawson would confront death up close. He had a hard time coping with the fact that this man—whom he'd grown to know—had recently walked into the building under his own power only to come out in a body bag. "It was the first time I'd ever seen death," Dawson later recalled. At the time, one of the more seasoned NCOs tried to put his troubled mind at ease by saying, "It's part of life. Look at what that man did. That's his punishment. He dealt with it. It's over. It was a mission."

Still, Dawson couldn't shake the memories of those afternoons he spent outside with Saddam as he relaxed in the outdoor rec area. Images would come to him of the old man calling him over to ask him about his girlfriend back home.

Months later, the interpreter, Joseph, would say simply, "Will I miss Saddam the brutal dictator? Of course not. But will I miss sitting in the evening with him as a human being? Yes, I will."

When he was deployed to Iraq in 2006 Steve Hutchinson might have seemed an unlikely candidate to be the member of the Super Twelve *most* troubled by the way in which the execution unfolded. But he may have been. In the months afterward, he thought about being in front of the "Big Man upstairs" on Judgment Day, and he worried about explaining why he didn't try to restore order that morning. He said that watching the Iraqis spit on Saddam was akin to their "spitting on my Army service." When he went home on leave a few days after the execution, he was still so disgusted and shamed by the episode that he felt cleansed only by taking his uniform off.

Hutch later reflected: "I feel like I have to explain why it bothered me so much; for an American to be upset. But for us to stand by and let them treat another human being that way—I thought that's what we were over here to stop, the treatment like that. I truly felt that I was just as guilty as anybody else. I've never really had a conscience about anything I've ever done over here. As far as humanity goes, I've seen some pretty bad things, but it's what I had to do, it's what was required of me, it was my job. But my job had never before said that I had to stand there and watch people spit on and kick a person's body. And you know what, I'm glad I feel that way, I really am. Because if I didn't feel that way, I would think something was wrong with me."

After enlisting immediately after 9/11, and serving honorably for six years and four deployments, on the day Saddam was executed Hutch resolved to get out of the Army.

CONCLUSION

I saw battle-corpses, myriads of them,
And the white skeletons of young men, I saw them,
I saw the debris and debris of all the slain soldiers of the war,
But I saw they were not as was thought,
They themselves were fully at rest, they suffer'd not,
The living remain'd and suffer'd.

> —Walt Whitman, "When Lilacs Last
> in the Dooryard Bloom'd"

CHAPTER 37

The soldiers' transition from being the Super Twelve, bound together by the "mission of a lifetime," to the "Regular Twelve," as Specialist Rogerson would observe with a tinge of bittersweet nostalgia, had begun. As time went by, though, some would discover that transitioning to "regular" life was harder than expected. Just as Saddam Hussein affected the lives of everyday Iraqis in ways that are indelible—ways that, for those who survived his reign, no amount of time can erase—he also affected the lives of a small group of Americans in ways that will last for a lifetime.

CHRIS TASKER

It was a chilly St. Patrick's Day, gray and cold, when, two months after Saddam's death, Chris Tasker's girlfriend, Amanda, picked Chris up at Cleveland's Hopkins International Airport. It was the conclusion of a long trip home from Baghdad for two weeks' leave. The hours had passed quickly, though, filled as they were with images of all the firsts Chris would experience when he got home—his first drink, hopefully a Jack and Coke, his first kiss with Amanda, and his first visits to Hot Dog Heaven and the West Side Market, where he'd order a brat sandwich. (Maybe he'd even hit both places on the same day.)

Earlier in the day, Amanda had sent a text to Tasker's parents saying she was going to drop by and say hello, executing the first part of Chris's plan, which was to get her there before he arrived without triggering any warning bells. He always liked to surprise his parents with goofy stunts, and was hoping that appearing on their doorstep unannounced—when they thought he was thousands of miles away in Baghdad—would be his best yet. Nice idea, but Amanda's text had only served to plant a seed in the mind of Chris's dad, Steve. A team leader at General Motors who'd spent much of Chris's childhood working long overtime hours to make ends meet, Steve found himself nurturing the hope that just maybe his son would surprise them. Otherwise, why would Amanda be coming over? He knew she hated the corned beef he always prepared for St. Patrick's Day. Quietly, Steve went ahead and made extra just in case Chris did show up.

Shortly afterward, Chris had Amanda drop him off at the end of his street so that he could walk the final block toward his house. He sent her ahead alone.

Arriving first, Amanda offered a cheery hello to Chris's father and brother, but then the family dog, Pepper, a German shepherd mix, began barking furiously. The Tasker men rushed to the window to figure out what was causing the racket, and spotted a tall figure in a uniform approaching. It was Chris. As soon as Chris set foot in the front hall, he caught sight of his mom coming down the stairs.

She froze, and began to cry.

As everyone assembled in the dining room and prepared to dig into Steve Tasker's special St. Patrick's Day corned beef, they showed eager curiosity about Chris's experiences in Iraq. What are you up to over there? Steve asked.

Though clearly happy to see everyone, Chris was reluctant to talk about his deployment. Eventually, though, after parrying more questions, he volunteered: So, remember I was telling you I was just doing guard duty? Sounded kind of boring, right?

They nodded, still partly in shock that here he was, sitting right in front of them.

Well, I was actually guarding Saddam Hussein.

Silence.

You mean, like, *Saddam* Saddam, the leader of Iraq? his mom asked.

Yeah, Saddam, the big dude, Tasker replied.

No way!

Chris could see that everyone at the table was having trouble absorbing what he was saying. He immediately interjected: I'm not supposed to talk about it, and I don't even like to, but I thought you should know.

What was Saddam like?

Well, he really wasn't a bad guy—to us, at least, Chris responded. I mean, he'd play chess with us, sometimes he'd invite us to have a cigar with him. He was even kind of funny, always joking that he was going to get "strong like gazelle" on his exercise bike so he could escape.

No shit, they said.

Chris offered a few more audience-friendly anecdotes, but even as he did he recognized that they didn't quite capture the surreal existence from which he'd emerged.

It felt good to break the silence his mission had enforced on him, but at the same time there was something about the difficulty he had articulating the nature of his relationship with Saddam—and something about his family's responses—that led him to conclude that no one would ever really understand what it had been like.

Chris would go on to complete the rest of his deployment with the Super Twelve and get out of the Army in 2008, when his contract was up. Unsure of what to do next, he went home to Amherst.

His parents were relieved to have him home and out of harm's way. But at the same time they began to detect that in some ways their son had changed. They weren't sure when the change had occurred or what had caused it; they even had a hard time putting their finger on exactly *how* he was different. Chris used to be such a sweet child, his mom observed wistfully, but now there are times when he isn't so sweet. Other family members noticed that he was drinking more heavily, and there were whispers of other troubling behaviors. His parents' fears that they'd receive a devastating knock on the door from Army casualty notification officers had been replaced by fears that they might receive a call from local first responders.

These days, Chris says he has enjoyed being home and returning to small-town Ohio life with his old buddies. He likes being able to keep up more closely with the Browns and the Cavaliers. He has even obtained a pilot's license, of which he and his family are quite proud. But, years later, he still hasn't found regular work. His father can't figure out why, observing that Chris was always a smart kid, capable of achieving anything he set his mind to.

Though Chris still rarely speaks to his dad about Iraq, Steve recalls one thing he said that stood out. Chris told him that Saddam, as his execution approached, had said, I forgive you, you're just doing your job.

For Chris, it almost would have been easier if Saddam had acted more like the murderous tyrant they'd expected to find.

PAUL SPHAR

A few years after Saddam's execution, Paul Sphar was no longer a guard. Now he was an inmate, his new home the Hays County Jail in central Texas. No longer was he responsible for the world's most famous detainee in a converted palace-turned-prison. Now it was *he* who was the prisoner, and, like Saddam, he was forced to adapt to a new routine over which he had little control.

While in the Army he'd struggled with his weight and the regimented military life, but still, he'd taken pride in his service. Upon returning home, that pride dissipated as he descended into a numbing routine of drug and alcohol use. He was diagnosed with post-traumatic stress disorder (PTSD), and had developed an addiction to painkillers that he'd initially been prescribed for chronic pain from leg and ankle injuries. About that period, Sphar says he "dropped off the face of the earth for a while," admitting he was "pretty far gone" before eventually landing in the Hays County Jail for writing bad checks to support his drug habit.

Now, mornings were spent in the prison's common area, usually watching the television show *Supernatural*, followed by a workout, a game of cards, a nap, and then more TV with the other inmates—maybe *CSI* or *Hawaii Five-0*. There was a predictable rhythm to his days, just as there had been in Baghdad.

Sphar first knew something was wrong when he experienced a crushing panic attack behind the wheel of an F-250 in Texas while at work for the state highway department replacing signs. He didn't know exactly what triggered the attack, but suspected that what he'd done in Iraq to help "lead an old man to his death" may have contributed to it.

Not only did he take no pride in the execution of an older man whose company he'd grown to enjoy, but when he *did* finally open up and try to explain to people what had occurred, he found that few believed him at first. Even Sphar's mother seemed skeptical. And if some did believe him, not many were inclined to feel sympathy for a guy who questioned his role in ending the life of one of the twentieth century's most notorious dictators.

The tattooed gamer from California was at rock bottom when he found inspiration from a most unlikely place. As he marked the hours in his central Texas prison cell, Sphar found that, at a visceral level, he had a new appreciation for what the former Iraqi president had gone through. Sphar, who has since completed his prison sentence, says, "You can be on top of the mountain one minute and tomorrow you can be, like, the worst person on the planet. I saw Saddam like this: an unstoppable force reduced to having a nineteen-year-old bossing him around all day. I experienced this a little, too. One day I was a soldier on this high-profile mission and the next I'm fighting some teenager in prison who thinks I've stolen his Ramen noodle soup."

As he sat in his prison's rec area, mindlessly staring at the CW network, Sphar found himself reflecting on Saddam's ability not only to survive his fall from power, but to even find pleasure in his reduced circumstances. Rather than succumb to depression, Sphar worked to summon a resolve similar to Saddam's to get through the nine months he'd spend in jail.

Sphar eventually made it through his jail time and was released. One day, he emerged from the prison into the harsh Texas sunlight and was back to feeling adrift. He had no support network to help him overcome the challenges of his PTSD and addiction. Soon, he found himself homeless and living under bridges around Austin, Texas.

Life was very difficult for a while, but he finally found help from a therapist with the Veterans Administration and today he has discovered a degree of stability working as a waiter at Logan's Roadhouse just off I-35 in Texas. He's come a long way from the Austin highway overpasses that he once lived under. He has the upper hand over his drug and alcohol challenges. Sometimes, though, his mind still wanders back to how, not too long ago, he was guarding Saddam Hussein. He's no longer waking up each day to work in a Baghdad palace. Instead, his job features a view of a Long John Silver's, an IHOP, a Motel 6, and an office park. The office park lies half empty but houses an Armed Forces Recruiting Center, where the next generation of Paul Sphars will step through a portal to another world.

ROBERT "DOC" ELLIS

Though not part of the Super Twelve, Robert "Doc" Ellis was one of the Americans closest to Saddam during his incarceration. When he returned to the modest home he shared with his wife, Rita, in St. Louis following his deployment, he realized that the two of them were overdue for a vacation. He decided to use some of his "deployment money" to take her on a cruise in the Caribbean. They would island hop through the western Caribbean, with stops in the Caymans, Jamaica, and Cozumel.

Despite the idyllic ocean setting, on the ship part of Ellis's mind was still held hostage by Iraq. In the evening especially, pleasant memories of sharing cigars with Saddam kept returning. He kind of missed the man.

He was alone with these conflicted emotions, though. They certainly weren't something he expected his fellow Hawaiian-shirt-clad cruise patrons from middle America to understand. To cheer up, he assigned himself a new mission as the ship stopped for a brief port call in the Cayman Islands. He needed a good cigar and sought out the island's version of the hajji mart. Eventually, he found the item he was looking for, and sometime later, ensconced once again on the ship's deck, he took out a Cohiba, puffed contentedly on it, exhaled, and squinted into the sunset as he sorted through his memories.

Unfortunately, the pleasant daily rhythms of his cruise foretold nothing of the life Ellis would soon be living. Stricken with aggressive cancer a short time later, he was suddenly thrust into a war as grim as the one he'd left behind. His chemotherapy regimen left him bald, gaunt, and fatigued, and adding to his gloominess, he felt himself increasingly bothered by his memories of his military service. His innately sunny disposition was clouded by a sense that his mission in Iraq—and indeed the entire American enterprise there—was a "gigantic waste of time, money, energy, and lives."

"I did my job," he said, "but it was bullshit. It's heartbreaking to see what's happening there now—it would have never happened under Saddam."

Retired in the modest suburban home he shared with his wife, Ellis was worlds away from the projects where he grew up, as well as the Baghdad prison cell where he'd spent so many hours with Saddam. But life hadn't gotten any easier. He was initially confused by why he felt "so cold and distant," resentful of his wife's affection. He chalked it up to just needing some time "to get his groove back."

But it wasn't happening. He found himself buffeted by compounding regrets: regret at not having been home for the final days

THE PRISONER IN HIS PALACE

of his mother's and brother's lives, as well as a sense of complicity in the death of a man whose company he'd grown to enjoy.

"I know I should hate Saddam, but it's not easy," he said.

Ellis felt more distant from his wife, Rita, than he did when they were thousands of miles apart, exchanging old-fashioned letters of affection. He began having "suicidal thoughts, homicidal thoughts, and sleep problems."

Ellis was proud and strong, though, and unwilling to surrender to despair. As he fought to reclaim a measure of happiness, he found himself marveling again at how Saddam seemed to effortlessly transition from "silk sheets to an Army cot," how he could seemingly find satisfaction in a prison cell merely by mixing old Folgers coffee packets into water with his finger. Encouraged by those memories, Ellis still snuck puffs from a Cohiba cigar from time to time, trying to make the most of life's simple pleasures.

Ellis kept the poem Saddam had written for Rita tucked away in a scrapbook, the one that had compared her beauty to "the stars and moon in the sky."

He'd always dreamed of going back to Iraq someday and visiting the mountainous north, a region whose beauty Saddam had often described to him. Ellis was waiting for things to "settle down" enough for him to do so. He wouldn't get that chance, though.

After putting up a brave fight, Ellis succumbed to his cancer on March 21, 2016, at the age of sixty-six.

ROD MIDDLETON

On the night of December 29, 2006, FBI Agent Rod Middleton and his thirteen-year-old son bellied up to the bar at the Fox and Hound in Tucson, Arizona. They must have seemed an odd twosome. Thousands of miles to the east, as the sun rose over Baghdad on Saturday morning, the Super Twelve had just delivered Saddam to the gallows for his execution. Middleton wanted to get out of the house and do something to mark the occasion, and so he called a number of friends to see if they wanted to meet him for a drink. None were free, so he and his son headed to the bar and asked the bartender to change the channel on one of the TVs from college football to CNN to catch the breaking news.

Watching CNN, Middleton's mind was a swirl of conflicting emotions. Sympathy for Saddam wasn't one of them. As the Super Twelve stood at the execution site on that cold morning in Baghdad and struggled with having just delivered a pleasant old man to his death, Middleton sat at the bar, nursing his beer. He wasn't afflicted with doubt, but rather felt a liberating sense of closure and finality. He'd played a critical role in the interrogation of one of the century's most prominent dictators, and, because of that, he'd missed some of the final months of his young wife's life. He was proud that he'd helped gather evidence that would lead to Saddam's death sentence. The way Middleton looked at it, he hadn't made the decision to go to war, but he'd honorably carried out his mission to investigate human rights crimes, and he'd helped bring the perpetrator to justice.

In a few days it will be 2007, he thought, *and it's going to be a good year*. He wasn't even sure why he was suddenly convinced of this. But as the "Breaking News" ticker crept across the bar's TV screen announcing Saddam's death, Middleton experienced something of a catharsis. A horrible person who'd brought to his people decades of misery and suffering, and had proven a slippery interrogation subject, was finally dead. His good mood led to other pleasant thoughts, such as the upcoming second date he'd be enjoying with a woman he'd met. After Barbara's death, it had taken him a long time to consider seeing other women, but, as he looked down at his son, who'd already gulped down his Shirley Temple, he couldn't help but feel that he and his children had earned some happiness.

Middleton would go on to marry the woman he'd been thinking about at the bar that night—and he'd feel real pride at seeing his daughter join the Navy, and his son the Army. These days Middleton still takes masochistic pleasure in running long distances. He especially enjoys the 120-mile Baker to Vegas Law Enforcement

Relay Race. As he glides determinedly across the desert landscape of western Nevada, the same unforgiving sun bears down on him that had tormented him during those solitary afternoon runs across the base in Baghdad. Undeterred, he strides east into the sun and away from the shadows.

ADAM ROGERSON

Jeff Rogerson knew that his son Adam had changed in a fundamental way as soon as he came home. He could see it in his face. "You know your kids," Jeff Rogerson says. "I could tell something was wrong by looking at him, just like I could tell if he was tired."

Jeff had been shocked, yet encouraged, when seventeen-year-old Adam had shown up at one of his masonry job sites years before and announced to his father that he'd joined the Army. He thought it would be good for his son, who, he says, while a tough kid, still "couldn't have found his butt with both hands before enlisting." Adam would be continuing a family tradition of military service, as his grandfather had earned a Distinguished Flying Cross serving in the Army Air Corps in World War II and Jeff had served in the 82nd Airborne Division.

Jeff couldn't have imagined, though, what Adam's mission would ultimately be, or the impact it would have on him.

After the countless hours he'd spent getting to know Saddam in the subterranean Crypt and on the Rock, Rogerson says that the execution was "like losing a family member." Recognizing how this might sound to someone who didn't share his experience, Rogerson explains, "You shoot someone on an overpass in combat, you keep going, who cares. You care for a second, and then it's like 'Eliminate the threat, and keep moving.' But getting to know someone, and getting close to them . . . as time passes, it hasn't gotten any better for me."

Rogerson slowly began to notice signs of psychological strain as he readjusted to life in America. The symptoms weren't immediate, and may have been delayed by the initial flurry of activity following his return from Iraq and resumption of duties as a military policeman at Fort Campbell. He was quickly thrust back into alternating twenty-four-hour shifts. It wasn't until things slowed down, and he had time to reflect, that he began to suspect something was wrong.

The difficulty of coming home after such a psychologically challenging mission was made worse by orders he'd received not to tell anyone about it. His own father didn't even know what to believe when, years after his son had arrived home, he finally started volunteering details of the Saddam mission. Until then, Adam had always been careful to invent cover stories to conceal what had really happened on the deployment.

"I almost feel like a murderer," Rogerson says, "like I killed a guy I was close to."

These days the popular, cocky high school jock has been replaced by a subdued man who keeps to himself and passes time at home with his wife, seven-year-old daughter, and one-year-old son. His weeks are marked by frequent VA appointments, where he receives treatment for the PTSD he was diagnosed with and is on disability for. Rogerson is stoic about his situation. He doesn't ask for sympathy or attention; rather, he recognizes that he's just one of many who've come home from war and been forced to grapple with the consequences of it.

Things aren't all bad. Rogerson appreciates the opportunity he now has to spend more time with his wife and young children. He also enjoys the company of his father-in-law, with whom he likes to play horseshoes and darts. He even hopes to soon resume coaching the defensive line for his younger brother's semipro football team, the Lorraine Nightmares.

Rogerson rarely talks to his former buddies from the Super Twelve, though. He suspects that this may be because he "doesn't want to bring the memories back." Recently, at a Cleveland Browns game, he was stunned to run into his former sergeant, Tom Flanagan—whom he and the rest of the Super Twelve had always admired—in a tunnel leading into the stands. He was surprised at how awkward the encounter was. The two men, who'd been through so much together, struggled to find something to say. They hugged, said that they missed each other, and traded numbers.

Neither would dial the other.

"I just sort of stick to myself," Rogerson says. "Maybe one day if we have some sort of reunion I'll talk to the guys, but for now it still feels too fresh, even though it has been ten years."

STEVE HUTCHINSON

"To this day, I still hear that fucking metal trapdoor slam," Steve Hutchinson says. "I always believed in everything I did in the military, but the moment that floor dropped open, I knew I was done with serving, even though I would continue to wear the uniform until my time was up."

Hutch now splits his time between running a firearms and tactical training business back in Georgia, and doing periodic security contracting work overseas. His wife encourages him to focus on his stateside business, eager to have him spend more time at home after their having been apart for much of the previous fourteen years. Hutch acknowledges that maybe it's time to consider throttling back his adventurous lifestyle, which has had psychological and physical consequences. He sometimes wakes up with a jolt during the night, expecting to see Saddam. And there are days when his wife, a nurse, takes his blood pressure, and it's as high as 155 over 90. The deployment stress, the memories, the Monster energy drinks, the cigarettes—all have taken their toll.

Hutch has come a long way from the hungover bouncer who enlisted in the Army following a surge of post-9/11 patriotism. He's now a proud father of three, and his days of late-night carousing are over. However, gone, too, is his hopeful idealism.

"I felt the obligation to serve after 9/11, and whether I liked the missions or not, during all my deployments, I never questioned them." The combat didn't especially bother him, he says, recalling in an offhand way the insurgents whose lives had been ended by 5.56mm rounds he and others had fired. Everything changed, though, when he led the old man he'd grown to know to his execution and was forced to stand by as his body was desecrated.

On that morning of December 30, 2006, Hutch says, "I resolved to never be that rube again, allowing the government to twist my faith." Reflecting on the overall U.S. mission in Iraq, he muses, "How many years of my life did I devote to this?" He stops for a moment and then adds, "I wish it had turned out better."

The Raymond Weil watch that Saddam Hussein took off his wrist to give Hutch on the eve of his execution rests quietly in a safe in his pleasant Georgia home. It has steadily marked the passage of time since Saddam's own time ran out. Time keeps ticking, until it doesn't—for self-professed reincarnations of King Nebuchadnezzar, his innumerable victims, or those who stood watch over his final days.

SADDAM HUSSEIN

Saddam Hussein has now been dead for a decade. The face whose gaze could induce panic in the bravest of men has long since decomposed. Even in death, though, he hasn't found rest. His Albu Nasir tribesmen, fearing that approaching Shiite militias would try to desecrate their leader's grave, dug up his remains and moved them to a secret location in 2014.

The tribe's concerns were well founded.

Shiite militiamen would eventually break into the tomb—which had grown into something of a shrine to the former president—destroy everything in it, and burn it to the ground.

ACKNOWLEDGMENTS

I was working at the Pentagon when I decided to walk away from a rewarding job and steady paycheck to write this book. It was a leap of faith, for many reasons, not the least of which was that, though I'd been serving as an infantry officer in Iraq at the same time Saddam was executed, I didn't participate in any of the events described, nor could I be confident that anyone who had would speak to me.

I could not have succeeded without the help of so many. First and foremost, I would like to thank Paul Sphar, Steve Hutchinson, Chris Tasker, and Adam Rogerson for agreeing to speak with me about their experiences guarding Saddam. This is their story, not mine, and I couldn't have written this book without them. I am immensely grateful for their patient answers to what must have seemed like my endless questions. Thank you also to Robert "Doc" Ellis and his wife, Rita, Rod Middleton, Jeff Green, Dave Manners, John Maguire, William Wiley, and Iraqi general Ra'ad al-Hamdani for agreeing to spend so much time answering my questions. Thanks as well to Marianna Riley, for introducing me to Robert Ellis, and for encouraging me to expand on some of the material that can be found in their excellent book, *Caring for Victor: A U.S. Army Nurse and Saddam Hussein*.

Jane Fleming Fransson deserves special thanks for believing in me, and this story, from the beginning, for her valuable guidance the entire way, and most of all for serving as an informal therapist when I needed a boost. Thank you to my agent, Zoë Pagnamenta, for her steadfast support, and for shepherding me into the hands of

ACKNOWLEDGMENTS

Rick Horgan, my fantastic editor at Scribner. Rick put me through the literary equivalent of Ranger School, and for that I will always be grateful, even if, like Ranger School, the process itself could be painful. Most of all, I thank them both for taking a chance on me.

Thank you to Shameem Rassam, who not only shared her own experiences with me, but introduced me to others in the Iraqi expatriate community whom I would later interview and whose insights were important to this book.

Thank you to Omar Feikeiki for his translation assistance, and to Kevin Woods for helping point me in the right direction as I began my research.

Ranya Kadri was the consummate hostess on my visit to Amman, and provided invaluable help making introductions to the Jordanian officials I needed to interview while there. The coffee and cookies she served were as fantastic as her translation during my interviews, and for all that, I thank her.

Thank you to Eric Schmitt, Sebastian Junger, Richard Clarke, and George Packer for taking time out of their busy days to share their accumulated wisdom as writers with this first-time book author. Thank you to Steve Wells for reading the entire manuscript and providing such valuable insights. I could always rely on John Bellinger and Alejandra Parra-Orlandoni to provide sound legal advice.

Thank you to the staff at Misha's Coffee and Northside Social in Northern Virginia for always serving the bearded guy in the Mets cap steaming cups of hot coffee, day in and day out, for what seemed like an eternity as I inched forward on this project, and to O'Sullivan's Irish Pub, where I could always find a pint of Guinness at week's end. Lest I forget, thank you to Parker the cat, for spending so many hours at my side, napping contentedly as I worked. You helped calm my nerves when the stress of various setbacks threatened to overwhelm me.

Thank you to my parents, Walter and Patricia, my brothers, Tad and Buddy, and my sisters, Nelly and Annie, for their support and advice. I'm especially grateful to my parents and to Annie, all writers in their own right, for reading so many drafts and generously sharing their editorial talents with me. I'll probably never be able to properly put into words my gratitude, or repay them for their time.

Finally, I'd like to thank my beautiful and patient new wife, Marcy, for also taking a chance on me. Most women wouldn't be thrilled to learn that their boyfriend was quitting a good job to embark on an uncertain journey that for so long looked like it would never end. I'm sure she must have had some doubts about the wisdom of her decision as she went off to work each morning and left me to do whatever it is that writers do, but if she did, she never voiced them. Instead, she provided unwavering support. I hope I've made her proud.

SOURCES

Army historians conducted interviews with each member of the Super Twelve, as well as Joseph, the interpreter. I was provided copies of these interviews by Michael Gordon in 2010 while helping research his 2012 book *The Endgame: The Inside Story of the Struggle for Iraq, from George W. Bush to Barack Obama.*

ADDITIONAL INTERVIEWS

Note: I interviewed many of these individuals multiple times.
*Indicates pseudonym

Robert Baer—Former CIA case officer
Amatzia Baram—Professor of Middle Eastern History, University of Haifa
Samih Batthiki—Former senior Jordanian government official
Chris Belles—One of Saddam Hussein's guards from a unit prior to the Super Twelve
Frank Byers*—FBI agent who worked on interrogation of Saddam Hussein
Ramsey Clark—Member of Saddam Hussein's defense team
Jesse Dawson—One of Saddam Hussein's guards from a unit prior to the Super Twelve
Paul Delacourt—FBI agent who served as program manager for the Regime Crimes Liaison Office and helped establish the Iraqi High Tribunal
Charles Duelfer—Former CIA official who also led the Iraqi Survey Group responsible for the search for Iraq's weapons of mass destruction
Robert Ellis—Master sergeant who provided Saddam Hussein with medical care while in U.S. custody
Jeff Green—FBI agent who worked on the interrogation of Saddam Hussein
Leena Haddad*—Friend of Raghad Hussein
Ra'ad al-Hamdani—Former general under Saddam Hussein
Steve Hutchinson—Specialist with the Super Twelve
Todd Irinaga—FBI agent who worked on the interrogation of Saddam Hussein
Marwan Kasim—Former Jordanian foreign minister
Kent Kiehl—Neuroscientist and expert on psychopathy

SOURCES

Juman Kubba—Author of a memoir of what it was like to grow up in Saddam Hussein's Iraq

Nelson Lee*—Former special operator who helped capture Saddam Hussein

John Maguire—Former CIA officer and deputy chief of Iraqi Operations Group

Kanan Makiya—Professor of Islamic and Middle Eastern Studies, Brandeis University

Dave Manners—Former CIA station chief, Amman

Abby Marsh—Professor of Psychology, Georgetown University

Rod Middleton—FBI agent who worked on the interrogation of Saddam Hussein

Tom Neer—FBI behavioral profiler who worked on the interrogation of Saddam Hussein

Najeeb al-Nuaimi—Member of Saddam Hussein's defense team

Jerrold Post—Founded the Center for the Analysis of Personality and Political Behavior at the CIA, and "profiled" Saddam Hussein

Shameem Rassam—Former TV host in Baghdad during Saddam Hussein's rule

Adam Rogerson—Specialist with the Super Twelve

Jeff Rogerson—Father of Adam Rogerson

Sammy*—One of Saddam Hussein's interpreters while in U.S. custody

Joseph Sassoon—Professor of Arab Studies, Oxford University and Georgetown University

Ali Shukri—Former head of Jordanian Royal Court

Paul Sphar—Specialist with the Super Twelve

Chris Tasker—Specialist with the Super Twelve

Steve Tasker—Father of Chris Tasker

William Wiley—Advised Saddam Hussein's defense team as part of the Regime Crimes Liaison Office (RCLO)

Kevin Woods—Historian, Institute for Defense Analyses

Judith Yaphe—Former senior Middle East analyst for the CIA

BOOKS

Aburish, Said. *Saddam Hussein: The Politics of Revenge*. Bloomsbury, 2012.

Balaghi, Shiva. *Saddam Hussein: A Biography*. Greenwood Biographies, 2006.

Bashir, Ala. *The Insider: Trapped in Saddam's Brutal Regime*. Little, Brown, 2005.

Cockburn, Andrew, and Patrick Cockburn. *Out of the Ashes: The Resurrection of Saddam Hussein*. Harper Perennial, 2000.

Coughlin, Con. *Saddam: His Rise and Fall*. Harper Perennial, 2005.

Duelfer, Charles. *Hide and Seek: The Search for Truth in Iraq*. Public Affairs, 2009.

Ellis, Robert, with Marianna Riley. *Caring for Victor: A U.S. Army Nurse and Saddam Hussein*. Reedy Press, 2009.

Hare, Robert D. *Without Conscience: The Disturbing World of Psychopaths Among Us*. The Guilford Press, 1999.

SOURCES

Hussein, Saddam. *Zabiba and the King.* Virtualbookworm.com, 2004.

Karsh, Efraim, and Inari Rautsi. *Saddam Hussein: A Political Biography.* Diane Books, 1991.

Kiehl, Kent A. *The Psychopath Whisperer: The Science of Those Without Conscience.* Crown Publishers, 2014.

Mackey, Sandra. *The Reckoning: Iraq and the Legacy of Saddam Hussein.* W. W. Norton, 2002.

Maddox, Eric, with Davin Seay. *Mission: Black List #1: The Inside Story of the Search for Saddam Hussein—As Told by the Soldier Who Masterminded His Capture.* HarperCollins, 2008.

Makiya, Kanan. *Republic of Fear: The Politics of Modern Iraq.* University of California Press, 1989.

Newton, Michael A., and Michael P. Scharf. *Enemy of the State: The Trial and Execution of Saddam Hussein.* St. Martin's Press, 2008.

Post, Jerrold M., ed. *The Psychological Assessment of Political Leaders with Profiles of Saddam Hussein and Bill Clinton.* The University of Michigan Press, 2003.

Russell, Lt. Col. Steve. *We Got Him! A Memoir of the Hunt and Capture of Saddam Hussein.* Pocket Books, 2012.

Salbi, Zainab, and Laurie Becklund. *Between Two Worlds: Escape from Tyranny: Growing Up in the Shadow of Saddam.* Avery, 2006.

Woods, Kevin, Williamson Murray, and Thomas Holaday, with Mounir Elkhamri. *Saddam's War: An Iraqi Military Perspective on the Iran-Iraq War.* National Defense University Press, 2009.

Woods, Kevin, David Palkki, and Mark Stout, eds. *The Saddam Tapes: The Inner Workings of a Tyrant's Regime, 1978–2001.* Cambridge University Press, 2011.

ARTICLES/REPORTS

Agence France Presse. "Man Who Oversaw Hanging Recalls Dictator's End." December 27, 2013.

Anderson, Jon Lee. "Saddam's Ear: An Iraqi Doctor Had a Unique Role in Saddam Hussein's Life." *The New Yorker,* May 5, 2003.

Associated Press. "Bush: Saddam's Execution Will Not End Violence in Iraq." December 30, 2006.

Associated Press. "Saddam Hussein's Tomb Destroyed as Battle for Tikrit Rages." March 16, 2015.

Associated Press. "Thirty Five Killed in Bombing Near Iraqi Shrine." August 10, 2006.

Associated Press. "U.S. Troops Among Nearly 50 Dead in Iraq." August 13, 2006.

Bennett, Brian, and Michael Weisskopf. "The Sum of Two Evils." *Time,* May 25, 2003.

"Bomb Kills Head of Saddam's Tribe." BBC.com, June 10, 2008.

Bowden, Mark. "Tales of the Tyrant." *The Atlantic*, May 2002.

Burns, John F. "Hussein Video Grips Iraq; Attacks Go On." *The New York Times*, December 31, 2006.

Burns, John F., and Kirk Semple. "Hussein Is Sentenced to Death by Hanging." *The New York Times*, November 6, 2006.

"Bush Challenged to 'Duel' with Saddam." *BBC News*, October 3, 2002.

Bush, George W. "President Bush's Statement on Execution of Saddam Hussein." December 30, 2006.

Cordesman, Anthony. "Iraq's Sectarian and Ethnic Violence and the Evolving Insurgency." Center for Strategic and International Studies report, December 14, 2006.

"Declassified FBI Notes on Interrogation Sessions with Saddam Hussein." Available at www.fbi.gov.

Duelfer, Charles. "Comprehensive Report of the Special Advisor to the Director of Central Intelligence on Iraq's Weapons of Mass Destruction." September 30, 2004.

Esterbrook, John. "Rumsfeld: It Would Be a Short War." CBSNews.com, November 15, 2002.

"FBI Interrogation of Ali Hasan Al-Majid Al-Tikriti." January–June 2004. Available at www.fbi.gov.

"FBI Prosecutive Report of Investigation Concerning Saddam Hussein." March 10, 2005. Available at www.fbi.gov.

Filkins, Dexter. "In Hometown, Hussein's Glory Is Quickly Gone." *The New York Times*, April 15, 2003.

"Genocide in Iraq: The Anfal Campaign Against the Kurds." Human Rights Watch report, July 1, 1993.

Habjouqa, Tanya. "Saddam H. Christ." *Vice Magazine*, March 1, 2007.

"Iraqi Leader's Koran Written in Blood." *BBC News*, September 25, 2000.

Joscelyn, Thomas. "Saddam's Stenographers." *The Weekly Standard*, July 7, 2009.

Joshi, Vijay. "Bomb Kills Two U.S. Soldiers in Baghdad." *The Washington Post*, August 12, 2006.

Martin, Paul. "'As I led him to the gallows, I hoped Saddam Hussein would show remorse. There was nothing'—Dr Mowaffak al Rubaie on the Dictator's Last Moments." *The Independent*, April 8, 2013.

McDonald, Mark, and Jonathan S. Landay. "Saddam Not Found When Marines Knocked at Tikrit Palace." *Knight Ridder*, April 14, 2003.

"Saddam Hussein's Iraq." United States State Department report, September 1999.

"Saddam Outburst Follows Hidden Testimony in Trial." *USA Today*, December 6, 2005.

"Tour of Prison Reveals the Last Days of Saddam Hussein." CNN.com, March 27, 2008.

NOTES

CHAPTER 1

The account of Steve Hutchinson deciding to enlist following 9/11 is based on interviews I conducted with him.

The account of the soldiers' arrival in Iraq is based on interviews I conducted with Steve Hutchinson, Adam Rogerson, Paul Sphar, and Chris Tasker.

CHAPTER 2

8 *Upon arrival . . . containerized housing units:* Author's interview with Steve Hutchinson, September 3, 2015.

8 *It was now the summer of 2006 . . . troops were being rushed in:* Vijay Joshi, "Bomb Kills Two U.S. Soldiers in Baghdad," *The Washington Post*, August 12, 2006.

8 *Just days before . . . blood and collect body parts:* From account of the bombing in "Thirty Five Killed in Bombing Near Iraqi Shrine," Associated Press, August 10, 2006.

9 *In a peculiar way . . . had it pretty good:* Author's interview with Adam Rogerson, May 18, 2015.

9 *"Our squad was good" . . . "twelve-mile ruck marches":* Ibid.

CHAPTER 3

10 *The twelve MPs were tasked with . . . hemorrhaging wound:* Author's interview with Chris Tasker, February 21, 2015.

10 *Many of the squad members . . . "had to see them":* Author's interview with Adam Rogerson, May 15, 2015.

11 *Already in his mid-thirties . . . perfect foil:* The descriptions of Perkins and

his unfortunate episode on patrol are based on interviews with Adam Rogerson, Steve Hutchinson, and Paul Sphar. I include this scene not to embarrass Perkins (which is a pseudonym), but rather because it provides a revealing illustration of the unforgiving nature of life in a combat environment among a group of young men.

12 *After one especially long and hot patrol . . . "I'd just had enough"*: Author's interview with Adam Rogerson, September 2, 2015.

13 *Their transition from an ordinary squad . . . how did I get chosen to do this?*: The soldiers' accounts of how they were informed of their change in mission varied, perhaps because they were first informed in smaller groups by their noncommissioned officers as opposed to receiving the notification at the same time as a larger group. My description is a composite account based on the recollections of Adam Rogerson, Chris Tasker, Paul Sphar, Steve Hutchinson, and the February 2, 2007, Army oral history interview with Tucker Dawson.

CHAPTER 4

The episode of Steve Hutchinson being startled by the cat while on overnight guard duty at the IHT is based on interviews I conducted with him on April 28 and 29, 2015, and September 3, 2015. The description of the subterranean "crypt" under the IHT where Saddam and the codefendants were held, and where the Super Twelve stayed, when trial was in session is based on interviews I conducted with Adam Rogerson, Chris Tasker, Paul Sphar, and Steve Hutchinson.

17 *The IHT was a massive facility . . . "you were so inclined"*: Author's interview with William Wiley, March 12, 2015.

18 *According to Baath Party records . . . "obtained from them"*: "FBI Prosecutive Report of Investigation Concerning Saddam Hussein," 36.

18 *Ali Hassan al-Majid may have been responsible*: Cockburn and Cockburn, *Out of the Ashes*, 144.

18 *He'd even donated blood*: "Iraqi Leader's Koran Written in Blood," BBC News, September 25, 2000.

18 *"I wish America would bring its Army"*: Woods, Palkki, and Stout, eds., *The Saddam Tapes*, 116–17.

19 *"He looked majestic and peaceful"*: Author's interview with Paul Sphar, September 17, 2015.

19 *"the most traumatized leader I have ever studied"*: Author's interview with Dr. Jerrold Post, January 8, 2015.

CHAPTER 5

20 *Awja means the "turning"*: Coughlin, *Saddam: His Rise and Fall*, 2.

20 *It was rife with bandits*: Ibid.

20 *"the badlands" . . . "cunning and secretive"*: Aburish, *Saddam Hussein: The Politics of Revenge*, 13.

20 *A Middle East scholar . . . "mischievous young boy"*: The account of Saddam's brother's death and his birth is based on author's interview with Dr. Amatzia Baram, January 26, 2015.

21 *cramped one-room mudbrick dwelling*: Aburish, *Saddam Hussein: The Politics of Revenge*, 15.

21 *Forced to navigate the dusty alleyways*: Karsh and Rautsi, *Saddam Hussein: A Political Biography*, 9.

21 *"son of the alleys"*: Aburish, *Saddam Hussein: The Politics of Revenge*, 17.

22 *"Hassan the Liar" . . . "son of a dog"*: Karsh and Rautsi, *Saddam Hussein: A Political Biography*, 10.

22 *"When Saddam was a child . . . If he ever was a child"*: Author's interview with Judith Yaphe, January 27, 2015.

CHAPTER 6

The description of Chris Tasker's hometown of Amherst, Ohio, is based on my visit there. The account of Tasker's childhood is based on multiple interviews I conducted with Chris as well as with his father, Steve Tasker. The story of Chris Tasker and Adam Rogerson receiving a speeding ticket in Kentucky on their visit home to Ohio is based on multiple interviews I conducted with both of them.

CHAPTER 7

27 *It was located on a small island . . . columns and ceilings*: The description of "the Rock" is based on the Army oral history interviews with the Super Twelve, as well as author's multiple interviews with Adam Rogerson, Chris Tasker, Paul Sphar, and Steve Hutchinson.

28 *"yes, sirs" and "no, sirs"*: The description of the evolution of the soldiers' interactions with Saddam—from awkward and tense to relaxed and familiar—is based on the Army oral history interviews and author's multiple interviews with Adam Rogerson, Chris Tasker, Paul Sphar, and Steve Hutchinson.

29 *"I was like a little kid"*: Army oral history interview with Tucker Dawson, February 2, 2007.

29 *Hutch, veteran of . . . "violent people in the world"*: Army oral history interview with Steve Hutchinson, February 2, 2007, as well as author's interview on September 3, 2015.

30 *Sphar, in particular, felt cognitive dissonance . . . let me come back!*: The account of Saddam asking Steve Hutchinson about his heritage and telling Hutchinson and Paul Sphar about threatening his teacher is from the Army oral history interview with Hutchinson, as well as author's multiple interviews with Paul Sphar and Steve Hutchinson. The dialogue that has been recreated in this scene, and all of the scenes involving the Super Twelve's interactions with Saddam, is based on their memory of what was said. The dialogue is not verbatim, but does capture the essence of what was said—and how it was said—to the best of the soldiers' recollections.

32 *Curiously, he'd always stop tuning*: Army oral history interview with Art Perkins, February 2, 2007.

32 *If the water wasn't boiling*: Army oral history interview with Jeff Price, February 2, 2007.

32 *Khairallah was a former Army officer*: Coughlin, *Saddam: His Rise and Fall*, 15.

33 *An Iraqi woman*: Salbi and Becklund, *Between Two Worlds: Escape from Tyranny*, 104.

CHAPTER 8

This chapter is based on footage of the event that is widely available on YouTube. My interpreter, Omar Feikeiki, provided translation.

34 *Baath Party's secretary-general . . . spare his life*: Coughlin, *Saddam: His Rise and Fall*, 155–63.

35 *Saddam was a devoted student of Stalin*: Bowden, "Tales of the Tyrant," *The Atlantic*.

36 *The condemned included a deputy*: Coughlin, *Saddam: His Rise and Fall*, 160–61.

CHAPTER 9

37 *Tasker had been just days away . . . training to use*: Author's interview with Chris Tasker, October 21, 2015.

38 *U.S. secretary of defense Donald Rumsfeld*: Report by John Esterbrook, CBS News, November 15, 2002.

38 *The cigar tastes better after the fruit*: Army oral history interview with Steve Hutchinson, February 2, 2007.

39 *"someone in his security detail":* Author's interview with Steve Hutchinson, September 3, 2015.

39 *"a shitty old bike like you'd find at Goodwill":* Author's interview with Paul Sphar, November 2014.

39 *Saddam patted one leg . . . "from Sesame Street":* Author's interview with Chris Tasker, February 21, 2015.

40 *I escape from jail before:* Saddam seems to have enjoyed telling the story of his failed assassination attempt on then prime minister Abd al-Karim Qasim, and his ensuing escape that included swimming across the Tigris. His retelling of the story in this chapter is based on Army oral history interviews with James Martin, Steve Hutchinson, Tucker Dawson, and Andre Jackson, all on February 2, 2007, as well as numerous interviews I conducted with Steve Hutchinson and Paul Sphar. Additionally, Saddam joked to a number of the soldiers about "riding his pony," including Chris Tasker, Jeff Price, and Paul Sphar.

40 *He'd enjoyed Hemingway's* The Old Man and the Sea: Duelfer, *Hide and Seek: The Search for Truth in Iraq,* 405; and Bowden, "Tales of the Tyrant," *The Atlantic.*

40 *One of Iraq's most decorated generals:* Author's interview with Ra'ad al-Hamdani, July 30, 2015.

CHAPTER 10

A number of books, and countless articles, have been written about Saddam's capture, many of which I include in my list of sources. My account of Saddam's capture is based on these materials, supplemented by more specific detail provided by a special operator who participated in the capture, over the course of a number of interviews with me.

44 *"Saddam would never leave Iraq":* Author's interview with Judith Yaphe, January 27, 2015.

44 *"He was everywhere, yet nowhere" . . . they joked:* Russell, *We Got Him!,* 293.

44 *The palace complex:* Some of the details on the Tikrit Palace are from Filkins, "In Hometown, Hussein's Glory Is Quickly Gone," *The New York Times.*

44 *Where he had once swam and fished:* Author's interview with one of the special operators who was there, who wishes to remain anonymous, November 12, 2015.

45 *As the burly special operators . . . patting his leg:* The account of Saddam Hussein being led from his old palace in Tikrit to be transported to Baghdad following his capture is based on the author's interview with one of the special operators who was there and who wishes to remain anonymous, March 17, 2015.

CHAPTER 11

The accounts of Saddam Hussein's interrogation sessions by the FBI in this and subsequent chapters are based on the declassified FBI notes on the sessions, which are available at https://vault.fbi.gov. The National Geographic *Inside* documentary "Interrogating Saddam" also features extensive interviews with the lead interrogator, George Piro, and reenactments of the interrogation based on the materials declassified by the FBI. Finally, I conducted dozens of hours of interviews with members of the FBI interrogation team, including Jeff Green, Rod Middleton, Tom Neer, Todd Irinaga, and one who prefers to remain anonymous.

47 *After they began settling in . . . crimes against humanity:* Author's multiple interviews with the CIA's John Maguire and the FBI's Jeff Green and Rod Middleton.

48 *"malignant narcissist":* Author's interview with Dr. Jerrold Post, January 18, 2015.

48 *"If we'd instantly created an adversarial situation":* Author's interview with Jeff Green, May 14, 2015.

49 *"a conversation with a purpose":* Author's interview with Tom Neer, April 21, 2016.

49 *"I will discuss everything" . . . "not an interrogation":* From declassified FBI notes of Saddam Hussein's interrogation, available at https://vault.fbi.gov.

49 *"He really was a genius":* Author's interview with Jeff Green, May 14, 2015.

50 *"If I hear that you did not":* Woods, Palkki, and Stout, eds., *The Saddam Tapes,* 174.

50 *"They do not look scared":* From declassified FBI notes of Saddam Hussein's interrogation, available at https://vault.fbi.gov.

CHAPTER 12

The accounts of Saddam Hussein's relationship with Robert "Doc" Ellis are based on material found in Robert Ellis and Marianna Riley's book *Caring for Victor: A U.S. Army Nurse and Saddam Hussein,* as well as hours of interviews I conducted with both authors. Their cooperation was critical in my ability to write this and subsequent chapters that highlight Doc Ellis's experience caring for Saddam Hussein.

51 *"Act confident, don't be afraid":* Ellis and Riley, *Caring for Victor,* 23.

51 *"Saddam Hussein cannot die in U.S. custody":* Ibid., 24.

51 *"I had to fight all the time":* Author's interview with Robert Ellis, August 25, 2015.

51 *"He was once a street fighter like I was"*: Ellis and Riley, *Caring for Victor*, 182.

52 *One night . . . "not just their aches and pains"*: Ibid., 29.

53 *On a few occasions Saddam tried*: Ellis and Riley, *Caring for Victor*, 112; and author's interviews with Robert Ellis, August 24 and August 25, 2015.

53 *"My friends, three Cohibas"*: From Army oral history interview with Saddam's interpreter Joseph, March 13, 2007.

53 *As they sat outside . . . "a ha ha ha" laughs*: Author's interview with Robert Ellis, August 25, 2015.

54 *Saddam's lustier side*: Duelfer, *Hide and Seek: The Search for Truth in Iraq*, 409; and author's interview with Dr. Joseph Sassoon, February 25, 2015.

54 *When Ellis returned . . . "remainder of our lives"*: Ellis and Riley, *Caring for Victor*, 90–91.

55 *The man who . . . "They must have eaten earlier"*: Ibid., 70.

56 *"looked at the box skeptically" . . . "Papa Noel"*: Ibid., 70–72.

56 Watch your back, Ellis, he told himself: Ibid., 46.

57 *"silk sheets to an Army cot"*: Author's interview with Robert Ellis, October 17, 2015.

57 *"I remember how I grew up"*: Author's interview with Robert Ellis, August 24, 2015.

57 *"He actually lived a simple life"*: Author's email exchange with Dr. Ala Bashir, October 27, 2015.

57 *He'd been watching a goofy comedy on his computer*: Author's interview with Robert Ellis, October 17, 2015.

57 *Saddam told him his stomach hurt . . . "break them in half for her"*: Ellis and Riley, *Caring for Victor*, 81; and author's interview with Robert Ellis, August 24, 2015.

58 *"I'm so sorry, Mr. Ellis"*: Ellis and Riley, *Caring for Victor*, 46.

CHAPTER 13

The bulk of this chapter—an account of Rod Middleton's experience in Iraq, and his return home—is derived from hours of interviews, as well as email correspondence, I conducted with him.

59 *Tom Neer, the FBI's profiler . . . "manage his legacy"*: Author's interviews with Frank Byers, July 26, 2015, and Tom Neer, April 21, 2016.

60 *"obsessed with his personal relationship with Saddam"*: Author's interview with Frank Byers, July 26, 2015.

60 *"Eventually you have to change the tone"*: Author's interview with Rod Middleton, June 18, 2015.

61 *"It may have been" . . . "shells dropping on me"*: Author's interview with Rod Middleton, August 27, 2015.

CHAPTER 14

63 *"Why soldiers come?"*: Ellis and Riley, *Caring for Victor*, 147.

64 *Saddam took Ellis . . . "They'll wish they had me back"*: Ibid., 147–48.

64 *Late one morning*: Ibid., 135–42.

64 *He was angry . . . "I will be your brother"*: Ibid., 140–42; and author's interviews with Robert Ellis, August 24 and August 25, 2015.

CHAPTER 15

The account of the interaction between George Piro and Saddam is based on the declassified FBI interrogation notes that are available at https://vault.fbi .gov, as well as on the National Geographic *Inside* documentary "Interrogating Saddam," which includes an extensive interview with George Piro.

66 *"I am a believer but not a zealot"*: From declassified FBI notes of Saddam Hussein's interrogation, June 28, 2004.

66 *the "turbans" must never be allowed*: Author's interview with Charles Duelfer, February 24, 2015.

66 *Just before Piro . . . it didn't show*: This scene was recounted by George Piro in the National Geographic *Inside* documentary "Interrogating Saddam."

67 *"Saddam did win"*: Author's interview with John Maguire, May 27, 2015.

67 *"The truth is that . . . personal stenographer"*: Joscelyn, "Saddam's Stenographers," *The Weekly Standard*.

CHAPTER 16

The account of Raghad Hussein hiring Dr. Najeeb al-Nuaimi is based on a number of interviews I conducted with him.

72 *Her home had morphed into a shrine*: Author's interview with a friend of Raghad Hussein who wishes to remain anonymous, August 1, 2015.

72 *She still carried herself*: Ibid.

CHAPTER 17

The account of Dr. Najeeb al-Nuaimi meeting Saddam for the first time is based on interviews I conducted with him on June 10, 2015, and March 15, 2016.

78 *"When you talk to him, he listens"*: Anderson, "Saddam's Ear," *The New Yorker*.

78 *Can you speak with the Americans*: Dr. Najeeb al-Nuaimi was not the only one who explained that Saddam seemed more troubled by the method of execution—hanging—than by the prospect of execution itself. A number of the Super Twelve explained that he expressed frustration over this to them as well.

CHAPTER 18

Dialogue from the trial in this and subsequent chapters is based on pool media coverage provided by trial observers that reads like a trial transcript and is at times accompanied by accounts of the atmospherics in the courtroom. I have also relied heavily on Michael A. Newton and Michael P. Scharf's book *Enemy of the State: The Trial and Execution of Saddam Hussein*, which, despite their participation in the trial, provides a generally evenhanded account of its successes and shortcomings. Visual descriptions of the courtroom and the primary participants are derived from TV footage of the trial as well as open source photographs that are in abundant supply. Much of the trial was broadcast locally in Iraq, as well as regionally and internationally. Highlights are easily viewable on YouTube.

79 *The swagger of Saddam's courtroom entrances*: Author's interview with Paul Sphar, January 15, 2015.

80 *Five Iraqi judges . . . Salem Chalabi*: Newton and Scharf, *Enemy of the State*, 103.

80 *As the security situation in Baghdad . . . "taking it to the enemy"*: Author's email exchange with William Wiley, April 13, 2016.

80 *Most assumed that Saddam*: A number of Americans I interviewed attested to the fact that Saddam could hear occasional explosions and gunfire, and that this not only reinforced his awareness that there was an active insurgency but also may have fed his belief that they would mount an effort to free him. Among those who mentioned this were the CIA's John Maguire, the FBI's Tom Neer, the RCLO's William Wiley, and a number of the Super Twelve.

84 *For that he would pay an awful price*: Newton and Scharf, *Enemy of the State*, 120.

84 *two defense attorneys would be killed by gunmen*: Ibid., 114.

84 *a woman, speaking from behind a screen*: "Saddam Outburst Follows Hidden Testimony in Trial," *USA Today*.

NOTES

CHAPTER 19

The account of preparing Saddam for movement from the Rock to the Iraqi High Tribunal courthouse is based on accounts provided in Steve Hutchinson's Army oral history interview on February 2, 2007, as well as hours of interviews I conducted with Hutchinson, Paul Sphar, and Adam Rogerson.

88 *As Saddam showered:* Author's interview with Adam Rogerson, May 18, 2015.
88 *"Company Fun Day":* Author's interview with Steve Hutchinson, November 23, 2015.

CHAPTER 20

Dialogue from the trial is based on pool media coverage provided by trial observers. The description of the "hajji mart" is based on interviews I conducted with Chris Tasker and Paul Sphar. The description of Tucker Dawson and Paul Sphar going to purchase cigars for Saddam is based on multiple interviews I conducted with Paul Sphar.

93 *"I know you've treated me very well":* Newton and Scharf, *Enemy of the State,* 125.
94 *He extolled their virtues:* Author's interview with Paul Sphar, September 7, 2015.

CHAPTER 21

The account of Saddam discussing his family is based primarily on the Army oral history interviews conducted with Steve Hutchinson and Adam Rogerson, as well as hours of my own interviews with those two. The specific tale of Saddam burning Uday's cars is based on a conversation Rogerson had with him and recounted to me in an interview on May 18, 2015. The episode is also mentioned in Dr. Ala Bashir's *The Insider: Trapped in Saddam's Brutal Regime.*

95 *clustered around Saddam's "fire":* Many of the soldiers recalled how Saddam seemed to enjoy affectionately naming certain inanimate objects, such as calling his space heater his "fire" and his exercise bike his "pony." Rogerson, Hutchinson, Tasker, and Sphar all mentioned this to me during interviews with them, and a number of other members of the Super Twelve referenced this habit in their Army oral history interviews.

96 *"All I knew at the time about Uday"*: Author's interview with Steve Hutchinson, September 3, 2015.

96 *Uday descended deeper . . . make his selections*: These accounts of Uday's depravities are from Bennett and Weisskopf, "The Sum of Two Evils," *Time*.

98 *"If you went in there and you were intimidated"*: Author's interview with Adam Rogerson, May 18, 2015.

99 *The event that had triggered Saddam's frenzied immolation*: The account of Uday shooting Saddam's half brother Watban is based on descriptions of that night in two sources: Bashir, *The Insider*, 163–70; and Cockburn and Cockburn, *Out of the Ashes*, 163–65.

100 *"a Jerry Springer episode on steroids"*: Author's interview with Adam Rogerson, May 18, 2015.

CHAPTER 22

The story of Saddam and Steve Hutchinson discussing their daughters is based on the Army oral history interview with Hutchinson on February 2, 2007, as well as on many hours I spent interviewing Hutchinson. The account of Raghad discussing the necklace her father gave her is based on an interview I conducted with Ramsey Clark on April 16, 2015.

101 *"Happy birthday to you"*: The description of Hala's birthday party is based on video footage of it included in the documentary *Saddam Hussein: The Family, Parts I and II*, produced by O3 Productions and available on YouTube. I relied on Omar Feikeiki for translation.

102 *"flagging down a waiter"*: Author's interview with Paul Sphar, January 11, 2016.

103 *They've been dressing up . . . "Every daughter is a princess"*: Army oral history interview with Steve Hutchinson, February 2, 2007; and author's interview with Hutchinson, April 28, 2015.

103 *"I've never seen" . . . Raghad had tumbled from his shoulders*: Author's interview with Ramsey Clark, April 16, 2015.

CHAPTER 23

105 *Perhaps sparked by something . . . would have shown weakness*: Author's interview with Steve Hutchinson, September 3, 2015.

106 *The soldier approached General Ra'ad . . . scarcely imaginable*: Author's interview with Ra'ad al-Hamdani, July 30, 2015. This and subsequent, detailed accounts of Ra'ad al-Hamdani's interactions with Saddam are based on hours of interviews that I conducted with him in Amman, Jordan, in

person, as well as a lengthy follow-up interview that Ranya Kadri—who served as my fixer/interpreter in Amman—conducted with him for me. While I was at first hesitant to recount episodes so heavily reliant on one man's memory, my confidence in the veracity of General Hamdani's recollections was reinforced by Kevin Woods, a historian, Iraq expert, and Army veteran with the Institute of Defense Analyses. Finally, Hamdani's accounts were consistent and believable based on everything I read about him and about Saddam's interactions with his subordinates, as well as audio, video, and written documentary evidence provided in Baath Party archives that I was able to research at the National Defense University. While people are naturally inclined to present themselves in a favorable light to interviewers, I ultimately had no reason to doubt the veracity of General Hamdani's accounts, and plenty of good reasons to accept them.

107 *Dave Manners, the new CIA station chief:* The account of the Kamels' defection, debriefings in Jordan, and ultimate return to Baghdad is based on hours of interviews I conducted in Amman and Washington, DC, with many of the Jordanians and Americans who participated in the episode, including Dave Manners, as well as senior Jordanian officials Samih Batthiki, Marwan Kasim, Ali Shukri, and one who prefers to remain anonymous. I also gathered material for this chapter from various books and articles cited in the list of sources above.

109 *"something was off" about them:* Author's interview with Ali Shukri, July 31, 2015.

110 *Saddam Kamel boasted . . . brains came out:* Author's interview with Samih Batthiki, July 29, 2015.

110 *By the end of these meetings, Shukri was convinced:* Author's interview with Ali Shukri, July 31, 2015.

111 *"Do you think I could harm":* Cockburn and Cockburn, *Out of the Ashes*, 207.

111 *"You donkey":* Ibid.

111 *"I want Your Excellency to know":* Woods, Palkki, and Stout, eds., *The Saddam Tapes*, 320–21.

111 *On the day of their scheduled departure:* Author's interview with Samih Batthiki, July 29, 2015.

112 *"pace up and down as if he were making up his mind":* Cockburn and Cockburn, *Out of the Ashes*, 208.

112 *"Khallas," he said:* Ibid.

113 *house in a southern suburb of Baghdad:* Bashir, *The Insider*, 172.

113 *In keeping with tribal tradition:* Cockburn and Cockburn, *Out of the Ashes*, 208.

113 *real-time updates . . . bathroom of the house:* Bashir, *The Insider*, 172.

113 *Hussein Kamel fought on . . . "thought of returning":* The account of the shootout is based on descriptions provided in ibid., 172–73; and Cockburn and Cockburn, *Out of the Ashes*, 208–9.

CHAPTER 24

115 *If there was time . . . world stage:* The description of Saddam's routine upon arrival at the IHT and prior to heading into the courtroom is based on an account provided by Steve Hutchinson in his February 2, 2007, Army oral history interview and confirmed by author's interviews with Adam Rogerson, Chris Tasker, and Paul Sphar.

116 *Day eight of the Dujail trial:* As is the case with all of the trial accounts, the dialogue is based on pool media coverage/transcription provided by trial observers. There is also video footage of much of the trial from various media outlets that can be found on YouTube. For additional context on what transpired in the courtroom, I relied heavily on Newton and Scharf, *Enemy of the State*.

116 *the removal of Amin:* Newton and Scharf, *Enemy of the State*, 129.

119 *Chris Tasker was sitting . . . puff away contentedly on his cigar:* The account of Chris Tasker sharing a cigar with Saddam is based on author's interview with Tasker on February 21, 2015. Saddam shared the story of Fidel Castro introducing him to cigars with a number of the other soldiers in the Super Twelve as well.

CHAPTER 25

121 *Hutch was on duty . . . nearby man-made lake:* Steve Hutchinson's recollections in this chapter of Saddam telling him stories about fishing in the nearby lakes are based on his Army oral history interview on February 2, 2007, as well as many hours of interviews I conducted with him.

122 *Saddam knew exactly where he was:* Army oral history interviews with James Martin and Tucker Dawson, February 2, 2007; corroborated by author's interviews with a number of other members of the Super Twelve.

122 *taste for human blood:* Author's interview with Chris Tasker, March 27, 2015.

122 *"floaters" out of the lake:* Author's interviews with Steve Hutchinson, April 28 and 29, 2015.

122 *twelve corpses got caught in metal grates:* Associated Press, "U.S. Troops Among Nearly 50 Dead in Iraq."

122 *"you will need someone like me":* Author's interview with John Maguire, May 27, 2015.

123 *Saddam watched his fishing line:* The account of Saddam fishing with King Hussein is based on author's interview on August 1, 2015, with one of the king's senior ministers who participated in the fishing outings.

124 *My friend . . . couldn't help but smile:* Army oral history interview with Steve

Hutchinson, February 2, 2007; as well as author's subsequent interviews with Hutchinson.

CHAPTER 26

126 *If you play that damn song one more time:* The account of Paul Sphar wrestling Tucker Dawson comes from author's interview with Paul Sphar, May 4, 2015.

126 *"if we got sick of each other" . . . "we'd have each other's back":* Author's interview with Adam Rogerson, May 18, 2015.

128 *"My cage cannot hold me":* Author's email exchange with Paul Sphar, August 17, 2016.

128 *Tunisian philosopher . . . traveled to Amman:* Author's interview with Dr. Najeeb al-Nuaimi, March 15, 2016.

128 *Saddam then set his papers . . . "chess for years":* The account of Paul Sphar playing chess with Saddam is based on author's interview with Sphar, May 4, 2015.

129 *One afternoon Dawson . . . access his bank account:* Army oral history interview with Tucker Dawson, February 2, 2007.

130 *Late one night at the Rock:* Author's interview with Adam Rogerson, May 18, 2015.

130 *"I don't think he ever":* Army oral history interview with Tucker Dawson, February 2, 2007.

130 *It was Qusay . . . deserted late-night streets:* The story of General al-Hamdani being summoned to the palace and explaining why Iraq would not be able to defeat the American military is based on author's interviews with Hamdani on July 30, 2015, and Ranya Kadri's relaying the author's questions to him on January 15, 2016.

CHAPTER 27

136 *The Iranians . . . dismissing it as nonsense:* Army oral history interview with Steve Hutchinson, February 2, 2007; as well as a number of author's interviews with Hutchinson.

137 *As the Dujail trial resumed:* As is the case with all of the trial accounts, the dialogue is based on pool media coverage/transcription provided by trial observers. There is also video footage of much of the trial from various media outlets that can be found on YouTube.

139 *Chemical Ali oversaw the massive operation:* "FBI Prosecutive Report of Investigation Concerning Saddam Hussein."

139 *Testimony included . . . "all three were dead":* "Genocide in Iraq," Human Rights Watch report.

140 *Another Kurdish witness described:* "FBI Prosecutive Report of Investigation Concerning Saddam Hussein."

140 *"There are two faces of Saddam":* "FBI Interrogation of Ali Hasan Al-Majid Al-Tikriti."

CHAPTER 28

141 *BOOM! . . . still in power:* Army oral history interview with James Martin, February 2, 2007; and author's interview with Adam Rogerson, May 18, 2015.

141 *"This is a wild place":* Author's interview with John Maguire, May 17, 2015.

141 *"Saddam had no sense of worry":* Author's interview with William Wiley, March 12, 2015.

142 *Were your friends nearby? Are they okay?:* Army oral history interview with James Martin, February 2, 2007.

142 *For the Bushes:* Chris Tasker, Paul Sphar, Doc Ellis, Andre Jackson, and others recall Saddam speaking highly of U.S. soldiers and reserving his anger for President Bush, Secretary of Defense Rumsfeld, and Iraqi officials who cooperated with them. It is, of course, impossible to ever really know the extent to which this was sincere or an effort to ingratiate himself with his audience.

142 *"The people are used to being ruled":* Author's interview with Steve Hutchinson, November 23, 2015.

142 *"were just over there trying to stop something":* Army oral history interview with Adam Rogerson, February 2, 2007.

142 *"brutal tyrant who deserved to be wiped out":* Army oral history interview with Saddam's interpreter Joseph, March 13, 2007.

143 *"Saddam had no friends":* Author's interview with John Maguire, March 27, 2015.

143 *Terrible fates befell senior advisors:* Author's interview with Tom Neer, April 22, 2016. This episode was also recounted in the December 1990 congressional testimony of Dr. Jerrold Post, the CIA psychologist who "profiled" Saddam Hussein, as well as in a number of other periodicals and biographies.

143 *Joseph never saw this side of Saddam:* Army oral history interview with Saddam's interpreter Joseph, March 27, 2015.

144 *"take three days to get in touch with him":* Duelfer, "Comprehensive Report of the Special Advisor to the Director of Special Intelligence on Iraq's WMD," 11–12.

144 *General Ra'ad al-Hamdani . . . summoned to the palace in the first place:* The account of the generals being summoned to the Tikrit Palace, where they

encountered the gathering of poets and artists, is based on author's interview with Ra'ad al-Hamdani, July 30, 2015.

146 *"Isn't loneliness the worst enemy"*: Hussein, *Zabiba and the King*, 81.

CHAPTER 29

Dialogue from the trial in this chapter is based on pool media coverage provided by trial observers.

147 *Khamis al-Obeidi had recently been gunned down*: Newton and Scharf, *Enemy of the State*, 162.
147 *"terrified that Saddam would die"*: Author's interview with William Wiley, March 12, 2015.
147 *one of Saddam's deputies . . . not a political hack*: The account of Saddam's hunger strike, and its resolution, is based primarily on the author's multiple interviews with William Wiley.
147 *Ramadan had previously achieved notoriety*: "Bush Challenged to 'Duel' with Saddam," BBC News.
149 *Meanwhile, closing arguments . . . over their security*: Newton and Scharf, *Enemy of the State*, 167.
149 *Saddam had long considered the trial a sham*: Author's interview with Ramsey Clark, April 16, 2015. Other trial observers and participants, such as Dr. Najeeb al-Nuaimi and William Wiley, echo the view that Saddam was not interested in legal minutiae, instead focusing on using the trial as an opportunity for political theater.
151 *Saddam's fiery call to kill Americans*: Army oral history interview with Saddam's interpreter Joseph, March 13, 2007.
151 *"he left it in the courtroom"*: Army oral history interview with Tucker Dawson, February 2, 2007.
152 *"yelling and swinging his arms"*: Author's interviews with Steve Hutchinson, September 3, 2015, and November 23, 2015.
152 *"exhausted from the show"*: Author's interview with Steve Hutchinson, September 3, 2015.

CHAPTER 30

The account of the run-in with the lieutenant over who got to use the television in the Crypt is based on my interviews with Steve Hutchinson. The supporting details of what life was like while at the IHT are based on virtually all of the Army oral history interviews with the Super Twelve, as well as on my interviews with a number of them.

154 *Hutch noticed that Saddam's cell:* The account of some of the soldiers taking it upon themselves to create an "office" for Saddam at the Rock is based primarily on multiple interviews I conducted with Steve Hutchinson. The more general sentiment that the soldiers tolerated Saddam's eccentricities and found themselves impressed by the respect with which he treated them—and were therefore more eager to please him—recurred throughout the Army oral history interviews as well as the interviews I conducted.

156 *"the people . . . may know the facts":* "Tour of Prison Reveals the Last Days of Saddam Hussein," CNN.com.

156 *Hutch would later recall:* From Army oral history interview with Steve Hutchinson, February 2, 2007.

156 *"It's the palace calling":* The account of Shameem Rassam being summoned to Saddam's palace is based primarily on interviews I conducted with her on March 14, 2015, and January 15, 2016. Many of the details of her experience are consistent with descriptions provided by others of surprise audiences with Saddam that can be found in various biographies and articles.

157 *he was even reported:* Duelfer, "Comprehensive Report of the Special Advisor to the Director of Central Intelligence on Iraq's Weapons of Mass Destruction."

157 *the Anointed One, as he was sometimes called:* Bowden, "Tales of the Tyrant," *The Atlantic.*

CHAPTER 31

161 *The streets of Baghdad . . . an exhausting life's journey:* Some of the details of the heightened security the day of Saddam's sentencing come from Burns and Semple, "Hussein Is Sentenced to Death by Hanging," *The New York Times.* I relied on the website Weather Underground (www.wunderground.com) for historical daily weather conditions for Baghdad. Finally, I drew upon my own experiences as an infantryman deployed to Iraq to capture the sensation of what it felt like when enemy activity seemed likely.

162 *Anxious to get started, Judge Rauf:* As is the case elsewhere, the dialogue of the trial is based on pool media coverage/transcription provided by trial observers. Additionally, video footage of the sentencing from various media outlets can be found on YouTube.

162 *"Saddam was often charming":* Author's interview with a former senior Jordanian official who met with Saddam on many occasions and requested anonymity prior to discussing his experiences, August 1, 2015.

163 *As they rode down . . . what God wants, God does:* Army oral history interview with Tucker Dawson, February 2, 2007.

163 *I've been sentenced to death before:* Army oral history interview with James Martin, February 2, 2007.

NOTES

163 *"he was going to get out"*: Author's interview with Adam Rogerson, May 18, 2015.

164 *"He deserves credit for taking it like a man"*: Army oral history interview with Jeff Price, February 2, 2007.

164 *Shiite neighborhoods . . . unjust sentence*: Some details of Iraq's reaction to the sentence are from Burns and Semple, "Hussein Is Sentenced to Death by Hanging," *The New York Times.*

165 *"Any means are justified"*: Hussein, *Zabiba and the King*, 30.

CHAPTER 32

166 *As Hutch sat watching . . . "I was letting him talk"*: The key elements of this chapter—Steve Hutchinson's relationship with his grandfather, how his interactions with Saddam triggered these memories, and the time he fell asleep and Saddam gently woke him—all stem from many hours of interviews I conducted with Hutchinson.

CHAPTER 33

170 *Overnight temperatures dropping into the high thirties*: Weather Underground, www.wunderground.com.

170 *As Adam Rogerson sat outside*: The account of Adam Rogerson's wife sending him candles, and Saddam asking for one to carve poems and messages on, comes from the Army oral history interview with Adam Rogerson, February 2, 2007; additional interviews I conducted with Rogerson; and the Army oral history interview with James Martin, February 2, 2007.

173 *Saddam's odd observance . . . "pretty nice"*: The episode of Saddam asking to watch *The Passion of the Christ* is from the Army oral history interview with Jeff Price, February 2, 2007.

174 *"When I'd see the trial going on" . . . "more like a grandpa"*: Author's interview with Adam Rogerson, May 18, 2015.

174 *Saddam would write an additional poem*: Army oral history interview with Jeff Price, February 2, 2007.

CHAPTER 34

175 *Chris Tasker remembers*: Author's interview with Chris Tasker, October 21, 2015.

175 *Saddam had just enjoyed*: Army oral history interview with James Martin, February 2, 2007.

175 *Saddam had gained weight:* Army oral history interview with Steve Hutchinson, February 2, 2007.

176 *A few hours later, Saddam said good night . . . didn't bother him:* In piecing together the sequence of events on Saddam's final night, I relied on all of the Army oral history interviews—which focused heavily on his last hours—as well as my own interviews with Steve Hutchinson, Chris Tasker, Adam Rogerson, and Paul Sphar. The chronology as presented here is based on overlapping details in their accounts, which I found to be far more similar than different as I cross-checked them against each other. Unlike a few other events recounted in this book that relied heavily—by necessity—on the recollections of one or two individuals, the account of his final night is based on the collective memories of almost all of the participants.

176 *"more of a friendship than that of criminal and translator":* Army oral history interview with Saddam's interpreter Joseph, March 13, 2007.

177 *Stephen Hadley, President Bush's national security advisor:* Associated Press, "Bush: Saddam's Execution Will Not End Violence in Iraq."

177 *"last stand at the Alamo":* Author's interview with Chris Tasker, October 21, 2015.

177 *little more than "babysitters":* Army oral history interview with Jeff Price, February 2, 2007.

177 *two of them chuckled:* Army oral history interviews with Art Perkins and Andre Jackson, February 2, 2007.

178 *Saddam asked to bathe:* Many of the Super Twelve's accounts made note of how Saddam chose to bathe prior to dressing and preparing for his execution.

178 *finding the right pair of socks:* Army oral history interview with Andre Jackson, February 2, 2007.

178 *Saddam spent some time:* Author's interview with Steve Hutchinson, April 29, 2015.

178 *"My friend" . . . final night ran smoothly:* The account of Saddam giving his watch to Steve Hutchinson on the eve of his execution is based on a number of interviews I conducted with Hutchinson.

179 *"You could smell him from a mile away":* Army oral history interview with James Martin, February 2, 2007.

180 *Standing tall . . . tears sliding down his face:* Army oral history interview with Jeff Price, February 2, 2007. Price's account was echoed by a number of the other soldiers who were there as Saddam prepared to leave his cell for the last time.

CHAPTER 35

181 *one of the coldest mornings . . . descending step:* Many of the Super Twelve recall that the morning of the execution was one of the coldest they would

3434

spend in Iraq. Exact temperatures can be found at Weather Underground, www.wunderground.com. The details of the transportation to the execution site, as well as the security outside of it, are based on accounts provided by many of the Super Twelve in their oral history interviews, as well as in interviews conducted by me.

182 *Specialist Rogerson would later say:* Author's interview with Adam Rogerson, May 18, 2015.

182 *The Super Twelve waited:* Author's interview with Chris Tasker, June 11, 2015. Descriptive details of the execution site are also based on accounts provided by Tucker Dawson in his February 2, 2007, Army oral history interview, as well as interviews I conducted with Adam Rogerson and Steve Hutchinson.

182 *Rubbaie received . . . "Doctor, this is for men":* Agence France Presse, "Man Who Oversaw Hanging Recalls Dictator's End."

183 *The former president was then escorted . . . "The hell that is Iraq?":* The scene of Saddam being led to the gallows and hanged was filmed—despite what was supposed to be a prohibition on cameras at the execution site—and leaked to the press. His final words are audible and translated with subtitles. The execution can be viewed on YouTube and his final words were widely reported in media across the world (though English translations differ slightly).

183 *"preserve the last scene":* Author's interview with Ra'ad al-Hamdani, July 30, 2015.

183 *"typical Saddam":* Author's interview with Steve Hutchinson, April 29, 2015.

184 *"If you listen to the video" . . . "wasn't scared":* Ibid.

CHAPTER 36

185 *The Super Twelve were quiet:* The fact that the Super Twelve's reaction to the execution was one of somber silence was repeated by just about all of them during their Army oral history interviews—even those who did not grow as close to Saddam as some of the others did—and in interviews with me.

185 *like a bomb going off:* Author's interview with Steve Hutchinson, April 29, 2015.

186 *"A criminal? True":* Agence France Presse, "Man Who Oversaw Hanging Recalls Dictator's End."

186 *The Super Twelve stood by . . . " 'You've got to be kidding me' ":* The chaotic scene following the execution was described similarly by many of the soldiers in their Army oral history interviews and reinforced by Adam Rogerson, Chris Tasker, Paul Sphar, and Steve Hutchinson in their interviews

conducted by me. Rogerson's quote is from his interview conducted by me, May 18, 2015. There is also abundant open source media reporting that reinforces their accounts and describes the manner in which the Iraqis handled the execution and its immediate aftermath.

186 *"I was raised tough"*: Author's interview with Steve Hutchinson, September 3, 2015.

187 *grabbed the big man from behind:* Army oral history interview with Steve Hutchinson, February 2, 2015.

187 *The sectarian violence:* Descriptions of the violent aftermath of the execution are based on information provided by www.icasualties.org and details found in Burns, "Hussein Video Grips Iraq; Attacks Go On," *The New York Times.*

187 *The sun was beginning to come up . . . by his lawyers:* The description of the Super Twelve's departure from the execution site and return to the Rock to clean up Saddam's cell is based on accounts many of them provided in their interviews. They were generally consistent, though there were a few differences, notably over how Saddam's body was removed from the execution site. A few recalled that they loaded it into a vehicle and transported it to another base for onward movement to Tikrit, while others contend that it was immediately loaded onto a helicopter and that they returned to the Rock by themselves. These discrepancies can perhaps be explained by the fact that none of them had slept that night and that they had just participated in a traumatic and disorienting event. In this case, as well as with a few other discrepancies, I developed my narrative around the account that was most common and consistent with news reports.

187 *Meanwhile, a helicopter . . . "God bless you":* Agence France Presse, "Man Who Oversaw Hanging Recalls Dictator's End."

188 *he later asked for, and kept, the noose:* Martin, "Dr Mowaffak al Rubaie on the Dictator's Last Moments," *The Independent.*

188 *the head of his Albu Nasir tribe:* "Bomb Kills Head of Saddam's Tribe," BBC .com.

188 *"an important milestone":* President Bush, "White House Statement," December 30, 2006.

188 *"President Bush arose" . . . "pondering his next steps in Iraq":* Associated Press, "Bush: Saddam's Execution Will Not End Violence in Iraq."

189 *"It didn't really hit us":* Author's interview with Adam Rogerson, May 18, 2015.

189 *"It was the first time I'd ever seen death" . . . "It was a mission":* Army oral history interview with Tucker Dawson, February 2, 2007.

189 *"Will I miss Saddam the brutal dictator?":* Army oral history interview with Saddam's interpreter Joseph, March 13, 2007.

189 *"Big Man upstairs" . . . resolved to get out of the Army:* Army oral history interview with Steve Hutchinson, February 2, 2007.

NOTES

CHAPTER 37

193 *The soldiers' transition . . . to the "Regular Twelve":* Author's interview with Adam Rogerson, February 2, 2007.

193 *It was a chilly St. Patrick's Day:* The account of Chris Tasker's return from the Saddam mission and the impact it had on him is based on extensive interviews I conducted with Chris over the course of a year, as well as on an interview with his father, Steve, on March 21, 2016. Detail on his hometown of Amherst, Ohio, is based on my visit to meet Chris there.

196 *Paul Sphar was no longer a guard:* The account of Paul Sphar's return from the Saddam mission, and his subsequent struggles with substance abuse and PTSD, is based on extensive interviews I conducted with Paul. Detail on his new home and job in Texas is based on my visit to meet him there.

198 *When he returned to the modest home:* The account of Doc Ellis's return from the Saddam mission, and his struggles with its aftermath, is based on material found in the book *Caring for Victor: A U.S. Army Nurse and Saddam Hussein*, which he cowrote with Marianna Riley, as well as a number of interviews that I conducted with both of them.

200 *FBI Agent Rod Middleton and his thirteen-year-old son:* The account of Rod Middleton's return home from his role interrogating Saddam in Baghdad is based on extensive interviews and email correspondence that I had with Middleton.

202 *Jeff Rogerson knew that his son Adam:* The account of Adam Rogerson's return home is based on extensive interviews with him and his father, Jeff, as well as on his February 2, 2007, Army oral history interview. The descriptions of his hometown of North Ridgeville, Ohio, are based on my visit there to meet him and his father.

204 *"To this day, I still hear":* The account of the impact his time with Saddam had on Steve Hutchinson is based on numerous interviews I conducted with him, as well as on his February 2, 2007, Army oral history interview. The description of his Georgia home is based on my visit there to meet with him.

205 *His Albu Nasir tribesmen:* Associated Press, "Saddam Hussein's Tomb Destroyed as Battle for Tikrit Rages."

236

INDEX

INDEX

INDEX

INDEX

Moussawi, Jaafar al-, as chief prosecutor at Saddam trial, 79, 83–84, 92

Najaf, 8, 187
National Guard, U.S., 9
Neer, Tom:
  as FBI's behavioral analyst, 48
  phased approach to interrogation suggested by, 59–60
NFL 2K5 (video game), 154
Nida, Ali al-, 188
Nuaimi, Najeeb al-, 128
  blunt assessment of Saddam's fate by, 74, 77–78
  as lawyer for Guantánamo detainees, 71
  in meeting with Raghad Hussein, 71–74
  as member of Saddam's defense team, 75–76, 84
  Saddam's first meeting with, 75–78
  and Saddam's request for new clothes, 76–77

Obeidi, Khamis al-, 75, 147
Ocala, Fla., 5–6
Old Man and the Sea, The (Hemingway), xi, 40
101st Airborne Division, U.S., 9
Orland, Calif., 30

Passion of the Christ, The (film), 173
Perkins, Art (pseud.), 6, 7, 11–12, 98, 126
  in pants-wetting incident, 12
  Saddam's last interaction with, 176
  Super Twelve's teasing of, 12, 88–89
Piro, George, 50
  Arabic spoken by, 47, 48
  as lead FBI interrogator of Saddam, 47, 48
  low-key approach of, 59–60

Saddam interrogation concluded by, 66–67
Post, Jerrold, 19, 48
Price, Jeff (pseud.), 164, 173

Qasim, Abd al-Karim, Saddam's assassination attempt on, 40, 44
Quarles, Luke (pseud.), 98–99
  Saddam guard duty announced by, 13

Ramadan, Taha Yassin, 34, 123, 144, 177
  Saddam's hunger strike and, 147–48
Rassam, Shameem, in meeting with Saddam, 156–60
Reagan, Ronald, 64
Regime Crimes Liaison Office (RCLO), 141, 148, 149
Republican Guard, 130
  at Saddam's Farouq Palace poetry salon, 144–45
Republican Palace, 80
Revolutionary Command Council, 50
Rock (palace prison), 37, 87, 163
  outdoor recreation area at, 29–30, 95, 121, 124–25, 128, 141, 154, 168, 170, 172
  Saddam as sole prisoner at, 27
  Saddam in transfers between Crypt and, 87–91, 115, 167
  Saddam's cluttered cell at, 154
  Saddam's "office" at, 154–55
  Super Twelve in return of Saddam's possessions at, 187
Rogerson, Adam, 7, 9, 10–11, 25–26, 87, 126, 142
  on dichotomy between Saddam's brutal past and interactions with prisoner, 174
  in life after Saddam duty, 193, 202–4
  and Saddam execution, 176, 177, 182, 186, 189

ABOUT THE AUTHOR

Will Bardenwerper has contributed to the *New York Times* and the *Washington Post*. He served as an Airborne Ranger–qualified infantry officer in Iraq, where he was awarded the Combat Infantryman Badge and a Bronze Star. Following his army service, he worked for the Department of Defense and in the private sector, including assignments in the Middle East and Horn of Africa. He has an MA in international public policy from the Johns Hopkins School of Advanced International Studies and a BA in English from Princeton. Will lives with his wife, Marcy, in Denver.